GENERAL GEORGE WASHINGTON

This portrait was painted for the City of New York by John Trumbull in 1790. Familiar New York City scenes provide the background.

THIS WAS NEW YORK

THE NATION'S CAPITAL IN 1789

Frank
Monaghan

Marvin
Lowenthal

Doubleday, Doran & Co., Inc.

GARDEN CITY, NEW YORK

1943

PRINTED AT THE *Country Life Press*, GARDEN CITY, N. Y., U. S. A.

THIS BOOK IS
COMPLETE AND UNABRIDGED,
MANUFACTURED UNDER WARTIME
CONDITIONS IN CONFORMITY WITH
ALL GOVERNMENT REGULATIONS
CONTROLLING THE USE OF PAPER
AND OTHER MATERIALS.

Preface

GREAT events are on the march in this year 1789. A fresh and
invigorating spirit stirs the land. A grand new idea is loosed to
shake a trammeled world. Destiny is on the loom and the spinners are at work. New York City is full pregnant with the future.
Here the new government of the United States begins. Here the
first Congress sits and deliberates high matters of state and low
matters of ceremony. Here on April 30 George Washington will
be inaugurated as the first President of the united nation. Here
basic issues are determined and the new government will be
given not only form but vitality. New York is the center of activity, of experiment, and of hope.

The city is vibrant with excitement. It is thronged with expectant crowds from far and near. It is impossible to get lodgings
in the best places. Yes, even a simple bed (no questions asked or
answered) is at a premium. But somehow we shall manage. Not
every man can take his full ease at a turning point in history.
Never have we seen such a collection of notables: statesmen,
politicians, diplomats, . . . and their gracious ladies. And we
shall see it all—in spite of the fact that humble authors are not
highly esteemed and that all this talk about equality and democracy are not yet quite operating realities. But we have a few
friends of republican principles who command entry into the best
places. We shall do our best to maintain both dignity and com-
posure.

But (since it is true) we must candidly admit that there are
times when we feel more at home over at the Tammany Society

v

talking about the dangerous tendencies of aristocracy in a republic —or in the local pub drinking the strong ale and the small talk of the town—or haunting the shops of the city for a little bargain —or sitting in at the mayor's court to hear the woes and tribulations of the unlucky. Unless you greatly object, we shall go with you everywhere in this city. For it is the people who intrigue us—the people in whose hands a democratic experiment is about to be placed. And if it is to be, as has been suggested, the people who will give voice and meaning and substance to this new government—then we ought to know those people. Even if they were the source of nothing of high importance they are still people— and we are infinitely curious. For it is people and not statesmen, it is people and not diplomats, it is people and not "gentlemen and ladies" that make a city what it is. For New York was a city of no mean degree before it was the capital of a nation; and New York will be a city of even greater degree after the capital is removed to Philadelphia and then to the muddy banks of the Potomac.

The people are the heart of a city—great people and little people. We must know them all. Yes, the bawling fishwives and the decorous housewives, the quiet scholar with his midnight oil, the sailor staggering over the pigs that infest the night and clog the streets, the visitors ripe for the plucking, the virginal school ma'am, the tippler drooling in his cups, the magistrate in the dignity of his robes, the intriguing ladies of the night, the butchers, the printers, the officers of the watch, those just out of jail, those in jail, and those just about to enter. Yes, the tradesmen and the merchants and the tavernkeepers—men who yearn and covet some solid and some lovely coin, who love the chink of money, the good sound thumping coin. Yes, little people too with their little cares. We must catch the rhythm, the color, the smells— the feel of it all. In short we must know the high of it and the low of it—and the middle of it.

The city pulsates with life and with the strange aberrations of life. There is bright light and there are murky shadows and there are strange and distorted figures. There is much that is tattered and tawdry; there is much that is brave and good. But the totality of these molded the future. It emerged from their habits, their prejudices, their opinions, their circumstances. Democracy is beginning to emerge. Will it survive—and will it merit the survival?

Then listen to the testimony of a high gentleman of a far older civilization. He is the Baron Hyde de Neuville, a refugee from the tyranny of Napoleon. After seeing New York and Americans in many places he writes to a friend in Europe:

These rebel colonists are on the way to become one of the most powerful of nations. Only let them be wise; let them, quietly without revolution, infuse a little more strength into their administration; let them redress certain abuses, and we shall one day see them the astonishment of Europe. An immense vitality animates this growing state. One feels, on taking a near view of America, as if something unknown were stirring in the future; as if the tyranny that weighs down our unhappy country were not the last word of this opening century; as if a fresh breeze had passed over the world. . . . The exact consequences cannot be foreseen and are slow to develop; but it seems, sometimes, as if America had surprised the future and forestalled the hour.

Yes, it was the people of New York and the people of America. They molded the future. To know them is to know the shape of the future. And the future is worth the knowing. Thus a journey into the past may well become a voyage into the future.

Your two modest scriveners believe that we know them well. We have found materials that have never been made public. We have gone into the manuscript records of the courts of the city; we have (for hundreds of hours) perused and studied the charging-out records of the New York Society Library, in order to report accurately, and for the first time, on what New Yorkers really read. We have searched out unpublished letters and diaries. We believe we know all the things that previous reporters knew and said. We feel that it is worth the knowing and the saying.

But we have tarried too long with these poor, albeit honest, words. Great events are on the march, and the echoes of their footsteps will, some distant day, be heard around the world. Enough of words! Let us be "off to New-York" . . . with . . .

Your humble & obedient servants,
FRANK MONAGHAN & MARVIN LOWENTHAL*

New York City
December 14, 1942

---

*Who hope (perhaps against hope) that your esteemed patronage will be such that we shall never be forced to follow the melancholy example of our late, honored colleague, Mr. Noah Webster, and admit that "we shall now give up writing and go into a more lucrative business."

Contents

Preface v
I Off to New-York 1
II Your Room and Board 15
III The City on Show 27
IV Fourteen Miles Round 39
V Shopping Round the Town 46
VI The City at Work 68
VII Medical Arts and Wiles 85
VIII Woman's World 92
IX The Social Whirl 103
X Diversions and The Arts 123
XI News and Reviews 135
XII To School? 168
XIII The City at Prayer 180
XIV Preserving the Peace 195
XV Be It Enacted by the People 203
XVI Oyez! Oyez! 214
XVII Against Foreign Enemies 228
XVIII Municipal and Social Services 238
XIX Inaugurating a Nation 251
Appendix
Acknowledgments 285
The Sources 287
Bibliography 289
Notes 292
Index 304

Illustrations

General George Washington . . . . . . *Frontispiece*

FACING PAGE

The City from the Harbor 68

Wall and Water Streets 69

Advertisements from New York City Newspapers,
  April 1789 148

Columbia College 149

St. Paul's and the New Presbyterian Meeting 188

Old Federal Hall and Wall Street 189

CHAPTER I

Off to New-York

SETTING out on a journey to New York City in 1789, you consulted first of all not a timetable but a calendar. You reckoned on two full days to get from Philadelphia to New York by stage wagon, at least three days from Albany, and not less than six days from Boston. And a day's travel usually meant from three or four o'clock in the morning until ten at night. If you planned to go by boat, you did not reckon at all; you prayed. And when the wind favored your prayers, you might count on cutting the run from Boston to three days and lengthening the trip from Philadelphia by an additional twelve hours. With a healthy breeze blowing day and night, which you never got, you could drop down from Albany inside two days; although with a little bad luck in the matter of weather it might take you nine to get back.

Your plans, however, were simplified by the fact that roads and routes were few, for the good reason there were not many places to come from. Big cities—with five thousand or more inhabitants —were to be found only along the Atlantic coast. A hundred miles inland population ran thin and, at the first ridges of the Appalachian Mountains, ceased. The largest town west of the Alleghenies was Pittsburgh, which boasted of perhaps a hundred and fifty houses, mostly log cabins, and about fifteen hundred residents—and, even then, of smoke. "The Towne," a visitor described it in 1789, "was the muddiest place that I ever was in; and by reason of using so much Coal . . . kept in so much smoke & dust, as to effect the skin of the inhabitants." Beyond

Pittsburgh there was nothing but keelboats and pack horses and Conestoga wagons, laden with settlers and their frying pans and blankets, going the wrong direction from New York.

If you decided to head for Manhattan by land, you had the choice of driving your own chaise or taking the stages. In the first instance you did wisely if you bought a copy of that handy little book, Christopher Colles' *Survey of the Roads of the United States of America,* which appeared in 1789. "A traveller," writes Mr. Colles, "will here find so plain and circumstantial a description of the road, it will be impossible for him to miss his way."

The maps, on a scale of 1½ inches to a mile, were ingeniously schematized, much like the guides we moderns employed when automobiling was a novel adventure. Only the main roads were drawn in full. Bad hills, bridges, ferries, and such landmarks as trees growing in the middle of the road were depicted in miniature. A symbol which looked like a gallows, but probably represented a tavern sign, indicated an inn, and next to it was printed the name of the host. The symbol of a horseshoe located a blacksmith's shop; and should your horse cast a shoe or your "carriage be broke," you could decide whether it was shorter to go backwards or forwards for repairs. Asterisks denoted gristmills—the gasoline stations of your trip. Other symbols told you the whereabouts of town halls, jails, and two kinds of churches, Episcopal and Presbyterian. Important farmhouses and plantations were duly marked, so "a traveller will have the satisfaction of knowing the names of many persons who reside upon the road," a convenience too when it came to borrowing a bit of harness or even a little pocket money.

Traveling by stage was probably cheaper; anyway, it was more general. But before you climbed onto the bench that was your seat, many details had to be arranged. Packing was a problem. You could not carry more than fourteen pounds of baggage free; and for any amount over that, up to each 150 pounds, you paid an extra full fare. "An American," remarks a French tourist in 1788, "travels with his comb and razor, and a couple shirts and cravats." Some travelers did, nevertheless, indulge in the luxury of trunks; and one such trunk, we know from a lost-and-found advertisement in May 1789, contained "a dark green coat with plain silver buttons, a green striped waistcoat, one pair of nankeen and one of black satin breeches, a pair of silver shoe and knee buckles, seven shirts, seven neck-cloths, three pair of white silk hose, and sundry pairs of thread hose." You had only to add some soap, a bottle of Milk of Roses, "very fine after shaving," and a box of white powder for your hair, and you were ready to go to the tavern and wait for the horses.

This presumes that you had already arranged for money. Good currency, ringing coins of full weight, was scarce after the Revolution; and it was hard to find takers for bad. Therefore, a day or two before a traveler set forth, he bought a draft or bill of exchange from the local money broker or private banker or from some town merchant who did business in New York, leaving himself only enough cash for fare and living expenses on the road. One pleasant consequence of the scarcity of passable money was the almost complete absence of highway robbers; holding up a stage wagon seldom paid.

Even so, money provided one of the journey's minor vexations or amusements—depending on your temperament. The details will be spared you until you reach New York and have occasion to cash your draft. It is enough now to say that merely between Philadelphia and New York a traveler's pennies changed value four times. When he set out from Philadelphia, his copper pennies were worth fifteen to a shilling. By the time he reached Trenton, they had sunk to thirty; at Princeton they mounted again to twenty-four; at New Brunswick they climbed to twenty; and on Broadway it took twenty-one coppers to buy a shilling—and, before the end of the year, forty or more. And he would know, of course, without being told, that in Georgia five shillings made a dollar; in Virginia and New England, six shillings; in Maryland, Delaware, Pennsylvania, and New Jersey, seven and one half

shillings; and in North Carolina and New York, eight shillings—
and that the American dollar itself did not exist except as a
figment of bookkeeping, a fictitious standard for reckoning real
money.*

But at this pace you will never get your place bought in the
stage. Fares were usually fourpence (4¢) a mile, though rivalry
between competing stage lines sometimes brought this down to
threepence. There was no need to dispute the mileage; for,
years back, Benjamin Franklin had contrived a machine which,
attached to a chaise, had measured off the distance and indicated
where to plant the milestones to be found on all the main roads.
The old roads, however, wound and twisted and shied from steep
hills or deep streams; and the distances between New York and
such towns as Philadelphia, Albany, or Boston were more than
one tenth greater than today.

Your initiation into eighteenth-century travel could, in fact,
begin at no likelier place than Boston, for its post roads were
among the most famous in the land. The advertisements of Levi
Pease, who opened the first "line of stages" to New York as soon
as the redcoats went home in 1783, notified you to "leave name
and baggage the evening preceding the morning that the stages
set off, at the several places the stages put up, and pay one half
the passage to the place where the first exchange of passengers
is made." That done, you were free to be entertained by your
friends at a farewell dinner which, in view of your prodigious
journey to far-off New York, was elaborate and possibly tearful.
To make things easier, you no doubt suggested that the dinner
be held at Mr. Pease's own tavern, "At the Sign of the New-York
Stage, opposite the Mall," where the stages start; and there was
no need to halt the flow of Madeira or tears in order to sleep.
Why go to bed when you must rise before you have warmed
up the sheets?

*Unless otherwise noted, this book will use the New York rate of eight
shillings, or about ninety-six pence, to the dollar—that is, standard pence
and not fluctuating copper pieces.

If Josiah Quincy were among the guests to speed your departure, he could warn you what to expect. He went through the mill the year after the line was opened. He relates:

The journey to New York took up a week. The carriages were old and shackling, and much of the harness made of ropes. We generally reached our resting place for the night, if no accident intervened, at ten o'clock, and after a frugal supper went to bed with a notice that we should be called at three the next morning, which generally proved to be half-past two. Then, whether it snowed or rained, the traveler must rise and make ready by the help of a horn-lantern and a farthing candle, and proceed on his way over bad roads, sometimes with a driver showing no doubtful symptoms of drunkenness, which goodhearted passengers never failed to improve at every stopping place by urging upon him another glass of toddy. Thus we traveled, eighteen miles a stage, sometimes obliged to get out and help the coachman lift the coach out of a quagmire or rut, and arrived at New York, wondering at the ease as well as the expedition of our journey.

But that was five years ago, you might protest to Mr. Quincy hopefully. And if you were up on the latest news from the Ohio country, you would scorn a New England quagmire. . . . Why, 'way out West, somewhere beyond Harrisburg, there's a whiplash sticking up out of the road and, tied to it, a sign: "No bottom here." A family has been camping near by for three months; and when the mud dries, they expect to dig up the whiplash and, under it, their Conestoga wagon and two pair of horses.

It would have been cheering, though, to have that foreigner, M. Brissot de Warville, at your farewell dinner. He would have painted the journey in red-white-and-blue lights. Jacques Pierre Brissot de Warville was a Frenchman whose republican ideas impelled him to visit the United States in 1788 with much the same curiosity, hope, and lenient eye that American radicals once employed in touring Soviet Russia. "My main object," he said, "was to examine the effects of liberty upon men, society, and government . . . among a people who had just won their freedom." And he found the effects beneficent even in the humble backyard privies, where "a somewhat lower seat for children proves how everyone here is concerned with the smallest detail of education." Making allowances for his enthusiasm, you could do no better than follow in the tracks of M. Brissot. He too set out for New York on Levi Pease's line.

Before dawn you mounted the stage—a gaily painted wagon suspended on stout leather straps which served for springs. Its three benches held six persons; and if you were spry you seized a place in the rear seat, the only one with a back to it. The four horses pulled off smartly; and within three hours you had covered the fifteen miles to Weston, where you breakfasted (for two shillings) on meats, fish, eggs, pie, and cider. Here, as about every fifteen miles, two of the horses were changed—to little advantage, as M. Brissot observed, for the new pair were held down to the jaded pace of the old. Two in the afternoon brought you another thirty-three miles to Worcester and dinner; and if you didn't get that back seat, you limped sore and stiff to your meal.

M. Brissot claims you dined well *à l'américaine* at the United States Arms, "which was a wooden building with charming ornamentation." Washington likewise ate there during his Eastern tour in 1789, after "he politely passed through the town on horseback" in order "to gratify the inhabitants." By special arrangement for stage passengers your dinner cost you two shillings ninepence (35¢), with an extra beefsteak at one shilling sixpence (19¢), and a bottle of "Champaigne" eased your aching joints for ten shillings ($1.25).

Travelers differed as sharply about the quality of a meal in a road tavern as they do now in a dining car. M. Constantin Volney, the Frenchman who wrote that scandalous anti-Christian *Ruins of Empire,* growled that "the whole day passes in heaping one indigestive mass upon another" and thought the American diet devastating for anyone but a Tartar. On the other hand,

M. Brissot's favorable verdict deserves respect, for his father owned a cookshop in Chartres. But no doubt the attitude most beneficial to digestion was shown by young Thomas Fairfax, who journeyed from Virginia to Massachusetts in 1799. "I have often been astonished," he jotted in his travel diary, "to find such stress laid upon a good or bad dinner, as if that was the first, which should only be a secondary, object. When we have a journey on hand, the object in view is the accomplishment of it; and if we meet with food by the way as often as needful, though of an ordinary kind, it should be sufficient."

With sixty miles for the day's run, you supped and slept in the new tavern at Spencer. It was only half built, but its cleanliness delighted M. Brissot because "that means a degree of well-being and of moral and delicate habits" never seen in the villages of monarchical France. "The rooms were neat, the beds good, the sheets clean, the supper decent: cider, tea, punch, and all for two shillings a head." Sleep, the little there was of it, cost one shilling in a single bed and sixpence more in a double; and if travel was light or the tavern commodious, you had a bedroom all to yourself.

A new stage owner greeted you at four o'clock of the second morning, for Mr. Pease's "line" was an interlocking service conducted by several hands. The new wagon had neither straps—thoroughbraces they were called—nor springs; and, like M. Brissot, you soon learned why. The rough and steep roads—fifty miles of them—beyond Spencer would have broken the best springs a smith could forge. Even Washington in his de-luxe coach called "the part crossing the hills very bad." To M. Brissot's terror, as the wagon plunged down the first hill he discovered it had no brakes, either, nor chain or drag to lock the wheels. But that too was Yankee thrift: huge stones and boulders in the road made progress down hill as slow and safe as up.

Following a ride of an hour and a half in the dark to whet your appetite, you breakfasted in Brookfield at "one Hitchcock's," as Washington called it. Here you read the gazettes, as M. Brissot did, "while waiting for the broiled and roast meats, the tea and coffee, which all told cost ten pence in Massachusetts money [13½¢]."

Then came the twenty-mile stretch down the rocky valley of the Quaboag, where if the horses showed speed you bounced like corn in a popper. At North Wilbraham, while the spent team was changed, you could recompose yourself by "baiting" at the Bliss Tavern, another stopping place of Washington's. "Baiting" meant anything less than serious eating and drinking, so call it a dish of bacon and beef, a turkey leg, and three rum flips.

Beyond North Wilbraham the road, dropping into the Connecticut valley, was excellent. "We started off like lightning," said M. Brissot, "and arrived at Springfield, ten miles, in an hour and a quarter." The lightning effect may perhaps be credited to rum flips.

In Springfield you dined, around two o'clock as usual, at Zeno Parson's place. Then you were ferried across the river, wagon and all, on a flat-bottomed scow; and you discovered you had to pay your own toll extra. If dinner and the ferry did not consume more than a couple of hours, you reached the Adams Tavern in Hartford by nine-thirty, ready for supper and bed, with sixty-three miles to the day's credit. And your brief sleep was sweetened by dreams of the beauties of Connecticut, which M. Brissot called "the paradise of the United States."

Thus day followed day; and if you had M. Brissot's luck, the fourth midnight after leaving Boston you rolled up to the feebly lighted door of Sam Fraunces' tavern in Cortlandt Street, New York, the terminal of the Boston and the Albany stages. But M. Brissot traveled in midsummer, when roads and weather were at their best. If you intended to be in New York for Washington's inauguration on April 30, as you should, for it was quite an event, the ice and mud and rain of the season would add a good two days to the journey. Coming up to New York by stage from Alexandria the following spring, Thomas Jefferson found "the roads so bad that we could not go more than three miles an hour, sometimes not more than two, and in the night but one."

For stage passengers, however, time never hung heavy. The boredom born of Pullman comfort was unknown. Every turn of the road invited speculation as to its rocks, mire, sand, grade, and hazards. Every new passenger brought a store of local news; indeed, M. Brissot sat entranced at the democratic freedom with which a shoemaker talked with so exalted a personage as a congressman. Every new driver meant the negotiation of fresh diplomatic relations, concluded over toddy. Every new team of horses evoked lengthy technical appraisals. Every steep hill gave you the occasion to be kind to dumb animals, and likewise to yourself, by stretching your legs as you walked on ahead and then waited for the stage to catch up with you at the top. Every breakdown enabled you to air your cleverness or display your muscular tone.

The blacksmiths and stableboys, the millers and ferrymen, the postmasters and innkeepers, the villagers who crowded around the incoming stage, were to be depended upon for diversion. The folks you passed on the highway always provided a subject for gossip; and sometimes among them you encountered history, as M. Brissot did when he met, near Hartford, a caravan of wagons filled with household goods, and children playing on the mattresses, and men and women walking alongside. " 'Where are you going?' I asked them. 'Down on the Ohio,' they answered gaily. I wished them a safe journey with all my heart. Before they would reach their destination they had eleven hundred miles to walk." When rain or snow or night shut up the world, the leather curtains were dropped snug and tight, and you drowsed on your bench, aware of nothing but the bite and crunch of the wheels, the thud of hoofs, the snap of a spark struck from a stone; and if you slept, with your chin on your breast, you slept like the dead, for without back or head rest, sleep came only with exhaustion.

Landmarks were long anticipated and, when they hove in sight, greeted with delight: the great East Rock cliff, which heralded the approach to New Haven; the church spire of Stratford, which led you to prepare for the dangerous crossing of the Housatonic River on a round-bottomed boat so narrow that the wheels of the stage hung over its sides; the rocky "staircase" plunge of the road at Horseneck (now Greenwich), scene of General Putnam's leap into fame; the sawmill and bridge on the Byram River, which meant that it was not far to Mrs. Haviland's tavern in Rye, and Haviland's meant, says Washington, "a very neat and decent inn," and M. Brissot adds that it meant "an infinitely gracious hostess" and her "well-built and well-bred daughter who fingers the piano forte very nicely." As you bowled up and down dale through the farm lands of Manhattan, the first glimpse of the cupola of the new Federal Hall lifting above the Bowery hills was the final thrill. Unless, of course, your best girl drove out to greet you at the Kissing Bridge over Saw Mill Creek (where Third Avenue now crosses Seventy-seventh Street), five miles from town.

The gateways of Manhattan were various. Travelers from Boston and Albany way crossed Spuyten Duyvil Creek over a makeshift pontoon structure on the site of the old Kings-bridge, which had been destroyed by the British; and they refreshed themselves at either Halsey's tavern on the north bank or at Hyatt's on the south—or at both. Washington preferred Hyatt's.*

Two ferry lines plied between New York and the village of Brooklyn: the more popular one from the Fly Market Stairs at the foot of Maiden Lane, and the other from Peck Slip at the end of filthy Ferry Street. The fares ran from twopence a person up to one shilling sixpence for an ox and two shillings for a coach; and you were liable to get a wild ride for your money— the oared barges and tiny two-masted piraguas used in the service

*After eating or sleeping in a score of inns on a single trip merely between Boston and New York, you were not surprised that there was hardly an American tavern which had not fed or bedded the father of his country and the most energetic traveler of his day.

were playthings in a heavy sea. Six hours were sometimes spent
in crossing. Commuters to New Jersey, however, drowned more
frequently. A stage from Brooklyn to Jamaica summed up the
public transportation system of Long Island.

Up the Hudson rowboats furnished casual service to Fort
Lee, to Bull's Ferry Road in North Bergen, and from Greenwich
village to the neighborhood of Weehawken. Down in New York
proper, open boats and piraguas signaling their departure with
the shriek of a conch shell and the ferryman's cry "O-v-e-r!"
plowed from the foot of Vesey Street to "Hobuck" and from
Cortlandt Street to Paulus Hook, now Jersey City. The passage
on the latter and more patronized line was sixpence. Something
of the terrors aroused by the Hudson in stormy weather may be
read in a letter written by Mrs. Aaron Burr after her husband
set off for Jersey City: "Every breath of wind whistled terror,
every noise at the door was mingled with fear of thy perserverance,
when Brown arrived with the word *embarked,* the wind high, the
water rough. . . . A tedious hour elapsed when our son was the
joyful messenger of thy safe landing at Paulus Hook." Yet these
perils had to be faced, for all traffic west and south lay across
the river or the bay.

Westward there was but a single line. From the little stone
ferryhouse up the path above the wharf at Paulus Hook you
boarded a stage at six in the morning for Morristown, N. J., and
arrived there around three in the afternoon—fare, one dollar.

Travel between New York and Philadelphia was heaviest of all.
Whereas stages ran only thrice a week to Boston, they left for
Philadelphia twice every weekday and once on Sunday; and there
were, in addition, a number of land-and-water routes. The main
daily stage lines took you from Paulus Hook either through
Newark and Trenton, with tedious ferries over six rivers, or
through Staten Island, Woodbridge, and Camden, with five
ferries but greater mileage; and they deposited you at Market
and Second streets, Philadelphia, on the second evening or third
morning.

By Boston-line standards these stages were imposing: four-seated wagons holding twelve persons. But taverns were dearer than in New England. M. Brissot paid fifty cents, "Philadelphia money," for a dinner in Trenton and thought it exorbitant, "considering that little wine is served and the food comes from local markets." A friend of Samuel B. Webb made the journey in May of 1789 and, not being a touring French liberal, was freer still in his criticism: "Where I had been taught to expect a bowling-green road and most excellent inns, judge my surprise to find roads so deep and cut to pieces that the wheels sunk to the hubs . . . and nothing to eat but what would poison the Devil. All the way to Princeton, to say nothing of the Ferrys (which are infamous and extravagant) the roads are intolerable." But two days brought the torment to a happy end. "I've ordered chickens and asparagus for Supper," he wrote from his Philadelphia inn, "for upon my first entrance in this City Tavern I saw fifty chickens, big enough, and crying 'Come toast me!'" As you may have guessed and as young John Davis, an Englishman, demonstrated and recorded a few years later, it was cheaper, pleasanter, and almost as quick to walk.

Where Mr. Webb's friend was eating chicken, strange things had recently happened, of which he and his generation were nearly as unaware as were the chickens they ate. Every generation is blessed with a similar blindness; our own played ragtime and bragged about the new Twentieth Century Limited while curious 'doings took place in a desert spot on the Atlantic coast called Kitty Hawk. Just so, on the Delaware between Philadelphia and Burlington in 1788 a scow had run—back and forth time and again—by *steam*. No one cared, those who saw and knew laughed; and John Fitch took his own life by poison out in the wilderness of Kentucky and died, thankfully, long years before his momentous invention was appropriated and exploited by that ballyhoo artist, Robert Fulton.

But even before steam some of the discomforts of stage travel could be avoided by taking a boat part way if you were willing to cast your schedule literally to the winds. Every Saturday morning a skiff left Coenties Slip (near the present Pearl and Broad streets) for New Brunswick and might reach port the same evening; and something like a ferry line undertook to land you daily in Elizabethtown; and from either place you could proceed south by stage.

For the main land-and-water route you may consult the announcement of John Rattoone in your morning's copy of the *Daily Advertiser:*

NEW YORK AND PHILADELPHIA

STAGES THROUGH SOUTH-AMBOY, BORDEN-TOWN & BURLINGTON

The proprietors of the stages respectfully inform the public, that a commodious stage-boat will set off from the bason of the Albany Pier in New-York, four days each week, to-wit, on Mondays, Wednesdays, Thursdays, & Fridays, for South-Amboy; at which place convenient waggons with careful drivers will set out on Tuesday, Thursday, Friday, & Saturday mornings at 3 o'clock for Borden-Town & Burlington (each place to be taken alternately). At which place a commodious boat will, on their arrival, proceed the same day to Philadelphia; by which means they are but little longer in performing the route, than the land stages, and at less than half the expence—the fare of each passenger, in specie, from New-York to Philadelphia, is 13s—Goods at 9s.6d. per cwt.

JOHN RATTOONE

In addition you needed merely to know that the Albany Pier was at the tip of the island between Whitehall and Broad, that thirteen shillings meant $1.63, and that "a little longer in performing the route" meant any number of hours—or days. Young Thomas Fairfax voyaged from Norfolk to within sight of New York Harbor in four days, and then spent ten more in being blown backwards off the Jersey coast.

However, packet boats were often, as Mr. Rattoone advertises, "commodious." Consequently they were the favorite means of travel between New York and New Haven, Newport, Providence, and thence Boston. On the Providence run, M. Brissot found the boat clean and well-managed.

> The cabin contained fourteen berths in two tiers, one row above the other. Each berth had its own little window. The cabin was well-ventilated and nicely varnished, so you had nothing of those vile smells which haunt the packets of the English channel. Two small spaces were cleverly enclosed in the poop to serve as privies. The crew consisted of the captain, two sailors, and a negro cook. The food was good. All I could complain of was the lethargy habitual to seamen.

The fare was about seven dollars, including berth and meals.

Before paying your money, though, it were well to weigh the risks. After having to wait over a day in Providence because "the captain hadn't finished loading his boat," M. Brissot—en route from Boston to New York—spent eight hours sailing the thirty miles to Newport. There contrary winds condemned him to wait six days; "I would have died of boredom without my books, pen, and ink."* Samuel B. Webb "boarded Capt. Clark" in New Haven at eight o'clock of a Monday evening, struck a head wind Tuesday about twenty miles from Hell Gate, and did not land in New York until one o'clock in the afternoon on Wednesday—forty-one hours to cover some seventy miles. Shoe leather would have fetched him quicker. On one return trip to Boston in the winter of '89 he encountered head winds, gale, and fog, and after an all-night's drive from Providence arrived on the fifth day, "without having had four hours quiet sleep" from the time he left New York.

Taking it all in all, if you were off to New York for the inauguration, walking was probably best.

*M. Brissot died in a different manner. A victim of his devotion to liberty, he was guillotined in Robespierre's purge of October 31, 1793.

CHAPTER II

Your Room and Board

ANY street urchin could guide you to the few large hostelries of the city and lug your bag as you strolled from the stage office or dock to look them over. Perhaps, scanning the newspaper while coming in, your eye had caught the notice in the *Daily Advertiser:* "John Francis informs the public that he has removed from No. 3 to No. 49 Great Dock street, the corner house formerly kept by Samuel Fraunces, where gentlemen may be accommodated with genteel board and lodging." Samuel Fraunces—"Black" Sam, the best cook in town—was now steward in President Washington's household, and his wife ran the tavern on Cortlandt Street where the stage lines terminated; but John did well by you at that "corner house" (still standing) on Broad and Pearl. Toasting before one of its fourteen fireplaces, you were served good fare from its "most excellent large kitchen" and good cheer from its "fine dry cellars." Then as now you were invited to gaze with caught breath at the "long room" where Washington bade farewell to his officers when the Revolutionary War was won.

Tops, however, was the City Tavern. This was a two-story building, once James De Lancey's mansion, on Broadway just north of Trinity Church. Its many names—Province Arms, Burns's, Bolton's, Hull's, Cape's, State Arms, City Arms—were still remembered. Memories, too, of the patriotic rallies in its "long room" and of famous duels, routs, concerts, dancing assemblies, theatricals, and state dinners endeared it to the city's heart. Also, the stables were spacious—stalls for fifty horses.

"My name is Benjamin Franklin. I was born in Boston. I am a printer by profession, am traveling to Philadelphia, shall have to return at such a time, and have no news. Now, what can you give me for dinner?" Such was the way Franklin used to introduce himself, "as the first step for his tranquility," when he entered an inn. It forestalled an endless inquisition and brought "immediate attention."

If you followed these tactics at the City Tavern, and if you didn't have an eighteenth-century appetite, the landlord, Mr. Edward Bardin, would likely stagger you with his bill of fare. A first-class house provided the usual butcher-shop round of fowl and meats and, in addition, game that was no less plentiful and cheap—venison, bear steaks, wild turkey, wild ducks, wild pigeons—besides oysters, lobsters, terrapin, soups, plain and meat puddings, vegetables, and desserts.

While dinner was preparing, you looked over the appointments for the guests, mentally comparing them with the best you knew elsewhere. The City Tavern had, of course, its parlor for ladies, its taproom for gentlemen, with an almanac, the city directory, and the newspapers on file, its dining rooms and card-rooms. It boasted two "long rooms"—the name was borrowed from the Indian term for a council lodge—for public functions and monumental banquets. Perhaps Mr. Bardin, in competition with Mr. Francis, tried to catch your breath with an account of the last monumental dinner in *his* tavern, when, in celebration of the American victory and in honor of General Washington, his officers and the French minister, 120 guests consumed 135 bottles of Madeira, thirty-six bottles of port, sixty bottles of English beer, and thirty-six bowls of punch and broke eight decanters and sixty wineglasses.

For your personal needs you expected—and enjoyed—comfort without gadgets. Aside from the pump and its handle probably the only piece of machinery in the City Tavern was the spit driven by the draft of the kitchen chimney. The pump, moreover, did not supply drinking water, which was delivered daily in hogsheads from the Tea-Water well, up on Chatham Street. However, according to season, you were warmed or cooled by the two most effective systems ever devised by man. In winter the rooms were warmed by an open fire or a Franklin stove, and the air was circulated and humidified by a goodly number of chinks and cracks around the doors and windows. In summer the guests themselves were cooled and air-conditioned by the application of corn-leaf fans and iced rum punch.

When you retired for the night you called for a candle and, in winter, a warming pan. If you were delicate or suffered from cold feet, a hot brick wrapped in flannel or a lank jug of hot water was at your command. During the night you controlled the temperature as we do today, by piling the blankets on or off; and in the morning you got a pitcher of hot water by shouting for it— loud enough. Bathing was simple. When the occasion arose you ordered, a few hours in advance, a hot tub in your room. Or you walked to Henry Ludlam's bathhouse at the foot of Liberty Street and enjoyed fresh, salt, hot, or cold water for four shillings (50¢) admission.

In all likelihood, though, your stay at the City Tavern or any other large hostelry was brief. The rates were high—seven dollars a week for room and board; and the influx of strangers during the inaugural year taxed the capacity of the leading inns. M. Pecquet, a French innkeeper at Philadelphia, bragged that his tavern was "not like an American-run house"; that he did not put twelve beds in one room, but that every lodger had a room to himself. And he added: "At my place you don't have to get out of bed, *comme chez les américains,* to go to the window, for Jeanette never forgets the chamber pot." The chambermaids of New York were undoubtedly no less attentive; Philadelphia taverns, in fact, had a reputation for untidiness and for the multiplicity of bedfellows, not all of the human variety. Still, most visitors who intended to remain any length of time—congressmen and other government dignitaries—put up at boarding-houses.

Close at hand on Broadway, a moment's walk with your luggage, were the boardinghouses of Mrs. Sebring, Mrs. McCullen, the widow Culley, and the widow Bailey. But perhaps politics determined your choice. If you wanted to hear good sound conservative views at your breakfast table you put up at Mrs. Dunscomb's, No. 15 Great Dock (now Pearl) Street. There you enjoyed the company of Theodore Sedgwick, Fisher Ames, and other Massachusetts members of the new Congress. Besides hearing Mr. Ames decry pure democracy, with oratorical allusions to "Shays' mob," and expose the "extravagant hypothesis" of those who "considered the war with Britain as involving the fate of liberty," you might gather lucrative hints on how to speculate in paper money. The same advantages could be had at Mrs. Mary Daubigny's boardinghouse, No. 15 Wall Street, one of the best in the town, for gentlemen only, and patronized by a party of Southern congressmen. If, however, you were radical-minded and eager to know what farmers and backwoodsmen thought of Mr. Hamilton and his money schemes, you sought the company of Senator William Maclay, a gouty and rock-ribbed democrat from the Pennsylvania frontier above Harrisburg, who lodged at Vandalsen's, near Bear Market at the foot of Vesey Street, and, later in the year, with the Rev. Dr. Kunze, 24 Chatham Row.

If Mrs. Daubigny had no room, you could try Mrs. Cuyler's, Mrs. Sheldon's or Johannah Van Brugh Ursin's places, all on Wall Street in the heart of good society and right thinking and all within a stone's throw of Joseph Corre, the town's leading confectioner. Board and room cost four or five dollars a week (wood was extra at four dollars a cord and almost double for slow-burning hickory). The better-class houses set a table laden with seven to nine dishes and four sorts of liquor. And, as usual, people complained in the newspapers that the prices were too high, that unfair advantage was taken of congressmen, Federal jobhunters and tourists, and that the boardinghouse keepers were injuring themselves and the city.

Lodgings without board were naturally available, as a glance at newspapers told you. Peter Byvanck advertised "a front room and a bed room" at No. 75 King (Pine) Street, where "dieting may be had in the family" in the event the house were not rented. But you may sample these offers yourself:

> TWO ROOMS, to be Let, a front parlour, and bedroom, furnished or unfurnished, situated a few doors below the Federal building.—Enquire of the Printer. March 5.

There might be something to write home about in rooming a few doors from that balcony on Wall Street where, the following month, the first President of the United States took his oath of office.

> TO BE LET,
> And entered the 1st May next,
> A Genteel House,
> WITHIN five minutes walk of the Federal Building, fit for three or four gentlemen of Congress, with or without stabling for four horses, furnished or unfurnished. For further particulars, enquire of Mr. Huck, corner of Wall and Smith streets, or of the printer hereof. March 5.

Mr. Michael Huck kept a first-rate tavern and was already boarding a number of congressmen.

> To be Let,
> TWO elegant Front ROOMS, one on the first and the other on the second floor, and a BED ROOM, in a genteel new house. Enquire at No. 32, Beekman-street. April 20.

Beekman Street sounds dubious. This was getting close to the tan vats of Jacobus Roosevelt and the district known as Beekman's Swamp.

> TO BE LET, two handsome furnished Rooms, pleasantly situated, near the Coffee House. Enquire of the Printer. May 5.

To be near the Coffee House had, as you will shortly learn, many advantages.

And now, in conclusion, something ambitious:

> TO BE LET, a House in Cherry Street, No. 6, three stories high, seven fire places, a pump & cistern in the yard, a handsome garden, with a large yard. April 20.

But you are not prepared to lease and furnish an entire house? Too bad. Three days later George Washington moved into No. 3.

Possibly you came to New York on business. In that case you lodged as near as you could to the tavern that catered to men in your line. Cattle dealers and their allies in the leather, glue, tallow, wool, and meat trades gathered at the Bull's Head, 'way up Bowery Lane on the edge of town (near the present Canal Street). It was the last stop of the stages bound for Albany or Boston. The cattle market was close by, and it would pay you to ask the landlord, Richard Varian, to introduce you—in the taproom—to Butcher Henry Ashdor. Mr. Ashdor was an ingenious German immigrant who invented the "pernicious practice" of riding far out on the post road to meet the incoming drovers and bought the best of the stock ahead of his competitors and thus obliged them to purchase from him at an extra profit. Mr. Henry Ashdor was soon to own the Bull's Head. "And how is your brother Jacob doing?" "Jacob, he sells piano fortes and beaver pelts. The pianos are slow, but I think he'll do well with the furs." Jacob Astor will.

Mercantile and big business centered in the Merchants' Coffee House, kept by the Widow Bradford, at the corner of Wall and Water. Within its doors real estate, ships, cargoes, wholesale merchandise, and Negro slaves exchanged owners at "public vendue." Shares in Western land grants, insurance ventures, and factory mills or a flier in "Jersey money" were to be snapped up any noon hour. Where there are businessmen, lawyers will be found; and Alexander Hamilton, whose office was up the street at No. 58 Wall, or Aaron Burr, whose shingle hung at Nassau and Little Queen (Cedar), could always be consulted over a cup of Widow Bradford's coffee if it were properly sweetened. Besides the public prints, including London and Paris newspapers, a specialty of the Coffee House was its marine register. In it were entered the names of ships and captains on their arrival, the ports they hailed from, the vessels they "spoke" to on their voyage, and any other important item from the log— a valuable service to merchants and voyagers or whoever awaited news from the sea when Europe lay six to twelve weeks away.

The mere business of writing or receiving letters made it convenient for you to adopt a well-known tavern and live close to its door. A taproom, with its whale-oil lamps or fat candles, its blazing fire, and its other stimulants, was always a more cheerful place to write in than a boardinghouse bedroom; and something of its warmth would suffuse your letters home. In all history, though, there has never been a public pen a man could write with; and you will buy your own supply of quills from Francis Turner, quillmaker, at 93 Queen (Pearl) Street: cheap ones, four shillings (50¢) a hundred, and the finest, fifteen shillings. Any reputable tavern would seal and post the results.

Receiving mail in the days before there were letter carriers was an art. Here, again, a prominent tavern provided an address that usually worked, and the porter spared you from haunting the post office. Should you insist, however, upon attending to your mail personally, be advised that up till October 5 of '89 the post office was at No. 8 Wall Street, William Bedlow, postmaster; after this date it was moved to the house of the new postmaster, Sebastian Bauman, at Broadway and Crown (Liberty) Street; and a howl was raised against its remote location. For the greater part of the year Philadelphia and Southern mail arrived three days a week at 3:00 P.M. and departed on another three days at 10:00 P.M. Boston and other Eastern mail arrived the same number of days at 7:00 P.M. and closed at 8:00 P.M.

Postage was enormous—ten cents a single letter sheet from New York to Philadelphia, and thirty-three cents to Savannah.

Fortunately there were only seventy-five post offices in the whole country on which to spend your money—six in all New Jersey. Fortunately, too, you could run a charge account with Postmaster Bedlow, and you had months to pay. This may help explain why in the last quarter of 1789 the total receipts of the New York City Post Office were $1,067.08. And with the best part of tavern life still to be tasted, you would waste, more precious than money, your hours—and they could seem endless—waiting at Mr. Bedlow's for the Boston post rider who was himself undergoing repairs in some taproom beyond Kingsbridge.

After all, a tavern was chiefly a place to eat and drink in. You have already learned something of the substantial meals served at the City Tavern. M. Brissot is more explicit. A good American table provided "hot and cold punch before dinner, excellent beef or mutton, fish, vegetables of all kinds, Madeira or Spanish wines, and, in summer, claret." Spruce beer and cider, though, took the lead over wine. A porter brewed near Philadelphia was "as good as England's best," and there were "delicious cheeses which rivalled Chester and Roquefort." Desserts included ice creams, fool's trifles, floating islands, whipped syllabubs, and "twenty sorts of tarts." Still there were drawbacks. The milk— which M. Brissot was amazed to see "drunk in large quantities"— tasted of garlic, owing to the prevalence of this weed on Long Island. Senator Lee of Virginia complained of the loaf sugar: it was mixed with lime and other vile adulterants; he had "broken a spoon trying to dissolve it."

The local cuisine was famous for its turtle soup and its oysters. In summer turtle feasts were held at the country houses up the East River; and, as every participant knew, while water may be the native, Madeira was the divine predestined element of a turtle. Oysters and clams abounded in the waters surrounding the city. They had been the source of wampum, the currency of the original inhabitants, whose chief mint was Oyster Bay. And in the eighteenth century they were a staple food, to be had for the mere digging, of the common people or such as could not afford six cents a pound for beef. In name, at least, one of America's most characteristic dishes originated on Manhattan; *sickquatash* the Indians called their mixture of corn and beans, which Sir Henry Hudson said they stored in quantities "sufficient to fill three ships."

A serious dinner, carefully ordered in advance, meant a cargo with deep draught and took a lot of liquid to keep afloat. Brillat-Savarin, who lived in New York during the 1790s, describes the course of such a meal with two Englishmen at Little's Porter House. The solids consisted of an enormous roast beef, a turkey *cuit dans son jus,* vegetables, salad, tarts, buttered toast, cheese, and nuts. The liquids began with claret. After the claret came port. After port, Madeira "at which we stuck a long time." After the wines came rum, brandy, and whisky—with song. After the straight spirits, Michael Little, the landlord himself, brought in a bowl of punch "sufficient for forty persons." Finally the Englishmen, singing "Rule, Britannia" to the last, foundered beneath the table; and M. Brillat-Savarin attributed his victory to "eating a quantity of bitter almonds, recommended for such occasions."

It would be hopeless for you to undertake a comprehensive tavern-crawl of the city. In the directory of 1789, 169 taverns and public houses appeared; but the directory must have ignored the common run of grogshops and ginmills, for there were 330 licensed drinking places—more than one to every hundred inhabitants. It should suffice you to know where to find the best resorts and the "hot spots." Little's Porter House, at No. 56 Pine Street, was one. This was the "Friary" or rendezvous of the Black Friars, the only society in town which did not hide its intention of having a good time under a charitable or political cloak. If you were of the right sort, an introduction by the "Father" or by the secretary, John Fisher, would no doubt enable you to procure a ticket to one of its biweekly "festivals."

Captain Aaron Aorson's tavern at Nassau and George (now Spruce) was another. That is, if you didn't tire of hearing the captain talk about the war and tell how, fighting at his side,

Montgomery dropped dead, pierced with three bullets, and the storming of Quebec failed and Canada was still lost to the States. John Simmons' huge bulk loomed Falstaffian behind the service bar of his tavern at Nassau and Wall. You would be sure to find him there, because when he did finally leave they had to tear down the wall between the door and window to allow room for the passage of the coffin. At Nassau and Ann streets was Jonathan Pearsee's taproom, and at Nassau and John streets was John Battin's; in fact, you did very well on Nassau. Then there was Rawson's, at No. 82 Water Street, good for a quick glass between watching the auction sales which centered in that neighborhood. And there was no need for slighting the City Tavern, the Merchants' Coffee House, Sam Fraunces, John Francis, late of "The True American," or Michael Huck, already mentioned. After a bracing walk past the open lots out Broadway to Murray Street—across from the Bridewell, Poorhouse (or Almshouse) and Prison—you arrived at the sign of the Two Friendly Brothers, better known as Montagnie's Gardens, where it would be time for you to quit or begin ordering bitter almonds.

On this pilgrimage you oiled your way with potions as varied, outlandish, and prevalent as modern cocktails. Rum was the preferred base. Mimbo—generally called Mim—was rum and loaf sugar and occasionally water. Calibogus—Bogus for short—was rum and beer. Black-strap—Josiah Quincy said he wished the recipe for it reposed among the lost arts—was made principally of rum, molasses, and herbs. Casks of this "most outrageous of all detestable American drinks" had salt fish hanging alongside, at once to kill the flavor and to provoke an encore.

Punch was the most popular of elegant drinks, the kind Mr. Quincy could not scorn. Varying with its contents, it brandished as many names—personal, geographic, nonsensical, and romantic —as our cocktails. Five ingredients were fundamental: spirits, fruit juice, sugar, spice, and water—hot or cold. The spirits were commonly rum or brandy or both. The lemon, orange, and lime juice—*sourings*—as well as pineapple juice were imported in casks and demijohns. *Shrub*, the sweetened juices sometimes already mixed with rum, landed in hogsheads. The sugar was brown muscovado for light purses and double-refined loaf for discriminating palates. In New York it was healthier and quite as orthodox to use boiled tea instead of water. New Yorkers also liked to substitute arrack for rum; and if you liked it too, you called for a Rack punch. A good-natured landlord might give you his recipe, but you may as well be forewarned with the following standard: "Sugar, twelve tolerable lumps; hot water, one pint; lemons, two, juice and peel; old Jamaica rum, two gills [half a pint]; brandy, one gill; porter, half a gill; arrack, a dash." Add the ingredients in the order named.* Stir continuously and, if you pleased, hard enough to make the drink foam. One last essential, which holds true for all cookery: "A man can never make good punch unless he is convinced that no man breathing can make better."

Flip shared the popularity of punch, and if you came from New England you certainly demanded it. Whereupon a quart-size pewter mug or earthen pitcher was two-thirds filled with strong beer sweetened with sugar or dried pumpkin. To this was added a quarter-pint of rum. Then a red-hot poker, called a loggerhead, was plunged and stirred into the brew which, if possible, you drank while it foamed and mantled. A few spoonfuls of a batter made of cream, eggs, and sugar gave the flip, under the name "Bellows-top," something of the character of a Tom-and-Jerry.

Other congenial drams which have survived this last century and a half—toddy, grog, sling, eggnog—need no gloss. Whisky was used in the South, which had already elaborated the julep; but it had hardly as yet come over the Alleghenies to New York. Cherry bounce—cherry brandy with sugar—held the field.

*This should be obvious. As an Irish scientist long ago observed, if you put in the spirits first, every added drop of water worsens the drink; whereas, if you begin with the water, every drop of liquor you pour makes it better and better.

Of wines—the true rival to punch—Madeira was king. But all the heavy or fortified wines of Spain, Portugal, and the Azores were to be found on any decent wine list. Sherry, vidonia, red and white port, Lisbon, Malaga, Teneriffe, Fayal, London Particular (Madeira), Old Mountain, and Old Malvosio filled the tavern cellars with pipes, butts, hogsheads, and quarter-casks; and what pleasanter task than to order the potboy to fetch you a pitcher and pour it before the beads melted into the smoky air! If you may believe the advertisement of José Roiz Silva, a pillar of the newly opened Catholic church, his white port of '77 was "of a superior quality to any ever imported to this country." Light wine—claret, red Catalonia, tent, tentillia—lacked demand—except in summer when, diluted with lemon water, spiced, and cooled, it was sipped by ladies and young sprouts under the name of sangaree. Still Aaron Burr set great store by tent, a Spanish claret, and "despaired" of getting the genuine article. But when spring comes, Jefferson will bring some from abroad.

London porter, three and a half dozen bottles to the hamper, stood between the butts and pipes of a good tavern cellar, and imported draught porter in barrels. Appleby & Matlack, whose brewery lay "nearly opposite the Tea-Water pump," satisfied cheaper tastes in local ale and in "Spruce, Table, and Ship. . . ."

But we are not chronicling small beer.

CHAPTER III

The City on Show

For a session of six months," said grouchy Senator Maclay of Pennsylvania, "I have passed the threshold of no citizen of New York. I was never in so inhospitable a place." Yet not a month later, when he had finished packing his baggage, ready, together with Congress, to leave for good, he wrote in his diary: "The allurements of New York are more than ten to two compared with Philadelphia." It is idle to try to discover why the senator changed his mind. Certainly neither the size nor the looks of the town, smaller and drabber than the Quaker capital, were responsible. Nor had the doors of society opened to him. He left as he came—and as millions of its residents have felt since —a stranger. It could hardly have been "the fragrant odours from the apple orchards and buckwheat fields" which, for a week or two, blew in from the Jersey shore, about the only pleasant smell that ever greeted the nostrils of a native. All we can be sure of is that even in the crudities of its awkward age, untidy and gangling, the city possessed what no words can convey and what we still call the lure of New York.

In truth the New York of 1789 had little tangible to brag about. Its 30,000 inhabitants ranked it second for size in the country. Philadelphia, the largest city, numbered perhaps 40,000, while Boston trailed third with about 16,000. But New York was already cosmopolitan. Many of the peoples that were to make it great were, in rubbing shoulders, rubbing away the provincialism and smugness that survived, for example, in New England.

The Dutch were still going strong, even if they had long ceased to rule. Shop signs were frequently in Dutch; in Bear Market, the resort of the farmers from Jersey, a knowledge of the language was almost indispensable; and it was to resound for years to come in the pulpits of the Collegiate Church. One half the aldermen elected in the fall of '89 had Dutch names. Jews, English, French, Germans, Scotch, and Irish had moved in on the Dutch—roughly in the order cited, beginning with the Jews in 1654; and there was a sprinkling of Welsh, Poles, Portuguese, and West Indians. Trade, persecution, poverty, and, lately, the Revolutionary War had brought them, as all subsequent immigrants, through the Narrows into a new and wider life. Hardly to be classed as an immigrant, one out of every fourteen New Yorkers was a Negro slave. Bond and free, the Negroes comprised about one tenth of the population. Among these multiple breeds the English predominated; but down almost any business street the names of the tradesmen or artisans—James Roosevelt, Isaac Levy, Baptiste Gilliaux, Christopher Baehr, Collin M'Gregor, William Mooney, John Jones, Richard Cusack, David Cation, Francis Panton, José Roiz Silva—read like an all-American football team.

Sight-seeing did not need to take long. There wasn't far to go or much for a sophisticated eye to see. A mile above the Battery, Broadway ran into open fields, which were bounded by swamps and the oozing outlets of the Collect Pond. On the East Side a stroll of little more than a mile along the present Pearl and Cherry streets ended in Mr. Rutger's farm and more swamp. Up the center of Manhattan, less than a mile from Wall Street, the Bull's Head tavern and the neighboring slaughterhouse marked the beginning of rural life. Even allowing for the miserable condition of the streets and reckoning in the hills, a half-hour was the limit of a walk in any one direction.

The scars of recent disasters were visible at every turn. Two major fires—one in 1776, four days after the British seizure, and another in 1778—had swept the lower end of the town and

destroyed a quarter of the city's habitations. When the redcoats
marched in, the rebel half of the populace fled; and there was no
need to repair or rebuild. During the seven years of British
occupation trade was nearly at a standstill, the wharves crumbled
with disuse, the abandoned homes of the patriots rotted with
neglect, and on the outskirts weed and bramble invaded gardens,
yards, and lanes. The monuments of the city succumbed to fire
or decay: Fort George, which lorded over the Battery, was
dilapidated; of all the leading churches, only St. Paul's was un-
scathed. Finally, when the exiles flocked home upon the return
of peace and began to clear the wreckage, they fell victim to that
usual aftermath of war, a business depression.

However, by 1788 things took a sharp turn for the better.
The release of energy was terrific. Building boomed. New streets
pushed into the fields, old streets had their faces lifted, bulkheads
and fills wrested fresh land from the rivers and the sea. "What
changes within a few weeks!" exclaimed M. Brissot during that
summer. "The North River is thrust back 200 feet by a sort of
dike made of piles, logs, and stones. Everywhere houses are
going up and new streets opened. Everywhere you see workmen
cutting or filling the ground, paving the streets, and erecting
houses and public buildings." The noise of hammer and saw,
pickaxe and shovel, sledge and derrick, cart and barrow echoed
the hubbub of commerce. Touring the town in '89 was therefore
far from dull. Quaint antiquity—a gabled façade of old Holland
brick—peeped out between gutted ruins and the very latest thing
in English stoops.

But the tour, however short, would not be hurried; for,
wherever you went, there was much to engage the eyes—and feet.
For the purposes of transit the streets could be divided into paved,
being paved, and never paved. It was hard to judge which were
worst. In the few that were paved, the two-foot sidewalks were
interrupted by trees, pumps, hitching posts, stairs, stoops, open
gates, refuse piles, and low projecting bay windows; the roadway
slanted from the curbs to a central sunken gutter clogged with

sewage and filth, and its ancient cobblestones sprawled in anything but a sweet disorder. Benjamin Franklin claimed that over
in Philadelphia, with its smooth streets, you could always spot
a New Yorker by the way he shuffled. When Congress decided
to abandon New York, rhymester Freneau immediately thought
of the paving program:

> Our streets that were just in a way to look clever
> Will now be neglected and nasty as ever,
> Again we must fret at the Dutchified gutters
> And pebble-stone pavements that wear out our trotters.

Indeed, the number of streets undergoing improvement was
enough to daunt a pedestrian.* After visiting the President down
on Cherry Street, Senator Maclay complained: "The day was
hot, I was lame, and the streets were ripped up a great part of
the way"—making, all together, "a journey of consequence."

The remainder of the streets, the unpaved and the virgin, which
meant the majority, were in due season a succession of mudholes,
ice floes, and dust bowls. For "foot passengers" and their clothing
there was some mitigation in an ordinance which forbade carters,
draymen, and water carriers to drive faster than a walk—if it
was obeyed. The inhabitants of Mulberry and Catherine streets
—caught between a hill, the Collect Pond, and a swamp—begged
for relief from the floods that came "whenever it rains" and
suggested that matters be regulated "so as to Carry the Water
through Cross Street." Touchy New Yorkers might protest that
these streets were in the heart of the slums, so what could one
expect? But the Murray Street folks were admittedly a cut
higher in class; and yet, disregarding grammar and spelling in

---

*Commissioner Robert Moses might be interested to know that in 1789 a
list of the streets ordered paved or being paved would include, wholly or
partly, Greenwich, Vesey, Partition (Fulton), Church, Barclay, Cortlandt,
Lumber (New Church) streets and Oyster Pasty Lane (Exchange St.) on
the west side, and Queen (Pearl), Water, Little Dock (also Water), Front,
William, Chatham streets and Hanover Square on the east; and that his
ancestor, Isaac Moses of 21 Wall St., had nothing to do with the matter
except to pay his taxes.

their indignation, they too spluttered to the authorities: "This Street is hills and Vallies, in rainy weather parts of it are over the shoes in mud, the lower part is washed into such Hollows that it is not passable with Carts and dangerous for foot Passengers after dusk, other parts of the Street is higher than there lower floors by which means there property is Injured." Nor were passengers in sedan chairs spared these dangers, as witness the nasty throw Senator Pierce Butler received, along with Congressman Huger; two weeks later, Maclay reports, the senator was still lame.

"A Number of Citizens" told the newspapers what they thought of "two such gentell, delicate, and sweet smelling avenues" as Stone Street and Petticoat Lane, just off the Battery. The delicacy and perfume in question were prevalent. They arose from circumstances which demanded mention and then consignment to the background where, ignored by the average citizen, they pervaded the entire scene. In Edinburgh, Boswell tells us, the householders used to throw it out of the windows. New Yorkers spared the passers-by this hazard: the well-to-do had Negro slaves, tubs on their heads, bear it away nights; but the commonalty dumped it in the gutters, together with the garbage, and trusted to sun, rain, wind, and the hogs. "Corporation Pudding" the cynical called it. The hogs thrived. There were twenty thousand of them on the streets as late as 1817, and they were still rooting at large in 1825. Though occasionally an irate citizen, with no appreciation of the sanitary service rendered, wrote a satire in the press, and from time to time the Common Council passed stringent bans, there was nothing the porkers needed to fear except the strong competition of the dogs and goats.*

*The roving livestock presented an insoluble problem in higher sanitation. The New York *Journal* of March 26, 1789, published, for example, an accusation that in Cortlandt Street—"the key to the city"—the pigs were a nuisance. Some persons defended them by saying that "they kept the streets clean." Others, however, claimed "they only served to scatter the dirt and rubbish already collected in heaps." Hogs or heaps seemed to be the alternatives.

Barking dogs chasing squealing pigs dodging between bleating goats were only part of the choral accompaniment to street life. At the crack of dawn the cry of "Milk, ho!" and "Milk, come!" rang through the town. The milk man—it was often a maid—carried two buckets suspended from a yoke and made the rounds after a night's walk and row from Long Island or Jersey. Next came the chimney sweeps, wiry Negro boys crying "Sweep, ho! Sweep, ho! from the bottom to the top without a ladder or a rope, sweep ho!" Then the knife grinders, lamp menders, orange girls, Yankee notion hawkers, ragmen, and wood vendors swelled the chorus. The latter added instrumental notes of their own by sawing and chopping the wood at the customer's door. When the day's business got into swing, a traffic blockage—common enough in the narrow streets—evoked a caroling of profanity worth increasing the jam to hear.

The general racket was so great that chains were stretched before the Merchants' Exchange on Broad Street, where the courts met, in order that the judges might hear themselves. More chains ringed off Front Street from the Fly Market. Chains were hung before Washington's house during the President's illness. On Wall Street the rumble of traffic drowned the oratory of Congress. "Such a noise," said Senator Maclay, "I was not master of one sentence of it." The windows were ordered closed, and Senator Robert Morris had to have the matter repeated. Even funerals added to the din. The tolling of church bells during burial processions and services—frequent in that summer of '89, when twenty persons succumbed to the heat in one week—exasperated one sufferer to printed protest. "When a usurer whose whole life has been a scene of extortion; when an old maid whose life has been devoured with spleen; when an old bachelor whose putrid carcase has long offended the senses, dies," he demanded, "must their souls be rung to eternity with peals of bell-metal thunder?" Apparently his ill-tempered outburst was due to more than the heat, for the Common Council soon put a muffler on the clappers. The nights at least were quiet; the watchmen dozed in their boxes, and Negroes and tubs made their silent rounds.

Wall Street was the show street of the town; and it was there you would go first, to see and be seen. There, as elsewhere, church, tavern, shop, and residence elbowed one another in a way to make a modern realtor stare. Street numbers were likewise haphazard. They began, skipped, ended, and duplicated themselves anyhow: so, if you were looking for Samuel Otis, secretary of the Senate, who lived at No. 5, it wouldn't help to know that John Stephen's livery stable was No. 4. Alexander Hamilton at No. 58 might and might not be a neighbor of Joe Mitchell the shoemaker at No. 62. But whomever you wished to locate among the five boardinghouses, five auctioneers, five taverns, five grocers, two confectioners, two tailors, seven attorneys (including the Attorney General), or the sundry cobblers, farriers, tobacconists, wigmakers, hatters, haberdashers, upholsterers, and fashionable residents, the man to ask was Dan McCormick.

Daniel McCormick was well known as a merchant, a director of the Bank of New York, an alderman, and a bachelor. Any fair day he could be found sunning on his front stoop, at No. 39, surrounded by "his cronies and his toadies, the latter of whom generally stayed for dinner." Without stirring from his seat he knew every big deal transacted in the Merchants' Coffee House at the Water end of the street, and every time—with a guess why—Mr. John Jay called on Mynheer Van Berckel, the minister from Holland, at the Broadway end. He noted every beau—"There's young Remsen again, Jay's secretary. . . . *That* one? Don't you know Sir John Temple?"—who knocked at No. 50, to pay court to the young misses White, "so gay and fashionable, so charming in conversation, with such elegant figures." Had he wished, when he talked to Francis Childs—who published the *Daily Advertiser* a couple of blocks down—half the social ears in town would have burned.

Little went on in Federal Hall without his comment, if not his knowledge. And when Congress dismissed for the day, and statesmen and socialites took their Wall Street airing, Mr. McCormick and his cronies had a word about each. Let the Secretary of War lumber past that observatory stoop, and the latest quip would be whispered concerning General Knox's unfortunate bulk—"Mrs. John Adams' daughter says 'he is not half so fat as he was'; she means before he wore stays." And when chubby John Adams himself strutted by "like a monkey just put into breeches," the stoop recalled how Senator Izard proposed that the Vice-President be titled "His Rotundity."

It was gay, this parade of "the rich, the well-born, and the able"—to use Mr. Adams' words. Amid the swish of hooped skirts, the flash of powdered hair, and the clatter of a coach, perhaps Mr. Adams felt it was historic.

The "court end" of town had moved up from Queen to Wall, and it was edging into Broadway. But as yet this avenue was too broad for its own good. With much pains the expanse of pavement was pushed from the Battery to Vesey Street; but the low houses, some of them jerry-built and frame, many of them retired behind trees and yards, gave it an empty and suburban look. The illusion was enhanced by the ridge on which it ran; it was the highest street in town and "commanded," said Noah Webster, "a delightful prospect of the Hudson" and the Jersey hills. The Kennedy mansion, at the corner of Bowling Green, which escaped the fire of '76 and now housed the Spanish minister, Don Diego de Gardoqui; the McComb mansion, which next year was to house the President; the City Tavern, the ruins of Trinity, and the staid beauty of St. Paul's exhausted its architectural sights. For animated show pieces, however, there were the French envoy, Count de Moustier, and his relative with her pet pickaninny and pet monkey; living opposite him, Senator "Rafe" Izard of South Carolina and his wife, the handsome and witty De Lancey girl; General Knox, at No. 4, and his wife who matched him in bulk—her waist "at least as large as three" of Mrs. Adams'; the John Jays, at No. 133, Mr. Jay "plain in his dress and manners," and Mrs. Jay who dressed "gaily and showily"; Van Berckel, the Dutch minister, at the corner of Wall, "gaudy as a peacock"—all indubitably rich, well born, or able.

Another animated show was the "Old Swago" or Oswego Market, at the corner of Maiden Lane, where ladies in taffeta bought vegetables from Dutch farm wives in linsey-woolsey. A familiar figure, probably better known to the townspeople than Mrs. Izard or Mrs. Jay, was an old *vrow* from Bergen, who rivaled Mrs. Henry Knox for amplitude and who specialized in coffee and crullers; the butcher boys welcomed her morning arrival with the cry, "Here comes the big doughnut!" Earlier yet in the morning pampered cows from the stables of the rich on Wall and Queen streets sauntered up Broadway to the succulent Lispenard meadows—"Lepner's meadows"—which lay to the west of the Stone Bridge (at the present Canal Street). And sunset glowed upon these same cows ambling homeward down Broadway, their bells sounding a gentle vespers.

Despite its hills and dust and desolate width Broadway had its throngs, for it led from one popular resort of the townsfolk to another. At its lower end Bowling Green and the Battery were, to be sure, rather a mess. Fort George, never completed, was disintegrating. The pedestal which once flaunted the statue of George III was bare. The lawns were unkempt. The hulk of the good ship *Hamilton,* left over from the Federalists' celebration of the preceding year, looked ready for the junkman. Excavators, masons, engineers, and carts overran the waterfront in works of improvement. Nevertheless the sound and smell of the sea were there, the sails danced in the harbor breezes, and Washington made it his favorite promenade.

Northward, Broadway led to the Fields (now City Hall Park), enclosed with a wooden fence. Quite aside from the Liberty Boys and their patriotic antics, this civic center was much admired for its Almshouse, Bridewell, Debtors' Jail, and its Gallows. The latter was built to look like a gaudily painted Chinese pagoda. During 1789 it provided the spectacle of ten executions;

none, incidentally, for any crime more serious than burglary. October 23 was the gala performance—five hangings at a go. Close to the main pagoda side shows were offered by the whipping post and the stocks.

Across the street, or rather the dirt road, from these diversions stood the city hospital and a number of mead houses and tea gardens, including Montagnie's Two Friendly Brothers and culminating in Ranelagh. British visitors no doubt sniffed at New York's efforts to reproduce the giddy and elegant Ranelagh of London—"What a contrast," sighed M. Brissot, "to English gardens!"—but, for that matter, what was Wall compared to Fleet Street?

A bit farther north, after its dip to the Stone Bridge, the road that has since become Broadway mounted Buncker Hill, a choice spot for picnics and duels. To the south, a hundred feet below, Collect or Fresh Water Pond sparkled in the sun. Its reeds and ripples covered the seventy acres roughly centering around the present Tombs prison; and a great fuss was made over its fish, wild fowl, and unfathomable depths. The name Collect may have been derived from Kalch Hoek, meaning "Shell Point" in Dutch and indicating that the Manhattan Indians ran a kitchen midden and wampum mint on its shores. But *Kolk* is a common term in Holland for the enclosed portion of a canal; and it is notorious that the first Dutch settlers, who tried to dig a canal in Broad Street, were pathetically homesick for the sedative smells of old Amsterdam.

In winter the town used the Collect for a skating rink and hockey field. Hundreds of spectators—so one of them relates—covered the hillside which "rose like an amphitheatre, tier on tier" to Broadway, watching the skaters drive a ball with a "hurly." By '89 fish and wild duck had grown scarce, and in summer the pond served principally as a free public laundry. "It's like fair day with whites and blacks washing their clothes, blankets, and things too numerous to mention; all their sudds and filth are emptied into this pond, besides dead dogs, cats, etc.

thrown in daily" and, most odious of all, "many buckets" which should, of course, have been decently dumped in the streets.

On the east and south shores, behind the washerwomen, stretched industrial New York; a few tanneries and iron furnaces, a pottery, a brewery, and a "rope walk," the latter a length of ground devoted to weaving cable and ship's rigging. The combined assault of the washerwomen and the industrial revolution upon the one natural beauty spot of the city had the inevitable result. In a short while the citizens changed the name of the pond to Collick. Decades were to pass before the "stinking mud hole" was filled in and the Tombs reared as its no less unsavory monument.

Unsavory, too, was the district beginning east of the pond, across Chatham Square, and extending to the river. Here, in the swamps surrounding and percolating through Roosevelt, Bancker, Oliver, Catherine, and Rutgers streets (named after their well-born landlords), lived a portion of the population that was neither well born nor rich, and probably not able. The postwar building boom had failed to touch these slums, which made up a good part of Montgomerie Ward. It was sometimes called the Out Ward, though Down-and-Out would have been more appropriate. Another portion of the low-born and unable lived in Canvass Town—Topsail Town—the burnt region between Broad and the East River. Public-health committees talked about its "deep damp cellars" used as sailors' boardinghouses and grogshops. Grand juries talked about its "innumerable receptacles for the vicious and the abandoned," and the sheriff busied himself closing some of the more disreputable resorts. The press talked about "the abode of dissolute characters and scene of frequent disorders." What all of them meant was that at least one New Yorker out of every four was damnably poor and lived in unseemly squalor.

Except for the factories around the Collect and the shipping along the East River, business had no special district of its own. Retail stores, to be sure, dotted Nassau and William streets and were numerous on Pearl, Water, and Hanover Square. The great auctioneers—commission merchants we would call them today—congregated around the Coffee House at Wall and Water; and the block was known as Merchants' Promenade and Auctioneers' Row. The tallest secular building in town was the sugarhouse on Liberty Street, six stories high. Its rival was William Rhinelander's sugar refinery on King George (William) Street, four stories and a loft; and Mr. Rhinelander, the sugar boiler himself, lived next door at No. 21. Many men of affairs, in fact, lived above or close by their office, factory, or shop. But the pleasure of shopping should not be spoiled by this business of sight-seeing, and it will be deferred to another day.

Besides, it is growing late. The cows must be coming home down Broadway; it is time for the watchmen to don their varnished hats and march to their posts, for the lamplighters to fumble with their tinderboxes, and for a weary tourist to go to supper and bed. It is safer, too. The rare street lamps are lit only on moonless nights—that is, unless it rains, when of course nobody will be abroad—and a pump handle or a pig is something to remember if you hit it in the dark.

CHAPTER IV

Fourteen Miles Round

THE fairest sight New York had to offer was the island on which it stood. "The rides in the neighborhood of the city," Governor Drayton of South Carolina wrote home, "are for miles beautiful —every elevation of ground presenting some handsome country seat—with what pleasure have I often viewed them." If you wished to partake of the governor's pleasure, you would some bright morning hire a saddle horse—or, if there were friends to share the expense, a carriage—and set out to see the rural delights of Manhattan.

Livery stables centered around Wall Street, below the Coffee House and near the horse market. A saddle horse was liable to cost a stranger two shillings (25¢) an hour; and, if you were as Scotch as Senator Maclay, you might refuse to pay this "extravagant" price and vainly shop away the day for something cheaper. The canny thing to do, as Maclay discovered, was to let your landlord hire one for you at a dollar a day, even though it proved to be a plug "not worth more than seven pounds [$17.50]." A *good* horse, if you had a mind to buy one, cost thirty guineas, or about $140.

James Hearn's hackney stand, the first in town, was in front of the Coffee House; but if you preferred to patronize an advertised concern, you hired a carriage from the Warner brothers, whose stable was at No. 9 Great George. They provided a choice of coaches, phaetons, and sulkies. To go to the two-mile stone and around west by Cummings' Florida Gardens cost six shillings (75¢) for the party and two shillings an hour waiting time (while you sampled the tea and punch). The top prices were thirty-eight shillings to Harlem and forty shillings ($5.00) to Kingsbridge for the day. But this would be tiring.

For the most enjoyable excursion you had merely to tell the coachman you wanted to do "the fourteen miles round." He would understand that you wished to take the customary drive of the President. On a pleasant day you might indeed have the luck to pass General Washington en route, together with Mrs. Washington and the children. He would be easy to recognize, though it is doubtful if you would catch him riding along country roads in his imported canary-colored state coach, shaped like a half-pumpkin, ornamented with cupids, festoons, and flowers, emblazoned with the family coat of arms, and drawn by four white horses. After all, even if postage stamps were not yet invented, Americans in 1789 knew what he looked like.

In any case you will begin following the presidential dust by taking the only highway that leaves town and goes anywhere —the Post Road. (The one other road leaving town is a continuation of Greenwich Street which ends at Greenwich Village— with some detouring we'll get you back that way.)

The first delay will be met on Chatham Street (Park Row). The water carts laden with hogsheads and lined up before the Tea-Water pump are a nuisance to traffic. Swinging into Bowery Lane you may note, or the driver will point out with an appreciative wink, the site of the first kissing bridge over Old Wreck Brook. Not a block beyond, at Oliver Street (off Chatham Square), you will pass the "Jews' Burial Ground," its stones already overshadowed by the growing city. The last traffic hazard is encountered at the end of the first mile, where you may chance upon an unruly herd of cattle or a jam of butcher wagons by the Bull's Head tavern.

A mile farther Peter Stuyvesant's farm stretches away to the right. His old *Bouwerie* house, which was burnt during the Revolution, is a ruin; but two other Stuyvesant houses and the

famous pear orchard, planted a century and a half before, invite
a halt for contemplation and refreshment. Luckily the Dog and
Duck tavern is close by, "at the two mile stone"—so runs its
advertisement—and with "the best bed of asparagus on the
island."

No lover of gardens, vegetable or flower, failed to stop at
Baron Poelnitz' farm. Its twenty-two and a half acres, compris-
ing the old "Minto" place, lay just south of what is today Union
Square. Senator Maclay often "took a long walk to the gardens
of a Dutchman who lives beyond the Bowery" in order to view
"the harmless and silent beauties of his garden." Baron Frederick
Charles Hans Bruno Poelnitz was not a Dutchman and probably
not a baron. But Maclay found him "sensible and well-informed"
and possessed of more agricultural machinery than he had ever
before seen. It was annoying to the democratic senator that the
baron was "disrespectfully spoken of," but this was probably due
to "the force of our old habits, derived from the English, who
seldom speak well of a foreigner."

Washington was likewise favorably impressed by the baron
and his machinery. He admired the cultivation of madder, woad,
and "several kinds of artificial grass." He admired the Winlaw
threshing machine. He liked the way Baron Poelnitz himself
held and guided several of the experimental plows. He was
especially taken with a gadget of the baron's invention, which
measured the force a plow required for use in any given soil.
And he ordered a "Horse-Hoe," made on the baron's specifica-
tions, to be sent to Mount Vernon. However, Poelnitz apparently
could not live on the admiration of the discerning or he grew
tired of the disrespectful speech of the local gentry, for this year
of '89 he offered his farm for sale.*

Where Madison Square stands today, the road forked. To
the left Bloomingdale Road followed something like the course

*Next year he found a purchaser, Robert R. Randall, who bought it for
$12,500 and, a decade later, bequeathed it to a sailors' home. More lucrative
than woad or artificial grasses, the rent which the ground produces still sup-
ports Sailors' Snug Harbor.

of modern Broadway. To the right the Post Road meandered northward between undreamed-of Fourth and Second avenues; and since the best taverns lay that way, the driver would need no nod to follow it. You skirted the east slope of Murray Hill and admired, on its summit, the country seat of Robert Murray, where in '76 Mrs. Murray's wit and Mr. Murray's wine saved General Putnam's army from destruction. A bit farther (Second Avenue and Thirty-fifth Street) you passed the Kip house, built in 1655 and one of the oldest on the island. In less than another mile you caught sight of the Beekman house dominating Beekman Hill (First Avenue and Fiftieth Street). If you relished the pathos of history, you drove over to see the greenhouse where Nathan Hale was tried as a spy and Major André set forth on a trip that brought him a similar trial in far-off Tappan. For General Washington this detour—as he would explain to his children—meant, not history, but personal grief. The five-mile stone (Third Avenue and Seventy-seventh Street) heralded the one kissing bridge that was in active service; and if you had no use or occasion for it in your party, it was your loss. You could console yourself at either Adamson's or the Dove tavern.

For the next two miles your course shifted toward the site of Central Park. Just inside the park, which naturally you could not distinguish from outside, you left the Post Road—regretting that there was no time to see the rugged splendor of McGown's Pass or the spires of Harlem beyond—and struck west up and down a cross lane that led to the Bloomingdale Road (near present Broadway and Ninety-fourth Street).

Turning south and homeward, you passed almost immediately the Apthorp mansion, headquarters of every redcoat general from Howe to Cornwallis. Washington dined there in '76—on his way out as the British were coming in.

The return drive down Broadway-to-be was enlivened by a succession of those "handsome country seats" that delighted the South Carolina governor—Colonel Livingston's Oak Villa, the Somerindyke house, General Striker's mansion; but the coachman will give you their names and pedigrees. No drive, however, was complete without a glimpse of Richmond Hill, in 1789 the home of Vice-President Adams. It will mean an extra mile or two; but, taking Senator Maclay's hint, you are presumably paying by the day.

Immediately south of the junction of the Bloomingdale and Post roads you will therefore turn west and enter Love Lane (Twenty-first Street at Broadway). This pleasant-sounding lane led to Captain Clarke's country house, which he called Chelsea and which his widow, an ardent Tory who once won an apology from Washington, still graced. But you will turn off south again on Fitzroy Road (between Seventh and Eighth avenues) and then, driving down Great Kiln Road (at Fourteenth Street), will soon find yourself in the village of Greenwich. Anyone hanging about the Old Grapevine tavern will direct you to Richmond Hill.*

After walking through the estate and, like Senator Maclay, "sitting in the shade," you will probably agree with the opinion of its tenant. Mrs. John Adams thought about her place much as all city folk do the first year they occupy a country seat. She wrote:

> The house in which we reside is situated on a hill, the avenue to which is interspersed with forest trees, under which a shrubbery rather too luxuriant and wild has taken shelter [the familiar complaint of a tenant]. . . . In front of the house, the noble Hudson rolls his majestic waves, bearing upon his bosom innumerable small vessels. On the right hand, an extensive plain presents us with a view of fields covered with verdure, and pastures full of cattle. On the left, the city opens upon us, intercepted only by clumps of trees and some rising ground which serves to heighten the beauty of the scene by appearing to conceal a part. In the background is a large flower garden, enclosed with a hedge and some very handsome trees. On one side of it, a grove of pines and

---

*It would be futile to follow these directions today. The Adams home— and later the home of Aaron Burr—stood on the top of a hundred-foot hill, a spur of the low range called the Zandtberg, and it overlooked a brook and a pond. From its site, bounded by the present King, Varick, Charlton, and MacDougal streets, not a trace can be seen of pond, brook, hill, or house.

oaks fit for contemplation. . . . A lovely variety of birds serenade me morning and evening, rejoicing in their liberty and security, for I have as much as possible prohibited the grounds from invasion. The partridge, the woodcock, and the pigeon are too great temptations to the sportsmen to withstand. . . . In natural beauty it might vie with the most delicious spot I ever saw.

Such were MacDougal and Charlton streets in 1789.

But country houses and especially city tenants who dwell on their beauties can be wearing. You have not, moreover, been taken out of your way merely to look at flowers or listen to pigeons. Between Greenwich Village and the city, dotting the Greenwich Road, were the best and most fashionable of those gardens that furnished their birds cooked and their vegetation distilled into tea, mead, spirits, and wine. There was Brannan's in Lower Greenwich (now Spring and Hudson streets). "Here," reports an English tourist, "was a good greenhouse, with orange and lemon trees, a great quantity of geraniums, aloes, and other curious shrubs and plants," and "iced liquors are much drunk here by parties coming from New York." Maclay dined here one day, praised the "elegant improvements," and entertained his dinner party with an imitation of the Vice-President pompously addressing the Senate.

There was Williamson's, on the east side of Greenwich Street, its gardens extending three blocks above Harrison; Washington liked to drive over on horseback. There was Cummings' Florida Garden, likewise "pleasantly situated on the Greenwich road"; in May the Florida was sold to George Leaycraft, and Mr. Cummings opened a porter house at the Fly Market. There was Vauxhall at Warren and Greenwich streets, too far in town, run down and for sale. Of them all M. Brissot preferred Cummings': "It is tea that you go to drink in the beautiful garden of M. Cummings, the Florida Garden of New York."

You sip your tea or Rack punch. You nibble at comfits, pastries, cakes, and jellies. With an eye on the sinking sun and an extra tip to the coachman, you decide to linger on for Madeira and dinner. Perhaps there will be fireworks, Chinese lanterns, and tightrope dancing. Leaning back in anticipation, and satisfied that you have seen Manhattan, you light a segar. Always informative and in case you don't know it, M. Brissot explains that segars "are leaves of tobacco rolled in the form of a tube, which are smoked without the aid of any instrument." M. Brissot, like many of his contemporaries, detested smoking. "Yet it has one advantage . . . it prevents loquacity. If a smoker is asked a question, it will take him two minutes to answer, but the answer is to the point." Which is a virtue—but the Madeira is on the table! —no cigarette advertisement has yet exploited.

CHAPTER V

Shopping Round the Town

NEW YORK CITY in 1789 is a paradise for shoppers. Merchants have almost forgotten the recent depression. Money is again circulating more freely, and everyone says that the inauguration of the new national government is a happy omen for business. Tradesmen are busy again, and merchants have stocked their shelves with the best European importations. New shops are being opened. The city bustles with activity and with new people: the members of Congress, sundry dignitaries, speculators, and visitors. New York is both the capital of the state and of the nation. Its shops should be worthy of this exalted situation.

Certainly they are filled with a glittering array of things that have never been in the best establishments of Hartford or Albany or Trenton; at least they have never been seen in such rich profusion—some not at all. Here are tailors and stylists who know the latest from Paris and London, wine dealers, tobacconists, booksellers, and dealers in wallpaper, musical instruments, and birds—indeed, here is everything or anything we might want, either for ourselves or as presents for family and friends.

We are not now interested in fish or fowl and meats and vegetables, for we shall later tour the markets of the city in the company of a New York housewife. Nor are we primarily interested in the wholesale stores of the metropolis. We should be rather at a loss to take care of "a bale of Flannels" or "a Pipe of Geneva" (126 gallons of fine gin). We might be intrigued by the purchase of a pipe of good Madeira, if we wished to lay something by for posterity and had the necessary $200 to invest. But we cannot summarily dismiss the wholesalers from our attention, for they are often more than willing to sell at retail. Some of their bargains we cannot neglect.

The public auctions, or "vendues," merit a visit. They are conducted by some of the best-known citizens: James Barclay, A. L. Bleecker, James Smith, Thomas Franklin, Robert Hunter, Frederick Jay, Isaac Moses, John Ramsay, and Nicholas Low. Sale by auction is a favorite method of disposing of real estate, either a simple house and lot or thousands of acres of upstate land, and especially of the possessions of the lately deceased. But at the Coffee House or in the various auction rooms you may find anything: an elegant bay saddle horse, ten barrels of "mackerel," a feather bed, an eight-day clock, or $42\frac{1}{2}$ dozen ramrods. Nicholas Low and Frederick Jay largely confine their activities to real estate, but James Barclay at No. 14 Hanover Square sells household and kitchen furniture every Tuesday and Friday. If we follow the newspapers we can keep informed of the offerings of the various auctioneers.

And, unless we know our New York or are informed by our host or tavernkeeper, we must consult the newspapers to learn of the shops and their wares. The newspaper was the only advertising medium available to the merchant of 1789. What of the weekly and monthly periodicals? New York had none in that year, and those published elsewhere did not carry advertising, which may help to explain their brief periods of publication. Here and there among the thousands of newspaper notices we can catch the faint glimmerings of the spirit of modern advertising, but there is none of its insidious technique, no illustrations (excepting an occasional crude woodcut which never changed) and consequently none of the lovely and irrelevant sex appeal which seems indispensable to the sale of modern products. A candid tailor, Edward Moran, stated in the *Daily Advertiser* of May 6 that, "as self-applause is commonly the unerring mark of ignorance and consequently disgusting," he declines it and only offers "the following most reasonable terms"—which indeed *were* reasonable. Another "Merchant Taylor," John Bands of 13 Water Street, disdaining even the primitive advertising of his day, simply declared that his establishment contained "many other articles in his line too lengthy for an advertisement." The "ads" of 1789, like those of today, give us but the roughest of clues. To know, we must visit the shops themselves.

Before beginning our tour it would be wise to check up on our resources, or what was referred to among contemporaries as "the needful." Money is the most convenient medium of exchange, but it is possible to do some of our shopping without either coin or paper notes. Since many of the merchants are both importers and exporters, they are perfectly willing to accept, in payment for the wares they have imported, goods that can be either resold in the local market or exported in settlement of their accounts abroad. Besty & Goodwin, druggists at 228 Queen Street, are eager to trade their merchandise for "gensang" (ginseng). J. Jacob Astor, at 81 Queen Street, will exert himself to sell you a "Piano Forte," but failing that he "will give Cash for all kinds of Furs." Hugh Smith, at 22 Wall Street, will exchange some of his Madeira and linens just imported from London for "Pot Ashes," which he will receive at the highest market price. Several doors away, at No. 46, Thomas Buchanan & Company will take our "Pot and Pearl Ashes, Rice, Flour, Corn or Staves" and gladly send us off with some of the Jamaica spirits or Teneriffe wines which are just being landed from the brig *Polly* over at Hallet's Wharf. Or Abraham Wilson will furnish us with a parcel of Carolina reeds or an American-made felt hat for either cash or "otters, Red Fox, or Minks." But this is becoming somewhat complicated; perhaps we should look at either our cash or credit.

If our purse is filled with coins, we can open it and view a truly international and chaotic scene. There is no national American coinage, and any well-stocked purse may contain a motley collection of British, Spanish, French, German, and even Irish pieces —purporting to be gold, silver, and copper. Mingled with them are coins of various American states and, among the smaller pieces, coins of a most dubious origin and of uncertain value. No prudent person will accept the bald statement of value impressed upon the coin, for almost all of them have been generously clipped. So common was the practice that during the Revolution the American government officially *ordered* Timothy Pickering of the Quartermaster's Department to clip the new coins received as a loan from France and suggested that he do it himself with a pair of common shears. This was literal and direct action to reduce the gold content of the coinage. The gold and silver coinage has been so closely clipped that a pair of scales is necessary for every cash transaction. In New York a committee of the legislature declared, in 1787, that virtually all the copper coinage in circulation was counterfeit; the pieces were commonly known as "Birmingham coppers," and these spurious items were among the most lucrative of English exports to the United States.

But if we have come a long distance we have brought only gold coins. If we wish to simplify our transactions it would be well to reduce our holdings to a common coinage. The units of value generally accepted in exchange transactions are the Spanish-milled dollar and the English pound. These will remain so for some years after the new government has established a national currency for the United States. The Bank of New York will receive our various gold coins at the following rates:

Spanish Johannes (a joe)	$16.00
Half-Joe	8.00
Spanish Doubloon	15.00
Double Spanish Pistole	7.48
Spanish Pistole	3.72
British Guinea	4.64
Half-guinea	2.32
French Guinea	4.52
A Moidore	6.00
A Caroline	4.72
A Chequin	1.78

and for the numerous other coins there was a detailed and intricate rate of exchange. If we wish to offer any of the paper currency of the various states we plunge into a situation that might baffle an international financier. The daily fluctuations of this paper currency caused William Livingston to write from his New Jersey retirement to John Jay, his son-in-law:

> Considering how much your Speculators, & the rotten part of our own Legislature play the Devil with our paper currency, it is exceedingly prejudicial for an honest Man to purchase any thing from you with what we call money, & you call a merchant-able commodity which is daily fluctuating in value; & the amount of that fluctuation at your own arbitrary disposal.

In view of this situation it might really be simpler to bring some ginseng, flax, and a few beaver skins into the city and barter for what you wish. There is, however, a third method by which we can make our purchases. If our credit seems good we can buy on what is basically a primitive installment plan, for there are many merchants who are happy to accept "good notes at short dates." If we divide the total sum and stagger the notes we shall have what posterity will one day think is a great innovation—installment buying.

By this time we have *some* form of "the needful" and shall visit the shops. It is impossible to do much "window shopping," for only a few of the stores have windows in which to expose their wares to persons who are merely strolling by. Some of the merchants stock a wide variety of goods; others are specialists in some particular line. The shops of the former may resemble the "general store" of a crossroads hamlet of the twentieth century, but they are also the venerable ancestors of the modern department store.

Let us visit the shop of William Griggs. He is located at the corner of Maiden Lane and William Street, in the house formerly occupied by Joseph Henry. He has opened his business only in late April, and his merchandise ought to be fresh. He has bought considerable space in the newspapers, especially the New York *Gazette* of May 1, to announce his wares. He is indeed proud

of his "Plate and Plated Ware," and these are popular because
they are not only useful and ornamental but represent a sound
method of investing excess capital—unless, of course, we wish to
plunge into the newfangled speculation in stocks and securities.
Griggs presents us with a large assortment of "Coffee Pots, Sauce
Pans, Sugar Dishes, Punch Ladles and Strainers" and continues
through wedding rings, penknives, smallswords, curling irons,
shoemakers' hammers, carpenters' rules, combs, "Bread and
Fruit baskets, Plate Warmers, Knife Trays, Tumblers, Snuffler
Trays, Letter Trays and Ink Stands." But that is only the beginning, because Mr. Griggs also has for sale "a handsome assortment of PICTURES, framed and unframed." Also patent medicines,
shaving soap, perfumery, "Milk of Roses, Cephalic Snuff,
British Herb-Tobacco, Stoughton's Bitters, a variety of ladies' and
gentlemen's gloves lined with Fur, Flannel and Lambs wool." In
the same category, so it seemed to Mr. Griggs and to the printer,
were ostrich feathers, songbooks, spelling books, and "small
bibles." But in a separate and lengthy paragraph he describes his
numerous songbooks and "Violin Music." The concluding section is the most inclusive and intriguing of all, for there he presents violins, flutes, guitars, fifes and clarinets, dog collars, "camel
hair pencils," spoons, buttons, shoes and slippers, trunks, coat buttons, snuffboxes, artificial flowers, and "Checker Boards, Back-
gammon Tables, Dice, Money Scales and Weights, Spice Powder
and Shaving Boxes, and many other articles." Mr. Griggs also
adds that he is carrying on the business of buying gold and silver.
He probably maintains the most extensive of the general department stores, but he will soon discover that he has lively competition from many of the long-established firms.

His competitors seldom offer such a wide variety of articles, but
many of them advertise more frequently and with an equally
curious assortment of items. George Barnwell & Company, at 205
Water Street, have just imported some sugar, molasses, cocoa, and
a few "Cow-hides and Goat-Skins" on the schooner *Juno*. They
have received by the *Ann and Susan* from Dublin some choice

linen, "high and low priced DOWLAS; black *Lastings,* and a few
bales of FLANNELS." They also have on hand some fine Teneriffe
wine, tobacco from the James River as well as from North and
South Carolina, and "a few Tierces of new RICE"—all of which
they wish to sell for cash "or good notes at a short date."

Gouverneur, Kemble & Co., at 26 Front Street, are in the same
general importing business and advertise their wares as extensively. Here we can buy some "very excellent St. Ubes salt" and
teas of almost any variety: souchong, sequin, tonkay, singlo, or
bohea. Also available are London Madeira wine, sherry wine from
four to ten years old, Teneriffe and Malaga wine and "Holland
Geneva, in pipes and cases, of high proof." This company imports as well Brazil sugar and Muscovado sugar, Spanish salted
hides, Irish linen and sheetings, and "Ticklenburgs, Holland and
Russia Duck, of the very best sort."

Streetfield and Levinus Clarkson tend to restrict their imports
to Holland, whence the brig *Eliza* has just arrived with a cargo of
hyson and souchong teas, nutmegs, and Geneva in pipes. They
deal regularly in "Holland lintseed oil, gunpowder, Holland flax
hatchels, a large assortment of writing-paper and quills, ink-
powder, bar-iron, shot of different sizes," and many cloths. Le
Roy & Bayard, at 202 Water Street, offer rum, cotton, wines,
gunpowder, writing paper, skates, and cinnamon. If we wish to go
over to 18 Hanover Square, to the store of M. & H. Oudenaarde,
we can find many of the above-mentioned articles as well as Russia sheeting, Dutch linens, Marseilles quilting, Turk satin, diapers
and St. Croix rum, horn combs and frying pans, knives and forks
and fiddlestrings. John Ramsay, at 221 Queen Street, adds but
little to the usual offering of linens, wines, tea, and gunpowder,
but we should note that he does have some "Large Barcelona
Handkerchiefs, Men's white silk stockings and beaver hats" and
that he also buys and sells public securities. It is recently rumored
that the establishment of the new Federal government will have
a beneficial effect toward re-establishing the value of those bonds
for which there is already a lively market. James Saidler is doing

a flourishing business in Continental certificates in addition to exposing for sale, at 31 Water Street, cloths, buckles and buttons, and window glass. He is perfectly willing to do business on a barter basis—exchanging for his imports "country produce" which he will, in turn, export. We must not confuse James Saidler with the firm of Sadler & Bailie, up at 215 Water Street, dealers in cloths, wines, indigo, and tobacco. While we are here we might well visit the shop of Shedden, Patrick & Co., a few doors away at No. 206. We now have some new items: clean Petersburgh hemp, white Manchester goods, and striped waistcoat patterns, as well as some wines not previously known or encountered—red Catalonia, Old Mountain, and Old Malvosio—and some French brandy in hogsheads as well as "Old Jamaica spirits, crop 1783."

A general store is a convenient but also a bewildering institution. It is a place in which to browse as well as to buy—and probably to buy more than we actually need. If we have specific purchases in mind we had better repair to those shops which specialize in various commodities.

Certainly clothes stand high on our list of ordinary needs. Even if we are not in immediate want of a new habit, waistcoat, or breeches, the shops of New York offer us an excellent opportunity of obtaining the most modern materials, patterns, and colors—all, if we so elect, cut to the latest styles from Paris and London. Perhaps we shall not be wearing them for some months, but even then they will still be in advance of the current vogue in Hartford or Albany or Trenton. And, indeed, styles do not change greatly from year to year. Neither men nor women are yet so regimented that they must acquire new clothes and styles from season to season. Certainly the styles vary a little each year, but failure to keep up with the changes is not yet a subject for serious criticism. Dressmakers and tailors have hardly begun to suspect what rich profits the future might confer upon their imperious and subtle successors.

We can, if we wish, obtain a few ready-made garments. But if we are members of those small circles where dress counts for something, we had better act in a far more prudent fashion. Few care what the bulk of the citizenry use to cover themselves; their dress is almost an unfailing sign of the level to which they belong. Democracy has not yet invaded the realm of clothing. It is still possible to distinguish the tavernkeeper from the diplomat and the great merchant by their dress. It is still simple to differentiate the waiter from the diners. If we are (or imagine we are) one of the "right people," it is necessary to have the proper clothes. We can buy the materials and take them to a tailor or we can go to a tailor who offers the goods, his services, and his knowledge of the best fashions.

If we simply wish to buy materials let us first turn to the offerings of John Turner, Junior, at 79 William Street. Other shops may have more varied offerings, but Mr. Turner has advertised his goods in the New York *Gazette* of May 1, 1789. In spite of our social position we may profitably respond to his statement that all the following goods "will be sold low for cash":

Plain, striped, corded, checked, tamboured, needle-worked, loom-spotted, and figured Book and Jackinet-Mullins: Ditto Aprons and Handkerchiefs; a great variety of Lawns; light and dark grounded Chintzes, Calicos, and Cottons; Printed Mullins; Chintz trimming; Chintz Furniture Cottons; red, blue, purple-gold; and olive coloured ditto; 4–5 and 6–4 Shawls; Mullinets; corded and India dimities; Fustians and Jeans; Marseilles Quiltings; Draw-boys; Cotton Counterpanes and Palampoors; 7–8 and 4–4 Irish Linens; very fine yard-wide Ticking; Cambrics and Lawns; Wandtops and Long Lawns; Russia Diapers; Table-Cloths and Napkins; Striped Tickings; Flanders Bell-Ticks; Cotton and Linen Handkerchiefs, Checks and Stripes; Brown Hollands; Armozeens, Mantuas, Lutestrings, Tobines; Brocades; Silver Tissue, Sattins, Florentines, Modes, Sarsnets, Taffities, Persians; and Serge Desoy; rich black Genoa silk Velvet; Coloured ditto; rich thread Lacings and Edgings; Black and White Blond ditto; black patent ditto; black and white Mock Point ditto; Gauzes, Italian Crapes, ribbons, collar Velvets, Umbrellas, Fans, Feathers and Flowers; Ladies Stays; Chip and Leghorn Hats; Bombazeens and Crapes;

Ruffells and Calmancoes; Durants; Tammies, Moreens and Tab-
berets; Welbore and common Camblets; Broad-Cloths, Cashmers,
Coatings; Baizes and Flannels; Shaloons and Rattinets; Nan-
keens, Velt Patterns; gold and silver Laces; Buttons and Knee
Garters; Cotton Velvets; Imperial ditto; Corduroys and Thick-
sets; Royal Ribbs, Sattinets, Denims, and Worsted Florentines;
ribbed and plain; white and coloured silk hose; patent ditto;
ribbed and plain white and random Cotton and Thread ditto;
Womens Silk, Cotton and Thread ditto; Mens and womens
Worsted ditto; mens and womens white Kid and Linen Gloves;
womens coloured ditto; Wafli-leather, Beaver and Buckskin ditto;
black, white and coloured Silk ditto; black, coloured, Barcelona,
Bandanoes, printed Linen, Cotton and Check Handkerchiefs;
Cotton and Thread Fringes; Silk ditto, various colours; Scarf
twist, sewing Silks, white and coloured; Threads, Pins, Shoe and
quality Bindings; Tapes, Dutch Laces, Ferrets, silk stay Laces;
black and white Beaver Hats; Tambouring Cotton and Threads
Slacks; Japanned Waiters, Paper Hangings, green Black and
figured Oil Cloth, &c. &c.

Important among Mr. Turner's many business competitors
are three. DeLuze de Montmollin & Co., at 191 Queen Street, do
a thriving importing trade from Holland and from France. They
have many of the materials advertised by Turner; they also offer
Silesia linen handkerchiefs and "Horsehair for Mattresses from
Amsterdam" and a nice assortment of taffeties and French ribbons. Joshua Waddington & Company, importing principally
from London, offer the usual broadcloths, calicoes, chintzes, as
well as "plain and striped wildbores of different colors, shalloons
and rattinets, and black calmanicoes." James Saidler, whom we
have already encountered, advertises "Black Barcelona, Bandano,
cotton and Pulicat handkerchiefs; Ganzes and millinets; Calmanicoes, durants, tamies & camblets; Burdeyd and cross-bar'd
stuffs."

There are more than a dozen others in the field. Isaac Moses,
at 21 Wall Street, has public sales of articles of clothing "suitable
to the season." A. L. Bleecker drew his imported materials from

London; John Delafield, from Canton—which had first been visited by an American ship only several years earlier. David Galbreath, at 224 Queen Street, and James Haydock, Junior, at 155 Water Street, conduct respectable shops, but their offerings add little to the general profusion. Perhaps we might visit Robinson & Harvey at 81 William Street, because they announce that they "are determined to sell at a reduced price" their goods which are "warranted real London dressed, and of the very first quality." We need not revisit our old friends Sadler and Bailie, but if we are on Water Street again a visit to John M'Vickar at No. 210 would show us the "printed waistcoats, toilanets and corded dimities" which have just come from Liverpool on the brig *Friendship*. George Pollock, 28 Water Street, is eager to exchange Irish linens for flaxseed. Queen Street houses many of the dealers in dry goods. George Douglas holds forth at No. 236, and a few doors below is the "New Federal Store," conducted by Thomas Nixon for the sale of "the best English, French and Spanish *Superfine Cloths.*" But if we are imbued with the rising nationalism of the day, perhaps we shall choose to patronize Pope & Candle, who have just moved their "manufactory" to 12 William Street and who are more than willing to provide a "general assortment of goods suitable for the season." There are more than enough merchants in cloths; there are too many. So says John Ireland, of 68 Water Street, who has just announced his intention "to decline business" and retire.

We may take our materials home and entrust the cutting, the sewing, and the tailoring to the women of the family. Or we can take our cloths to any of the several good tailors and habitmakers who enjoy a thriving trade. They also have the necessary materials for sale, but they will not object too strenuously if we bring our own. Certainly Edward Moran, "Taylor and Ladies Habit-Maker from London and Dublin" (recently moved to 24 William Street), would not, because he is both honest and modest. It was he who declared, in the New York *Daily Advertiser* of May 6, that "as self-applause is commonly the unerring mark of ignorance

and consequently disgusting," he declines it and only offers "the
following most reasonable terms"—very reasonable with eight
shillings to the dollar:

FOR MAKING

> Plain coat, 15s.
> Fashionable do. 16s.
> Lappelled do. 17s.
> Waistcoats made fashionable, 6s.
> Silk and velvet breeches, 8s.
> Jean, nankeen, corduroy, &c. do. 7s.
> Double breasted surtout, 16s.
> Great coat, 14s.
> Ladie's Habit, fashionable, 16s.

Opposite the Coffee House on Wall Street (No. 22, to be
exact) is the establishment of Daniel Campion. He appeals only
indirectly to our esthetic sensibilities—more directly to our purse,
for he stresses not only "very moderate terms," but also "a very
cheap rate." Atchinson Thomson has just "declined the Tayloring Business in town" and moved to the country, where he hopes
to enjoy the continued patronage of New Yorkers. William Henson "from London" has bought Thomson's shop at 52 William
Street and is actively soliciting clients.

Posterity owes John Shepherd of 23 Hanover Square a debt
of gratitude for the details of the many charming colors and
shades that were available to the esteemed gentlemen (and ladies,
too) of the early Federal period. Men's formal attire, unlike the
drab formal clothes of later generations, was as gay and resplendent as that of the ladies. In the *Daily Advertiser* of May 5,
Mr. Shepherd sets forth his intriguing multicolored offerings, and
with some indication of prices:

> Best superfine Cloths of the following colors, viz. Black, bottle
> green, batswing, drab, new brown, new drab, do. olive, fashionable mixture, pearl, navy blue, ravens grey, London smoke, olive
> mixture, Devonshire brown, changeable pearl, light mixture, dark

mixture, Queens drab, scarlet, light blue, light green, Parsons grey, silver grey, purple, mulberry, garnet, sea green, mouse's ear, pea green, and a number of other colors, amounting to nearly a hundred different colors, all of which will be sold for 38s. per yard, particular high colors excepted, which will be regulated in proportion to the above.

CASSIMIRS.

Dark drab, dark olive, light drab, light olive, pearl green, sage colored, white, buff.—Striped Cassenets, excellent for summer coats.

VELT PATTERNS.

Jennets, muslinets, dimoty, cotton, silk velvet, cotton velvet, silk and cotton, gold tambour muslin, silver do. very rich, twilled satin Florentine, plain do. silk do. fine sattinet lasting undressed, Princess stuff, worsted florentine, cotton denims, jeans and fustians, gilt and plated buttons, imperial do.

N.B. The above assortment perhaps excells any that has been imported in this city (in one person's hands) these many years, and as the most of the above articles are fresh imported, consequently they are of the newest taste.

If the reader of today is somewhat troubled in visualizing bottle green, London smoke, Queens drab, batswing, mouse's ear, or Princess stuff, it may humbly be suggested that the present nomenclature (especially in materials for women) is equally fancy and perplexing.

Both men and women display a lively interest in the latest styles. However, the ladies have more time, more curiosity, and incur far more expense. Brissot de Warville, shocked by the display of the follies of English luxury in New York, further laments that "luxury forms already, in this town, a class of men very dangerous in society—I mean bachelors. The expensive upkeep of women makes men dread matrimony." Other French travelers note that English fashions seem to predominate in New York circles. But the styles from Paris are not neglected. The newspapers publish occasional fashion notes. On May 15 the New York *Gazette* reports:

NEW FASHIONS FROM PARIS FOR THE LADIES

The only variety since our last appears in the three following dresses.

First. A plain celestial blue satin gown, with a white satin petticoat. On the neck a very large Italian gauze handkerchief, with satin border stripes. The head dress is a pouf of gauze, in the form of a globe, the crenaure or headpiece of which is made of white satin, having a double wing in large plaits, and trimmed with a large wreath of artificial roses, which falls from the left at top to the right at bottom in front and behind contrary.

The hair is dressed all over in detached curls, four of which in two ranks, fall on each side the neck, and behind it is relieved in a floating chignon.

The second dress is a Pierrot made of grey Indian taffaty, with dark stripes of the same colour, having two collars, one yellow and the other white, both trimmed with a blue silk fringe, and a reverse trimmed in the same manner. Under this Pierrot they wear a yellow corset or shapes with large blue cross stripes. With this dress they have a hat à l'Espagnole, made of white satin, having a large white satin band, put on in the manner the wreath of roses is on the hat of the first dress; but this hat is relieved on the left side, and has two very large handsome cockades, one at the top, the other at the bottom, where it is relieved.

On the neck they wear a very large plain gauze handkerchief, the ends of which are hid under the shape. Round the bottom of the Pierrot is pinned a sort of frill à la Henry IV, made of gauze, cut in points round the edge.

The third and newest dress is a Pierrot and petticoat, both made of the same sort of grey striped silk, and trimmed all around with gauze, cut in points at the edges in the manner of the Herrisons.

These Herrisons are now nearly the sole trimmings used for the Pierrots, Caracos and petticoats of the Parisian ladies, either made of ribbons or Italian gauze, but chiefly the latter.

With this dress the ladies wear a large gauze neck handkerchief, with four satin stripes round its borders; two of which are very broad, and the other less. These handkerchiefs are an ell and a half square.

The head dress is a plain gauze cap, made in the form of those worn by the elders, or ancients in the nunneries.

Shoes are celestial blue satin, with rose colour rosettes.

Muffs are not yet left off, those worn most are Siberian wolfskin, with a large knot of scarlet ribbon.

For the ladies it is a day of gorgeous brocades and rich taffetas, luxuriantly displayed over "jaunty, flowing bellhoops" which were flattened before and behind and stood out two feet on either side. Hats are either very small or very large, utterly simple or highly ornate. There is no middle ground. Mary McCrea wears a gauze cap close-fitting as a nun's; to the rose-pink color scheme her Paris milliner has added a little "note of celestial blue." A few ladies prefer "a sweet airy cap with a white sprig," but the majority favor more imposing combinations of coiffure and hat. One style provides a mass at least a foot high and gives the effect of a churn turned upside down and decorated with lace and flowers. At the Inaugural Ball one headdress was a pouf of gauze in the form of a globe with a crown of white satin hung with artificial roses. There were also hats à l'espagnole, each with a great plume and two cockades. Other styles are designed to resemble towers bedecked with ribbons, artificial flowers, and plumes. While the flowing gowns sweep the floor, the hats seem to reach upward to sweep the ceiling. From time to time the headdress does sweep the lighted candles of a chandelier and there is a fire, but this is not a common disaster. Hats are growing to such huge dimensions that a recent letter in the newspapers advises the importation of larger umbrellas to cover them from the rain. Mrs. McCrea is content with the fetching charm of a simple cap; Mrs. Knox, buxom and resplendent, beams forth from beneath a vast pyramid. Perhaps because her husband was the Secretary of War she affected a military style in dressing her hair. In front it is "craped up at least a foot high, much in the form of a churn bottom upward, and topped off with a wire skeleton in the same form covered with black gauze, which hangs in streamers down to her back. The hair behind is in a large braid, turned up, and confined with a monstrous large crooked comb." When Mrs. Knox steps forth in dress regalia, she resembles a frigate under full sail.

The dressing of one's hair is both tedious and expensive. A lady of fashion complains in *The Contrast* that she "sat tortured two hours under the hands of my friseur." The rates quoted by Charles McCann of 40 Pearl Street are those that generally prevail. Ladies' "dress cushions" cost sixteen shillings, braids from ten to twenty-four shillings, and ringlets seven shillings a pair. If you wish to have the hair dressed daily the rate is £15 (almost $38) a year. A single dressing is five shillings. For the gentlemen the same daily service is available at £8 ($20) a year; three dressings a week cost £4 10s. For those who wish to do their own, they will find the shop of Nathaniel Smith, at 187 Queen Street, indispensable. Mr. Smith, at the Sign of the Rose, is a manufacturing chemist and perfumer. He is well known for his "superfine English white hair powder" and his "clarified hard and soft pomatums, on a new construction that was never introduced into this country before; they are rendered exceeding nutritive to hair, feels cool and pleasing to the head, and never causes the least heat or agitation, but on the contrary, strengthens and nourishes the hair, keeping it from turning grey, or combing off." Mr. Smith also offers tooth paste, toupees, powders, razors, likewise his "liniment for destroying nits in the hair, with printed directions" and a hundred aids to beauty—for both ladies and gentlemen.

Fashions for gentlemen are not so complicated, but a person who pretended to any importance was an elegant creature. The miniature painter, John Ramage, was a handsome, conspicuous figure. He was certainly not alone. A beau of '89 has penned his reminiscences of one of his own sartorial victories:

You must remember the Misses White, so gay and fashionable, so charming in conversation, with such elegant figures. . . . I can remember going one night with Sir John Temple and Henry Remsen to a party at their house. I was dressed in a light French-blue coat, with a high collar, broad lapels, and large gilt buttons, a double-breasted Marseilles vest, Nankeen-colored cassimere breeches, with white silk stockings, shining pumps, full ruffles on my breast and at my wrists, together with a ponderous white cravat with a pudding in it, as we then called it; and I was considered the best-dressed gentleman in the room.

I remember to have walked a minuet with much grace, with my friend Mrs. Verplanck, who was dressed in hoop and petticoats; and, singularly enough, I caught cold that night from drinking hot Port wine negus, and riding home in a Sedan chair, with one of the glasses broken.

The New York *Gazette* includes the gentlemen in its fashion notes from Paris:

In undress [they] wear a very long blue riding coat, with plain steel buttons, made full like a bomb or globe.

A scarlet waistcoat and yellow Kersemere breeches, quite plain without embroidery at the knees or buttonholes.

With this dress they wear gaiters made of black polished leather, which reach half-way up the thigh, and the shoes are tied with strings.

Jocky hats of a middling height in their crown, and the round very narrow. The hair is dressed on the sides in two long curls, and behind tied in a queue.

Round the neck a very full muslin cravat, the ends of which are tied in a large knot before.

The muff is black bear skin, with a large knot of scarlet ribbon attached to it.

All the concern about male beauty exasperates one old-fashioned gentleman, who thunders forth in a letter to the newspapers in November 1789:

The young ladies have totally laid aside all manner of deception [!]; cork and wool are no more necessary in the dress of a fine woman, and, to the immortal honour of the ladies of New York, let it here be recorded that they have adopted the most natural and becoming fashions, this winter, that we have ever seen; whilst the young bucks and petit-maitres are metamorphosing themselves into *lusus naturae* and their tailors into upholsterers.

If our purse permits we can safely visit several of the leading jewelers of the city. There is Francis Patton at 38 Wall Street who also deals in shell goods; Peter Ritter at 50 Broadway who mixes jewelry with ironmongery. Bessonet & Menkler conduct a shop known as At the Sign of the Dial at 32 Maiden Lane. William and John Mott (at 240 Water Street) have just issued a copper business token with an advertisement on each side.

Jewelry may not interest us, but we can hardly escape our need for gloves and boots and shoes. James Hays, "Leather Breeches Maker and Glover, at the sign of the Buck and Breeches, No. 18 Water Street, nearly opposite the *Coffee House*," promises punctuality and dispatch and feels certain that his "long Experience in Business in different Parts of Europe, as well as in the capital cities of America," enables him to offer the utmost satisfaction at the most reasonable rates. Thomas Garnis, at 72 Queen Street, between Peck's Slip and Cherry Street, describes himself as a "Boot and Shoe-Maker from London" and as one who "has been used to work for the first nobility in England for a number of years." At his shop he "makes and sells all sorts of Ladies silk, sattin, stuff and leather shoes, likewise all sorts of gentlemens boots, shoes and galloshes in the neatest manner, and most approved fashion on reasonable terms, and at the shortest notice." Charles Gilmore of 161 Queen Street presents, at the Sign of the Boot and Shoe, "a genteel assortment of gentlemen's boots and shoes at moderate prices; likewise, ladies silk and stuff shoes of the best kind—childrens shoes of all sorts." Footwear is moderate in price; a pair of gentlemen's boots cost about six dollars, and ladies' shoes a dollar and a half.

Certainly few visitors will come to New York and fail to purchase items needed for the home. Perhaps it is a mirror, some pottery, or a bit of china. Samuel Dunlap, at 13 Queen Street, has just imported an elegant assortment of looking glasses. From Newcastle the firm of Shedden, Patrick & Company has just received "a quantity of Flint Glass Ware, Crown Window Glass, and cream colored and brown Earthenware," to be seen at 206 Water Street. The leading dealer in the field is James Chrystie of Maiden Lane, who thus advertises his goods with great frequency:

CHINA

Tea-sets; nankeen, painted, &c. a great variety of cups and saucers; half-pint bowls of all sizes; enamelled, painted, penciled; and blue and white pudding dishes; plates; tureens; cake-plates; tea-pots; sugar-dishes; milk pots, &c.

GLASS-WARE

Complete table-sets, elegantly cut; best double refined flint; a large assortment of common tumblers, wines, &c. also of plain double-flint; bird fountains; globe lamps; small lamps for candlesticks; proof bottles, &c.

EARTHEN-WARE

A very general assortment of blue and white; French gray; variegated; queens, &c. a large assortment of flower pots, of different colors and sizes; likewise of home manufacture.

There is one plaintive appeal for the support of domestic glass manufacture. DeNeufville, Heefke & Walfahrt addressed the public from Dowesburgh on the subject of "Window and Green Hollow Glass, Being the first that has been brought to that perfection within this State, and not without great expense. The Proprietors therefore, would solicit the public for a generous encouragement of their infant manufactory, wherein not so much themselves as the community is interested." Their products are currently on view at the house of John Heefke in Cortlandt Street.

If it is furniture we seek there are numerous public auctions. At the moment Lewis Nicholas is selling his mahogany furniture at bargain prices. He is moving to the country and offers clearance sales both at his house at 90 William Street and at his shop on

Queen Street. Or we can visit Thomas Burling, next to the Chapel in Beekman Street. He is a cabinet and chair maker of established reputation. Another chair maker, James Hallet of 43 Broadway, also builds coaches and chariots. If our tastes run to music we shall find ourselves in the shop of J. Jacob Astor at 81 Queen Street, near the Quaker Meeting House. He has for sale "an assortment of Piano Fortes, of the newest construction, made by the best makers in London, which he will sell on reasonable terms." If we are interested in hardware, cutlery, guns, wallpaper, garden seeds, or birdseed we shall readily find a plentiful variety. We can even find one birdseller: Elizabeth Anderson, at the corner of Greenwich and Chambers streets.

Many of the great merchants of the city sell imported wines, gin (known simply as "Geneva"), brandy, and Jamaica rum. The traffic is large in volume and rich in profit. The eighteenth century was a period of excessive drinking. Even small children were given wine and hot and cold punches. The United States had, in 1789, a population well under four millions. There are no accurate figures on the consumption of alcoholic beverages, but an estimate of imports for 1787 is revealing: four million gallons of brandy, rum, and strong spirits, a million gallons of wine, and three million gallons of molasses (to be converted into rum by American distillers). These represent only the imports; there is no estimate of the beer, wines, hard cider, applejack, and whisky produced within the United States—and at a time when there was no internal-revenue tax to discourage either distillers or drinkers. It is interesting to note that in 1787 we imported a total of only 125,000 pounds of tea.

William Backhouse & Company, at 15 Duke Street, offer a choice variety of imported wine: Madeira, sherry, vidonia, red port, Lisbon, Malaga, Teneriffe, and Fayal, "by the Pipe or Butt, Hogshead or small cask." Madeira is the favorite wine. A pipe of it (126 American gallons) costs from £66 to £90, so that when purchased in quantity a gallon of excellent old Madeira is from $1.30 to $1.80. Port, when purchased in bulk, is only 90 cents a gallon, while Fayal can be had for 40 cents. Jamaica rum is listed at less than 60 cents a gallon, domestic rum at 32 cents. Tipplers who do not favor rum as their strong drink have available many variations of domestic whisky at about 50 cents a gallon. Beyond the mountains, in Pittsburgh, whisky is taken in trade at one shilling [12½ cents] a gallon. But this intriguing price would hardly justify the arduous expedition to the west.

Shedden, Patrick & Company, over at 206 Water Street, sell Spanish and French brandies, Granada rum, and red Catalonia, Old Mountain, and Old Malvosio wines. When Frederick Jay, brother of the chief justice, is not occupied with his many auction sales, he imports and sells London-bottled porter at about three dollars a dozen. Charles Tillinghast operates a distillery in Cherry Street and advertises "New-York RUM of excellent flavor and good proof." There are many other dealers in strong spirits, but they add nothing to the general variety.

We shall have little difficulty in purchasing tea or tobacco. There are many importers of tea and numerous "tobacco manufactories."

New York has more than a dozen publishers and booksellers. Each of them combines activities in several related fields. Robert Hodge, at the corner of King and Queen streets, publishes a few books, imports varied stocks from Paris and London, and offers for sale "an excellent assortment of stationery" which includes knives, message cards, and shoe buckles. The publishers of newspapers are often book publishers as well as general printers and stationers. In truth there is not yet enough profit in any single field to justify specialization.

We ought to pay a visit to old Hugh Gaine at the Sign of the Bible in Hanover Square. Some forty years ago this Belfast Irishman set up a printing press and launched the New York *Mercury*. For more than thirty years he was a newspaper publisher; during the late war he was a notorious Tory. He remained after the peace and now dispenses Bibles and religious tracts with the zeal of a fanatic—in both business and religion. Before ending our shopping tour we must visit James Rivington, that other arch-Tory and ex-publisher who is now a stationer and tobacconist at No. 1 Queen Street. There, snugly ensconced behind his counter, is an elderly gentleman in a rich purple velvet coat, full wig and cane, and ample frills. We purchase a bit of Rivington's special tobacco. As he wraps it for us he assures us, with a smile, that "the Gentleman's Twist is a constant Vade Mecum and hilarious Associate of the Cognoscenti and other Amateurs of our All-cheering, delicious Morceau." If so, we have finally made a real purchase.

CHAPTER VI

The City at Work

IN THE year that the United States embarked upon its "more perfect union," how did New Yorkers make a living and how much of a living was it? The answer is simple and was evident at almost every street end. As for well over a century before and almost a half century to come, they lived directly or indirectly from their waterfront and its ships.

When the brig *Polly*, Captain Green, tied up at Hallet's Wharf, fifty-four days out of Copenhagen, she brought more than bales of merchandise in her hold and gains for her owners on Cherry Street. She brought, as well, interest to the Bank of New York. She brought commissions to the auctioneers of her cargo on Wall Street. She brought profits to the wholesale houses on William Street and then to the retailers on Nassau. She brought an order of 200 feet of cable to the ropewalk out by the Collect. She brought wharfage fees—seven shillings sixpence a day—to the owners of the Slip. She brought repair jobs to the caulkers, sailmakers, sawyers, riggers, brass founders, shipwrights, carpenters, and joiners on Water Street, and, for her crew, other repair jobs to the brewers and distillers and to sundry "dissolute characters" in Topsail Town. She brought work to longshoremen, carters, blacksmiths, and wheelwrights. Before she was loaded again and had sailed, she distributed pounds or pence by devious channels not only to the butcher, baker, and candlestick maker, but to Aaron Burr, attorney at law, and to the Dutch doughnut woman in Old Swago Market. Hudson Valley farmers and Jersey millers used the *Polly* to turn their wheat and flour into

THE CITY FROM THE HARBOR

A view of New York City drawn by Robertson about 1793–94.

WALL AND WATER STREETS

This oil painting, done by Francis Guy several years after the inauguration, shows the newly established Tontine Coffee House, but the general atmosphere had other-

plows, knives, or cash. Old Hayman Levy and young Jacob Astor, fur merchants, and through them traders among the Iroquois and trappers beyond Detroit, managed to earn a living because the *Polly* docked at New York.

In 1789, 1,107 *Pollys*, seagoing vessels, entered the port; 770 of them were American, 308 British, 11 Spanish, 8 Portuguese, 5 French, 3 Dutch, and 2 Swedish. A few years before, China and Madras had been opened to American trade by vessels sailing out through the Narrows; and in May of '89 a ship returned to New York that was the first to fly the American flag on the Ganges.

But the sea accounted for only part of New York's shipping. Rivers and creeks which are regarded today as mere details of the landscape, and often not even decorative details, were channels of traffic. Scows, barges, rowboats—nearly anything that floated and could be poked along by poles or oars—carried freight to and from the upper reaches of the Raritan, Hackensack, Bronx, and Housatonic rivers. Creeks now almost buried in mud, the Sparkill at Piermont for a humble example, boasted of their yearly tonnage.

Then as now the Hudson was of course navigable to Albany. Indeed, in 1785 Captain Stewart Dean of that city had wearied of sailing his 80-ton sloop, the *Experiment,* up and down the river and set off for—China. He got there too, the second American ship to reach a Chinese port; and when he returned to Albany, proud and well heeled, the town named a street after him.

The maritime correspondent in the port of Poughkeepsie reports, December 30, 1788:

> In our last, we mentioned the sailing of the sloop *Lydia* for the West Indies, and Capt. North for New-York; and we are sorry to add that they were both froze up in the Highlands, without any prospect of getting out this season. We are told that upwards of twenty vessels have been catched in the ice between this place and Spiten Devil . . . we lament the unfortunate owners.

It was not so hard on the crews, who could skate to the nearest tavern.

In his introduction to the city directory of 1786 Noah Webster describes this inland commerce with lexicographical precision. New York, he observed, "imports most of the goods consumed between a line 30 miles east of the Connecticut River and 20 miles west of the Hudson, which is 120 miles. . . . The whole territory contains at least a half a million people or one-sixth of the population of the United States . . . besides some other states are supplied by goods from New York." Owing to the tradition of colonial independence and to the leisurely pace of transportation, the consumers of New York still thought of the other states as foreign parts. "Imported from Rhode Island," one merchant advertised his goods. A. L. Bleecker, of 208 Water Street, informed the public that he had "just imported an assortment of Broad Cloths, also a few chests of Hyson and Souchong Tea"— from Philadelphia!

The leading exports tell something of the livelihoods gained in the city and its hinterland: wheat, flour, flaxseed, potash, bread, furs, barrel heads and staves, and raw hides—to the tune, including minor items, of about two million dollars in 1788 and a half-million more in 1790. Most of these goods went to London—the West Indies trade was still hamstrung by English and French restrictions. M. Brissot says that "the English have a great predilection for [New York] and its productions; its port is always filled with English ships. They prefer even its wheat, so that the American merchants bring wheat from Virginia and sell it for that of New York."* Some member of the Chamber of Commerce must have given M. Brissot an earful, for he likewise asserts that in point of trade New York ranked first in the country. Although the city led in coastal trade, it was outstripped by Philadelphia as a whole until the middle of the 1790s. From then on—to the satisfaction of Messers John V. Glover, Peter Schermerhorn,

---

*This chapter makes no pretense at rivaling a Chamber of Commerce report; but the scale of trade may be judged by noting that New York in 1788 exported 322,000 bushels of wheat (at $1.00 per bu.), 183,000 bushels of corn (at 43¢ per bu.), and 10,000 bushels of rye (at 31¢ per bu.).

Thomas C. Pearsall, and their fellow shippers—New York kept increasing its lead.

After leaving the ship's hold, a cargo passed through the hands of auctioneers, commission agents, and wholesale dealers. These gentlemen conducted their business after the fashion of a trading post or country store. They handled anything and everything that could be bought or sold. Smith & Bradford, of 22 Wall Street, proposed to auction at the Coffee House Bridge barrels of wine, casks of rum, boxes of table and tea sets, tubs of Chinese bowls, hogsheads of tobacco, and "two bags of feathers." In a single advertisement Anthony L. Bleecker offered to the highest bidder Madeira wine "fit for immediate use," Carolina indigo and rice, China tea, a house and lot on Queen Street, thirteen acres up near Harlem, and "a neat post chaise, with harness for a pair of horses." Frederick Jay, opposite the Coffee House, relieved someone of a dozen city lots and someone else of "three hogsheads damaged tobacco." James Barclay sold at his auction room, No. 14 Hanover Square, lots and tenements, household and kitchen furniture—from andirons to bed curtains—barrels of mackerel and 42½ dozen ramrods. In fact the only limitation upon the auctioneers was their number; the state licensed but twelve of them to deal in imported wares.

Wholesale merchants did their business largely on commission, and except for the quieter manner of fixing prices differed little from the auctioneers. Certainly they were as versatile. A buyer from Hackensack, Albany, or even the West Indies could easily meet the demands of his local trade by walking into Robert Bowne & Co. at 39 Queen (Pearl) Street. There he could purchase—as advertised—raw hides, wine, lignum vitae, boxwood, eighty sets of mahogany bedsteads, turpentine, varnish, lampblack, wax, sheet copper, anchors, beef, pork, butter, lard, hams, flour, rice, furs, and a variety of dry goods. Peter Goelet, ironmonger, carried a line of saddles, hardware, pewter spoons, hair trunks, and playing cards.

The few specialized concerns dealt chiefly in furs or sugar.

Hayman Levy is remembered for his prominence in the fur trade, his sixteen children, and his having trained in the fur business young Jacob Astor. Dying in 1789, with glowing obituaries, he was succeeded by his nephew, Isaac Moses. The big sugar men, refiners and merchandisers, included Isaac Roosevelt, who set up the first refinery in the land, and members of the Livingston, Bayard, Cuyler, and Van Cortlandt families.

Indeed, many names now woven into the fabric of the city's political and cultural history or enshrined in its social register were painted over store fronts. Archibald Gracie, Robert Lenox, John Delafield, Nicholas Low, James Depeyster, etc., etc.—a list of the leading merchants is something for their blue-blooded descendants to be proud of. For most blue blood, in America or Europe, is extracted from the skill of a shopkeeping ancestor to keep out of the red.

In 1789, when modern industrialism and the stock market were not available, the favorite method for keeping and increasing the profits of trade was to invest them in real estate. This involved more than putting money in the ground and speculating on a rise in population; though speculation in the soil of lower Manhattan could hardly be counted a risk. But the boom in building, together with the grading and filling of suburban acres and the extending of the shore line, amounted to a major industry. It helped provide tradesmen and laborers with a livelihood on a considerable scale.

A hint of the scale may be seen in a few typical transactions. Prices are not recalled in an attempt at humor. They may serve as a rough index to the size of the profits—to the worth—of the storekeepers and their commerce. A lot on the corner of Broadway and Liberty Street—25 feet by 90 feet—together with a small parcel in the rear, brought $1,750. Down further, below Wall Street, a lot with 105-foot front on the west side of Broadway and extending clear to the Hudson River was purchased for $8,000. 'Way uptown, on the west side of Broadway, between Murray and Warren streets, it took $600 to buy a plot 25 feet by 108 feet. In the heart of the city, on Wall Street near Pearl, two lots, each possessing 57-foot frontage and over 100 feet in depth, together cost $4,500. The city authorities did not feel they were getting a bargain—no city administration ever got one—when they bought the corner house at Wall and Broad, with its 16 by 30 feet of ground, for $1,125; said plot with a somewhat different house is now the offices of J. P. Morgan & Co.

The year before, Earl and Lady Abingdon sold the Warren estate, fifty-five acres and a country house deemed to be the finest near Greenwich Village. It netted them $2,200. The city sold two hundred acres of common land in 1789 between the Post and Bloomingdale roads for an average price of $72.50 an acre. Baron Poelnitz must have cultivated his soil marvelously or sown it with gold to get $12,500 for the Minto estate.

Rentals may be judged, perhaps unfairly, from two examples. A city house, No. 27 Queen (Pearl) Street, three stories high, three rooms to a floor, was rented for $362 a year. As for the suburbs, Edmund Randolph of Virginia, the first United States Attorney General, wrote to his wife: "I have a house a mile and a half from Federal Hall, that is, from the most public part of the city. It is, in fact, in the country, is airy, has seven rooms, is well furnished, and gentlemanlike. The rent is £75, our money." Translated from Virginia pounds, this meant about $240 a year —and a year when the presence of Randolph and Congress had kited rents and prices.

Altogether the investment of New Yorkers in real estate was assessed, in 1790, at approximately $5,845,000. The average rate of taxation was 13s. 6d. on £100—or about 67¢ on $100. Within the next decade the assessed valuation increased fourfold, at which Isaac Roosevelt, George Janeway, Alexander Macomb, and other large purchasers of real estate, and the heirs of Moses Gomez, realtor and broker, shed no tears. It was gains such as these that led Jacob Astor to prick up his ears and started him on his way to become "the landlord of New York." Similar gains made an alchemist's dreams come true. About 1791 Jan Max

Lichtenstein bought a modest house on Wall Street for $825, and for thirty years he sweated there over a triple-chimneyed furnace trying to turn base metals into gold. Then, one day while he was absorbed in his usual researches into the "imbibition, solution, ablution, cohabation, ceration, and fixation" of metals, a stranger walked up to him and paid him $33,000 for his house. Later alchemists, though they did not call themselves such, who have come to Wall Street in an effort to turn paper into gold have not always been so lucky.

By and large a New Yorker in 1789 called himself affluent and fit for admiration if he possessed $50,000. Undoubtedly the wealthiest man in the city was a transient—the President of the United States.

The immediate beneficiaries of business were the lawyers. M. Brissot was repeating a complaint as old as the legal profession when he remarked that their fees "were excessive, as in England." New Yorkers claimed to have additional reasons for wishing to throw their 122 lawyers into the river. Opponents of the Federal Constitution pointed out that "of the men who framed that monarchical, aristocratical, oligarchical, tyrannical, diabolical system of slavery, the *New Constitution,* one half were lawyers." Furthermore, of the men who "misrepresented" the city at the convention that led to its adoption, *"seven* out of the *nine* were lawyers." The accusations if not the adjectives were correct. Among the attorneys eligible to practice at the New York bar, John Jay, Alexander Hamilton, Robert Morris, Gouverneur Morris, and Aaron Burr had a hand in making the nation; but it is hardly debatable whether the bill they sent to American history is excessive.

A young man, William Alexander Duer, who was studying law at the time liked to recall in later years his memories of the New York bar. He recollects:

> I have listened in blind admiration to the black letter learning of the elder Samuel Jones and with breathless emotion to the lucid and impassioned eloquence of Hamilton. I have sometimes

felt in danger of fascination by the imposing self-possession and sententious brevity of Burr and [was] captivated by the graceful rhetorick of the classic but sarcastic [Richard N.] Harrison, the candid ingenuity of Brockholst Livingston, and the legal acumen and *Nisi Prius* tact of the elder Ogden Hoffman. Nor did I less appreciate the more homely but not less forcible logic of [John] Cozine and [Robert] Troup.

All these gentlemen and their colleagues were especially busy not only in attending to the normal run of law work, but in arguing the numerous claims and suits arising from the British occupation of the city, the changed fortune of the Tories, and the advent of American independence.

The business of making a living by the law changes less, from century to century, than most professions or trades. Among the recognized trades of 1789 many of the commonest have now fairly vanished. Today a man would have to tramp the streets long hours to find a successor to John Amory the whipmaker, John Fawpel the peruke maker, James Hawlett the coachmaker, Thomas Gridell the pewterer, or John Smith the farrier. In a city as fantastic as modern New York it would be brazen to claim that there exist absolutely no tallow chandlers, chimney sweeps, spermaceti refiners, town criers, tinderbox repairers, sleigh-bell founders, tavern-sign painters, or makers of knee buckles, hair powder, snuffboxes, bootjacks, bustles, quills, candle snuffers, bed warmers, wine castors, and dinner-and-dance swords. The White Rock company would protest that even water carriers are not extinct. But in 1789 these were prevalent occupations.

A subtle change, however, was working within the ranks of all trades. Master, journeyman, and apprentice were terms still widely in use; but they had lost or were losing their old guild significance. In most trades a master had become merely an employer, free to hire or fire at will. A journeyman was merely an employee, and the apprentice a beginner, likewise free to take or leave a job. And as wages and working conditions grew flexible— a matter of tug and bargain between the hirers and the hired—

both groups tended toward a separate organization and defense of their own interests.

As befitted their superior economic position, the masters organized first. By 1786 a General Society of Mechanics and Tradesmen represented the employers' interests in the leading crafts and trades. But the "class struggle" lay so far in the future —free labor was cheap and plentiful—that the society and its affiliated bodies devoted themselves largely to mutual benevolence and social festivity.

Their annual dinners were an event. In '89 the General Society's banquet was held January 6 at "the House of Mr. Samuel Fraunces, Corner of John and Nassau Streets." The newspapers described it as "an elegant entertainment"; and among the customary thirteen toasts, one for each state of the Union, the loudest applause must have greeted the following: "A cobweb pair of breeches, a porcupine saddle, and a hard-trotting horse to all the enemies of freedom!" The Peruke Makers' Society held their anniversary dinner on January 2 at the house of William Ketchum and drank deep in response to the sentiment: "May contempt be the fate of such among us as struts in foreign foppery to the destruction of American trade and manufactures." The Society of Master Bakers met at their annual dinner in September at the house of Lawrence Heyer; and if their toasts omitted mention of the "staff of life" or "our daily bread," it set a record.

Often the beneficiaries of these events included men who had no seat at the table—the inmates of the Debtors' Jail who, next day, received the remnants of the feast. After the General Society's banquet, the debtors published in the newspapers a note of acknowledgment: "The prisoners confined in gaol for small debts return their most grateful thanks to the Society of Mechanics for their donations of bread, beef and cheese. Their benevolence gave a temporary relief to many persons now in want and poverty who formerly were in easy and comfortable circumstances." At a time when one out of every seven men in the city was jailed for debt—the figure for 1788—most tradesmen and mechanics must have wondered, as they met at their annual feast, whether they would eat it next year at a dining-room table or on the prison-cell floor.

The size of the livelihoods earned by these small businessmen was limited by a familiar squeeze play. An upswing in general commerce brought an increase of competitors; and if profits rose, rents increased. Whereas a downward turn might mean the Debtors' Jail for the tradesman, and a common laborer's job—if one could be found—for the bankrupt artisan.

The majority of New Yorkers were of course laborers. A skilled worker—carpenter, mason, or smith—earned four shillings (50¢) a day. An unskilled worker—ditch digger, hod carrier, or carter —earned two shillings (25¢) a day. A day's work lasted from dawn to dark—fortunately for the workers, the high price of candles prevented it from lasting longer. Strikes, moreover, were almost unknown.* The supply of labor was so plentiful that organized resistance to low wages and long hours was unthinkable. Yet some of the well-born and rich were not satisfied. John Jay complained that the "wages of mechanics and labourers . . . are very extravagant." How extravagant they were may perhaps be judged from a claim in the *Daily Advertiser* (of January 31, 1791) that "many of our industrious small tradesmen, cartmen, day labourers, and others dwell upon the border of poverty and live from hand to mouth."

A large part of the laboring population earned no wages at all, in the modern sense of the term. These were the indentured servants and the slaves. Indentured servants were white serfs who had sold themselves, or had been sold, into from three to seven years of bondage for a fixed sum—which they often failed to get. Most of them were "redemptioners" from Europe, immigrants sold at the wharves into years of labor for about fifty dollars, a sum which just covered the price of their ocean passage. When they had

---

*In 1785 journeymen shoemakers went on strike, and in 1788 the journeymen printers won an increase in wages. Such are the brief annals of labor conflicts in the decade; but this hardly proves that if labor had no history, it was happy.

served their "times" they were as penniless as the day they landed. But foreign labor, even at bargain prices and with a whole continent to exploit, was opposed by shortsighted men on, as usual, the noblest grounds. Immigration, the New York State Council of Revision declared in 1785, would be "productive of the most fatal evils" for the reason that it would be impossible to assimilate the immigrants "ignorant of our Constitution and totally unacquainted with the principles of civil liberty." This was an attitude that infuriated Senator Maclay. "We Pennsylvanians," he declared, "act as if we believed that God made of one blood all the families of the earth; but Eastern people seem to think that He made none but New England folk. It is strange that men born and educated under republican forms of government should be so contracted on the subject of general philanthropy."

The remaining indentured servants were native-born unfortunates—men jailed for debt, dependent women, orphans, public charges, presumed vagrants. The authorities sold them into service to pay off their upkeep or debts, and when their years of servitude were over they had little or no cash to show for it. Bond servants were forbidden to buy or sell anything, to go more than ten miles from their masters' homes, to gamble, or to marry. A bondwoman who bore a child was required to serve an extra year. Captured runaways had five days added to their term for each day's absence.

Finally, as we have noticed in touring the city, one out of fourteen inhabitants was a Negro slave. As few of them were skilled, they served largely as domestic help, roustabouts, and scavengers. They were bought and sold privately—the old slave market, part of the Meal Market in the middle of Wall Street near Water, had vanished; and almost any morning's newspaper carried advertisements offering likely human flesh. By "enquiring of the printer" you could buy "A STOUT active NEGRO LAD, 17 years of age—Also, a NEGRO GIRL, aged 14." Or "A NEGRO WENCH, about 25 years of age, sold for no fault—Also, an excellent house Negro, and a very good Spinnet." If you maintained bachelor's

quarters, you might have been interested in "A stout healthy
NEGRO MAN, about 22 years of age—He is sober and honest,
a good coachman, understands attending at table, and will
answer very well for a single gentleman." If you lived on the land,
what about "A YOUNG NEGRO GIRL, twelve years of age, strong
and healthy, bred in the country, used to the business of a farm"?
Even without money you could purchase "An active, well-set,
strong NEGRO LAD, of 19 years old. He is handy—bred to farm
and house-Work, can plough, cook, and washes well—perfectly
sober and honest. . . . West-India or New-York Rum, Sugar, or
Molasses (if more convenient than Cash) will be taken in
payment."

In 1775 it took about $150 to buy an adult male and about
$100 for a woman. But after the Revolution prices varied ex-
cessively. In the face of cheap free labor the value of slaves must
have declined sadly, if the rewards offered for the capture and
return of runaways can serve as a gauge. David J. Johnston
promised ten dollars to anyone who would take up a "Negro
Man named GEORGE, about five feet eight inches high, remarkably black, his teeth very white, with ill looking red eyes" and
"deliver him in Bridewell in the city of New-York." Five to seven
dollars was the usual reward, often less than the value of the
clothes the runaways had the foresight to borrow when they lit
out. Joe, the property of Ebenezer Legget of Westchester, walked
off clad in "a short blue coatee, with metal buttons; a red
flowered velvet jacket, linen trousers, a new felt hat." A Negro
woman named Annie, "though she sometimes calls herself
Molly," took, along with her freedom, "one new striped calico
long gown, one red short ditto, and petticoat, one black calimanco
petticoat, three homespun ditto; black hat, and sundry other
things." Yet all a man would receive for "taking up" Annie and
delivering her to Isaac Vanderbeck, Jr., of Hoboken was four
dollars. Presumably Mr. Vanderbeck Jr. felt that the chances
of seeing Annie again were slim, and as for getting back Mrs.
Vanderbeck's wardrobe the chances were nil.

In fact the initial outlay required for purchasing an indentured servant or a slave, plus the subsequent maintenance charges, was so large that free labor—free to be hired, fired, or starved—won the day. By the end of the eighteenth century slave and indentured labor was doomed in New York as throughout the North. Modern factory production and the great waves of immigration that came later merely gave the death blow to already dying institutions.

What kind of living did the wages of freemen buy? At almost any price level twenty-five and fifty cents a day seems meager; and, if life is thought of in the light of modern needs, it means no living at all. A workingman could not travel for pleasure when it cost him a week's labor to buy a ticket to Philadelphia. He didn't go to the theater if he had to work two days to earn the privilege of hissing from the gallery. Even cheap entertainments, Bowen's Wax Works or a lecture on "The Divinity of Jesus Christ," at two shillings sixpence and one shilling respectively, were beyond his means. He had a hard enough time buying bread at three cents and beef at three and one half cents a pound. At that it must have been wretched beef; for it took ten cents—almost a half-day's work—to pay for a pound of salt pork.

A worker's standard of living cannot, in fact, be reckoned or described in modern concepts. The simplest food, drink, and clothing and the meanest hovel were the terms of his existence. In 1795 it cost ten cents a day to maintain a pauper in the Almshouse; and this sum was naturally based on the wholesale purchase of provisions, clothing, and fuel, and it excluded rent. Yet in that year, as in 1789, a common laborer blessed with a wife and child had less per head with which to provide for the three of them than an inmate of the poorhouse.

Still, hard as it may be to conceive, he did live. The 330 taverns and grogshops could not have catered only to the well-to-do. Fishing was free, plentiful, and occasionally fun. Cock-fights, dice, and cards were good sport, however low the stakes.

Swimming, sledding, and skating were healthy and gratis—a handy man made the family sled and skates. In the days before refrigeration quantities of food—farm produce and fish—were to be had a little overripe but edible and monstrously cheap. Children meant, through the seasons, a free supply of mushrooms, salads, berries, and nuts. A wife could be counted on for dressmaking, tailoring, and, after a Sunday's excursion in the country, lugging home a sack of corn or potatoes bought for a penny. M. Brissot, coming from the squalor of Paris, its hungry mobs on the eve of revolution, was probably right from a contemporary standpoint when he said of the New Yorkers: "There are no poor, meat and fish being so cheap." European emigrants were amazed to discover that in the New World a plain worker ate three meals a day.

But the omens of a revolution, peaceful though it was, were many. Wherever a man turned, if he had eyes to see, he could find evidences, as yet mere wisps and scraps, of the coming machine age which has so altered the conditions of life, for good and evil, that no worker today could by any stretch or shrinkage put himself into the skin of a journeyman one hundred and fifty years ago.

Turn first to the newspapers. In January of 1789 appeared the following advertisement: "Coal Tar—and Black Varnish Extracted from Coal—to be sold for ready money by Charles Wilkes, No. 12, Hanover-Square, the sole agent in America for the British Tar Company." Industrial chemistry was under way. Another advertisement announced "the New Invented Friction Cogg for Blocks—cast and sold by John Youle at Beekman-Slip; being a new and easy method for hoisting a heavy weight." So too was industrial engineering.

Inventions were popping up everywhere. Leonard Harbah, a Baltimore mechanic, came to New York and exhibited to Congress models for a grain cutter, a dock cleaner, and a threshing machine. With his reaper, he claimed, one man could cut five acres of wheat in a day, and his thresher could do the work of forty farmhands. Up in Hudson, N. Y., Benjamin Folger was devising a water mill for roping and spinning combed wool and flax. Mr. Torrey of Lebanon was preparing to amaze the fishermen of New London by donning a strange apparatus and walking on the bottom of the sea four fathoms deep. President Washington, who loved to examine the new gadgets at the Poelnitz farm, took time off to design a castor for serving four bottles of different wines at once—a valuable invention, he thought, for when bottles are passed separately "it often happens that *one* bottle is moving, *another* stops, and *all* are in confusion."

Someone set up a linseed-oil factory on the hill north of the Collect Pond and ran it with "wind sails." The state legislature passed an act "securing to James Rumsey the sole right of making and employing for a limited time the several mechanical improvements by him invented." One of these improvements was "an Engine far superior to any other for supplying Towns with Water"; and throughout the year the New York Common Council had his engine under consideration, but in the end they clung to the Tea-Water pump. Peter T. Curtenius & Company, who operated the New York Air Furnace, must have been alarmed to hear Congressman Clymer of Pennsylvania boast that down in Philadelphia a single furnace was making 230 tons of steel a year and, with a little encouragement from the government, could "produce enough for the whole country."

Turn again to the newspapers. On May 12 the New York *Packet* related that a "company of forty-three ladies" in East Greenwich, Rhode Island, "spent the day in spinning." Of "no party and no creed," they spun "$173\frac{1}{2}$ knotted skeins of good linen yarn." And "sundry gentlemen waited on them with wine, cakes, etc." This was no romantic revival of a New England spinning bee. It was part of a patriotic country-wide effort to make America independent of English manufactured textiles.

In New York the effort was a bit more practical. A Society for the Encouragement of American Manufactures was organized in January, with "wine, cakes, etc." at Rawson's tavern. In

February a fund, labeled "The Test of Patriotism," was raised for the establishment of a textile factory. By the end of December fourteen weavers and 130 spinners were at work in a linen mill on Vesey Street.

But the New York manufacturing society was not quite practical enough. To compete successfully with England, a factory needed to use the Arkwright spinning jennies; and England not only forbade their export but guarded the secrets of the invention as though it were more valuable than a crown jewel, which indeed it was. Rude or imperfect imitations of the Arkwright and allied machines were set up in a number of American cities and failed to work.

Then, in the last week of November 1789, an immigrant landed at New York who carried in his head more than the wealth of the Indies. Samuel Slater, a mechanic from Derbyshire, had memorized, to the last cog and cam, how to make a jenny, a billy, a carding machine, a stocking frame, an entire English textile mill. The day he docked he went to the plant on Vesey Street and, after one look, urged the manufacturing society to throw their machinery into the Hudson. They refused. By January Slater was in Pawtucket. In less than a year after, Almy & Brown of that city had the first Arkwright plant going full blast. And New England—not New York—became the textile center of America.

Manufacturing—the new machine age—took more than far-seeing promoters, skilled mechanics, cheap labor, and patriotic stockholders. It took practical men of science, and they were as yet a rarity. In New York the best-known was Christopher Colles. Born in Ireland of English stock, he had emigrated to America in 1765. He tried his hand at designing almost everything from a mouse trap to a steam engine. He proposed a canal to connect Lake Ontario with the Hudson. He developed a plan for the water supply of New York City. He projected a telegraphic system by semaphores for the whole Atlantic coast. During the

Revolution he gave the American artillery forces lessons in gunnery. Then he turned to chemistry.

In January of 1789 he was trying to make a living by exhibiting scientific curiosities and electrical experiments at Halsey's tavern, near Kingsbridge, "so long as the sleighing lasts." When the snow melted he exhibited a "solar microscope" at his home in No. 3 on the Lower Battery. His instrument magnified a common louse "to the length of twelve feet" and thereby, so he calculated, increased its bulk 644,972,544 times. (Admission, three shillings, with the privilege of a second visit free, provided you brought another customer.) In August he petitioned Congress for the patent rights to a meter that could measure the revolutions or movements of any machine or its parts. After his road book appeared, he proposed to Congress a survey of the entire three thousand miles of main roads in the United States and offered to do the job for $375.

But the life of a practical scientist was as unremunerative and hard as that of any other pioneer. Colles was ever rich in ideas and often distressingly poor in purse. His closing years—he died in 1816—were somewhat cushioned against adversity when his friends secured for him the appointment of superintendent to the American Academy of Fine Arts. Science, like the machine age, fine arts, and belles lettres, was still a thing of the future.

CHAPTER VII

Medical Arts and Wiles

THE doctors of New York, if we accept the cursory judgment of M. Brissot, charged moderate fees. But their patients, he further explains, were few and their pickings were consequently meager. He observed that the only widespread and popular malady was "bilious fevers," which he attributed to excessive colds and to simple carelessness. These fevers may have been the influenza which Maclay said "rages all over the city" and which Trumbull, the author, called "a Federal disorder bred out of the new Constitution and communicated by infection from Congress."

Senator Maclay's experience with New York doctors has a familiar ring. He was urged so "incessantly" to see a doctor for his gouty knee that he "unfortunately said yes." Drs. Malachi Treat and J. R. B. Rodgers, well-known practitioners, with offices at No. 19 Cedar Street, called on him—both "very well dressed." Continued the senator in his diary:

> The sole point I wished them to attend to was my left knee. I could hardly get them to look at it. They said it was immaterial. Aren't you a good hand at taking medicine? No (faintly). You are all over indisposed; you must undergo a course of physic; you must take a course of antimonials to alter your blood. A vomit, said the other, to clean your stomach.
>
> I begged leave to observe that I was well circumstanced in my body, both as to urine and blood; had not a high fever. My knee, gentlemen, my knee. And I showed it to them, flayed as it was with blistering. Here is my great pain.
>
> Poultice it with Indian mush, and we will send you some stuff

to put on the poultice, and the antimonial wine; the drops and the laudanum, etc. They seemed to me like storekeepers with their country customers: won't you take this, and this? You must take this, and this.

Three days later: "The doctors did not call today, and it seems like delivering me from half my misery."

Such calls cost, for an ordinary visit, $1.00; for a visit with a single dose of medicine, $1.25; verbal advice, $5.00; dressing the blister, 50¢ to $1.00.

Other charges, according to the table of fees agreed upon by the Medical Society in 1790 (and again in 1798), included $1.00 to $2.00 for dressing wounds; $4.00 for cupping; $1.00 to $5.00 for bleedings; $5.00 to $10 for attending in smallpox; $50 to $100 for amputations of limbs, breasts, or eyes; $25 for "extirpating" the tonsils; $125 for a hernia operation; $15 to $25 for an ordinary case of midwifery and $25 to $40 for a difficult or tedious case. It took $10 to $20 to cure a simple or virulent gonorrhea, and $25 to $100 to "cure" confirmed syphilis.*

The income of a doctor naturally varied with his skill, clientèle, and reputation. As a body the doctors of New York were held in high esteem. Dr. John Bard was the dean of the profession and the first president of the Medical Society of New York when it was reorganized in 1788. He was an old-fashioned bedside practitioner with a host of living friends whom on occasion he had relieved of sundry ailments. He gave you a purge, a cupping, or an hour or two of diverting conversation which took your mind off your ills. His son, Dr. Samuel Bard, was even more eminent. He had gone through the hospitals of London as an assistant to Dr. Russell of St. Thomas'; he had received instruction from Dr. Else, the famous surgeon, from Dr. Grieve, and also from the poet Akenside; at Edinburgh he had won the Hope Prize for his compilation of the indigenous herbs of Scotland; and he had published a handbook of midwifery. He organized New York's

---

*People who like to talk about ills and operations may consult a complete list of these charges in Pomerantz, pp. 403–04.

first medical school in 1768 and in the summer of '89 attended Washington when he fell ill of a malignant carbuncle.

Dr. Richard Bayley was a formidable surgeon who had studied under Dr. John Hunter of London. He lectured on surgery in New York and illustrated his findings with specimens of morbid anatomy which edified his students but consternated some of the more weak-stomached citizenry. Any operation, even if skillfully performed, was a dangerous venture. Opium and laudanum were the only anesthetics in use, and antiseptics were unknown. The typical diet which followed a successful operation consisted of tapioca, buttermilk, rennet whey, a good pear, and four or five prunes.

Among other well-known physicians were Dr. Charles Mc-Knight, surgeon and Columbia professor; Dr. George C. Anthon, a German, who bought a house on Broad Street from Alexander Hamilton in April; Dr. Charleton, who was said to have confined his practice largely to his relatives; Dr. Orsi, an Italian; and Drs. Seaman and Romayne. Presumably most of these doctors did as well as that Negro in Philadelphia who, after winning his freedom and mastering medicine, earned fees, according to the *Daily Advertiser,* "to the amount of $3,000 a year."

These gentlemen were, by and large, esteemed and reputable members of the New York medical profession. But, then as now, there were others.

While most doctors were given to pills, phlebotomy, and purges, one of the most successful practitioners of the day, Dr. Elisha Perkins, loudly condemned and discarded them all. His method of treatment was mechanical, external, and so simple that anyone equipped with Perkins' Metallic Tractors—at a beggarly five guineas the pair—could cure himself. The tractors looked suspiciously like horsehoe nails, but they were forged of metals which, possessing strange chemical powers, were alleged to bring almost instant relief when gently stroked over the seat of complaint. Agents sold these metallic healers from Vermont to South Carolina; but New Yorkers were privileged to consult Dr. Perkins in person at No. 1 Gold Street and find relief from rheumatism, boils, ague, cancer, burns, crushed bones, tuberculosis, bellyaches, and toothaches.

Midwifery was usually practiced by elderly women, and the rate of infant mortality was high. Mrs. De Lespine, an advertiser among the sisterhood, had indeed considerable difficulty in delivering herself of the King's English. She presents "respectful compliments to the ladies in general; is thankful for their encouragement as a midwife; and hopes they will not be offended at her requesting, that in future such as mean to employ her will apply prior to the time they wish for her attendance; inconveniences may then be put aside what from short notice cannot be avoided; her place of bode is at No. 66, William-street."

Dentists, according to their advertisements, did about everything to be expected of them. The best in the city was John Greenwood, at No. 56 William Street. He undertook to preserve the teeth and gums, make them adhere, remove tartar, cure "scurvy in the gums," destroy bad breath (and without intimidating his public by declaring that one of every five had it), and insert "artificial teeth in so neat a manner as not to be perceived from the natural," thus imparting "a youthful air to the countenance" and rendering "the pronunciation more agreeable and distinct." In 1789 Mr. Greenwood forever enhanced his reputation by making a full set of "sea-horse" teeth for President Washington. However, dental art did not measure well with dental advertising, and Senator Maclay found Washington's voice to be "hollow and indistinct, owing, as I believe, to artificial teeth before his upper jaw." The honorable senator was more than correct, because more intimate friends of the President realized that Washington's long periods of silence during dinners arose, not from any innate taciturnity, but from a fear that his false teeth would fall out and thus compromise his dignity.

Mr. Greenwood's fees were four guineas (a little more than $18) for transplanting natural teeth, which he furnished for two to five dollars each on silver or gold plates. He charged one to two dollars for artificial teeth, three dollars for "grafting" a tooth into the gums, and one to two dollars for cleaning the teeth and removing tartar. He sold his own tooth powder for two shillings sixpence a box and paid a guinea each for live teeth. His office hours took up most of the day, and since his advertisements mentioned that he had a room set apart for dentistry alone, it may be inferred that, unlike some of his colleagues, he was not simultaneously practicing the art of a barber or a blacksmith.

His chief competitor, M. Gardette, formerly of Philadelphia, called attention to himself by inserting in the newspapers long essays on the care of the teeth. More to the point, he undertook to pull the teeth of the poor free of charge. His rivals were soon compelled to do likewise, and by 1792 something like a public clinic for dental treatment was opened by Richard Cort Skinner. Thereafter dentistry progressively ceased to be a common trade and slowly rose to the rank of a mystery and a profession.

Meanwhile patients could resort to Dr. Ogden, a fireman who fixed teeth on the side; to Mr. Fisher at No. 114 Queen Street, who combined dentistry with surgery, phlebotomy, and the tonsorial arts; or to Dr. G. Ruspini, formerly "surgeon dentist to His Royal Highness the Prince of Wales" and now resident at No. 42 Hanover Square. Dr. Ruspini modestly stated that his own make of mouthwash, a "most extraordinary styptic solution," was sovereign for "all kinds of hemorrhages."

Despite M. Brissot's cheerful report on the salubrious nature of the city enough New Yorkers fell ill and enough doctors failed to cure them or charged them so royally for it that home remedies flourished and patent medicines were far more popular than they are today. For the former you had only to consult the druggist, the tavernkeeper, your newspaper, the current (or any other) *Almanac,* a friend, or your grandmother. The cures for certain ailments were beyond the realm of argument. The time-honored remedy for a cough was turnip broth. A blister on each arm, reinforced in serious cases by a vomit, took care of a fever.

Cupping did for asthma, a cow-dung poultice for bruises, quicksilver water for worms, a rotten apple for a sty. For the colic you had a choice of catnip tea, peppermint water, "Daffys Elixir," or a draught of sweetened gin and water.

The newspapers gave frequent advice to the ailing, both in the advertisements and in the news columns; and their offices were as well stocked in patent medicines as the pharmacies. The New York *Journal* for August 6 gave an infallible cure for the bite of a mad dog:

> Take six ounces of rue, picked from the stalk and bruised, four ounces of garlic, picked and bruised, four ounces each of Venice treacle, scrapings of pewter or tin and mithridate; boil them in two quarts of strong ale or porter in a pan close stopped until one quart is consumed, then strain the ingredients from the liquor and give nine tablespoons to a man or woman, warm, fasting; to children in proportion, according to their age; ten or twelve to horses or cows; four or five to sheep, hogs, or dogs; this even if taken in nine days by God's blessing will not fail.

Thomas Greenleaf, printer of the New York *Journal* (at 196 Water Street), did a brisk trade in patent medicines. He stocked "a lotion for all kinds of ulcers" at eight shillings the bottle, with full directions. Testimonials were offered as proof of the virtues of Dr. Cowan's "Aetherial Anodyne Spirit for asthmas, dropsies, fevers, consumptions, etc."—ten shillings the bottle. For the toothache there was "Dawes's famous Golden Tincture . . . with which any Person may cure themselves of that afflicted sensation of Torture . . . also keeps the breath sweet . . . and cures sore eyes, ulcers, and headaches." Dr. Ward, self-described as "Occulist to his late British Majesty," offered "his famous Eye Water, a perfect cure for all defilements or Vices of the Eyes." An "electuary for destroying Worms in children and grown Persons" was sold in Wainwright's Apothecary Shop for four shillings a pot.

Remedies for cancer and venereal diseases were advertised on the equitable principle of "No Cure—No Pay." Mr. Leonard R.

Leland, "bred as a physician," assured the world that "he can totally eradicate cancer without cutting—the terms are No Cure, No Pay—the Poor he cures *gratis.*" But he took the precaution to add that "his stay in this place will be short."

Sheed's Specific Solution, to be bought at No. 94 Queen Street on the no-cure-no-pay plan, was "much approved for its quick effects in the cure of a certain *unfriendly disease.*" Travelers and sailors in a hurry could procure it "with printed directions, on half an hour's notice." One advertisement of this "valuable medicine" contained an irrefutable endorsement. "Many persons," it read, *"could* vouch for its quick effects were it admissable, but the nature of the complaint forbids the idea." If Sheed's didn't work, the patient could always fall back on Leak's famous pills, of which two or three boxes at five shillings each were claimed to suffice; or on Dr. Walker's "Jesuit Drops" at five shillings the bottle—but the number of bottles necessary was never specified—undoubtedly a bit of discreet restraint.

But whether you called in the most eminent doctor or placed your faith in a metallic tractor or simply relied upon the curative wisdom of your grandmother or your *Almanac*—if you were ill, your life was equally in danger.

CHAPTER VIII

The Woman's World

AFTER thumping on the knocker, what you found inside the door of a New York house depended on whose house it was. In the best homes a lackey or a maid, a whale-oil lamp, an elaborately knobbed hatrack, a pier glass, and a cane stand helped prepare you to meet the hostess. You had already removed the dirt from your boots with the aid of a scraper on the stoop.

In many of the better homes, however, social life did not begin at the front door. The front room on the ground floor was often set apart for business. If the tenant was a tradesman, it served as his shop. A merchant or a banker used it for his counting room, and a lawyer for his office. It was there a doctor felt pulses and compounded drugs. In the rear was a combined dining room and kitchen, or the summer kitchen might be in an outbuilding; and the family spent a great deal of time in both.

The prevalent middle-class dwelling comprised two or three stories and a basement. The latter contained the kitchen and cellars. Above, a single large room stretched the length of the main floor. The name of this room depended largely upon the social pretensions of the occupant. It might be described as the tearoom, the drawing room, or, more vulgarly, the parlor. Its prim gloom was broken by an occasional reception or tea party. The hostess sat alone at the mahogany table and poured. To the guests scattered about the room, servants brought tea with rusks and cakes, and sometimes wine with fruits. Glass doors, thrown open on these gala events, set off the rear of the parlor as a dining room. Less formal gatherings were held downstairs in the room behind the shop, and then hosts and guests sat around a long oak table and possibly dunked. The upper floors contained the bedrooms, usually three to a floor—two big ones and a little hall bedroom. Servants slept in the garret or, if the dwelling included an outhouse, in the small rooms above the summer kitchen.

The Secretary of War, General Knox, a man whose spending habits were as extravagant as his waistline, lived in a truly elegant house. It was a four-story brick mansion, $31\frac{1}{2}$ feet wide by 60 feet deep, on the west side of lower Broadway. Two of its rooms were 30 feet long, three were 23 feet, two were 20 feet, and one was 26 feet. In addition there were eight small rooms, half of them with fireplaces. A large servants' hall and a kitchen, 20 by 30 feet, occupied the ground floor. A piazza, 10 feet deep, stretched across the rear of the house. The back yard contained a good well—one of the few in the city—a cistern, and an ash house. The land, prettily gardened, extended 500 feet to the coach house and a wharf end on Greenwich Street.

To be perfect, a dwelling of this luxurious type had garrets capable of storing generations of outmoded heirlooms, and a series of cellars respectively appropriate for fuel, wines, vegetables, smoked and pickled meats, preserved fruits, and eggs packed in salt. It included a detached summer kitchen, a stable, a smokehouse, and an arbor for contemplation and garden parties. Perhaps General Knox's place had them all. In any event the upkeep proved such a burden—the general was learning that to have a million western acres valued at a dollar an acre did not mean that he had a million dollars—that he advertised his home for sale before the end of the year.

On the other hand General Washington found a similar house too cramped. The Franklin mansion, on the corner at No. 3 Cherry Street, several doors east of the present Franklin Square, was something of an architectural show piece. It had been built by Walter Franklin, a substantial merchant, only eighteen years before Washington moved in. Its four stories with five windows on each side, its Georgian doorway facing the square, its stoop with two graceful flights of steps fronting Cherry Street, its plastered attic façade, and its fine proportions in gross and detail made it a monument to good taste but did not go far enough toward rooming the President's family, an executive staff, numerous servants, and the army of callers who weekly "waited upon the President at his levee" or who every Friday evening partook of Mrs. Washington's tea. Next year (February 1790) the President moved into the McComb place on Broadway. Even there he was put to the necessity of building a stable to accommodate his "six Virginia bays," his saddle horses, his canary-colored state coach, his chaises, phaetons, baggage wagons, and other vehicles. Back in the Cherry Street house, which had no such accommodations, his livery-stable bill ran to $80 a month.

To be sure, maintaining a coach in a city as small, ill paved, and crowded as New York was an extravagant nuisance. Like a private automobile in the city of a later day, it flattered your pride but frayed your nerves. Maclay observed that one of his fellow senators "affords a striking proof of the inconveniency of being fashionable. He set up a coach about a month ago, and of course must have it come for him to the [Federal] hall. But behold how he gets hobbled: the stated hour for the Senate to break up is three, but it often happens that the Senate adjourns a little after twelve, and here a healthy man must sit two or three hours for his coach to take him three or four hundred yards." This became so embarrassing that the senator finally got to pretending he was lame and had to wait. "Thus," concluded Maclay, "Folly often fixed her friends."

The furnishings of a well-to-do home were still "Georgian." An inventory of the house owned by Stephen and Mary McCrea at 129 Cherry Street revealed in the drawing room a dozen Sheraton chairs with needlework seats, a mahogany sofa, two card tables, two tea tables, and several easy chairs. Above the mantelpiece were a pair of French gilt mahogany mirrors set off by sconces, and two oil lamps with tinkling crystals.

The dining room contained a grandfather clock which looked down upon a slender-legged mahogany dining table with rounded ends, bar-backed William and Mary chairs, a solid serving table, and a curved Sheraton sideboard. The china was Nankin, and there were Lowestoft cups and saucers among the numerous tea sets. There were pairs of fluted silver candlesticks of "Egyptian" design, a hand-beaten silver bowl (dated 1720 and a precious heirloom), silver caudle cup and mugs, salt boats and a large coffeepot. The table sets—forks and spoons—were delicate and graceful. There was likewise an elaborate silver tea service; and assuredly the silverware included one or more tankards, decanters, salvers, chafing dishes, sauce boats, punch bowls, sugar bowls and tongs, shovels for the salt, snuffers and stands, mustard pots, bread baskets, dram bottles, tobacco dishes, and castors. It was not exceptional for a wealthy home to boast of a thousand ounces of "massy plate."

Pewter was going out of style. The best had been melted into lead bullets for the Continental Army; and silver, china, and porcelain now supplanted the "garnish" of pewter plates and porringers hung in a row along the wall or lined against the back of the sideboard.

The McCrea bedrooms bulged with dressing tables, cedar and oak chests, stools embroidered with needlework, sets of drawers, and vast beds. Even the biggest McCreas had to climb into these beds by means of steps set between the mahogany posts which rose to the ceiling. In the nursery the little McCreas had a mahogany cradle, a warming pan, and trundle beds. Brass-handled drawers, rolling gently at a touch, guarded the children's clothes; and a wardrobe shelved the linen. The master's study contained a severe mahogany desk, bookcase, and medicine chest. A "chariot, pair of bay horses, and pleasure sleigh" stood in the stable. The kitchen gleamed with "brass and copper cooking utensils."

Peculiar to New York, the Dutch cupboard called a *kas* lingered on until, in our day, it has become a museum piece.

Common to all America as well as New York were close chairs, Windsor chairs, feather beds, and corn or straw mattresses. Furniture was upholstered with rush, cane, matting, horsehair, leather, plush, silk, and damask. The august names of Chippendale, Hepplewhite, and Sheraton still ruled the styles. But next year, 1790, their reign was to be threatened by a young man who came down from Albany—one Duncan Phyfe.

To run an upper-class home, magnificent but machineless, took a great deal of care and labor. The care fell to the nerves of the mistress, the labor to the hands of the servants. The most extensive household in the city was the President's. The number of its servants was therefore hardly typical; but their character and pay reveal the complications of eighteenth-century housekeeping. Washington employed in his Cherry Street mansion five white general servants at $7.00 a month plus liveries at $29 each; five black general servants at no wages, but $46 each for clothing; two black maids at $46 a year each; a housekeeper at $8.00 a month; three other women at $5.00 a month; a valet at $162 a year; and the steward, Sam Fraunces, at $25 a month. He hired a Mr. Hyde to preside "at the second table" for $200 a year, and his wife for $100. He had a hard time getting and keeping a cook and a coachman—his want ads for them ran at least for a month. Dunn, the coachman who finally took the job, drank too much, overturned the wagons, drove the coach into the ditches, and "got the horses in the habit of stopping." From the fragmentary bookkeeping that has survived, Washington's household expenses in New York have been estimated at $12,317 a year. The President, a thrifty man, was not proud of the result. Perhaps, like so many of us, he overestimated his neighbors' gift for getting along on little, but he complains that "it is unaccountable to me how other families, on $2500 or $3000 a year, should be enabled to entertain more company, or at least entertain more frequently, than I could do for $25,000."

But this was living—and entertaining—in grand style. A Connecticut man, Oliver Wolcott, got the position of auditor to the Federal Treasury in the fall of '89; and, before accepting the position, he prudently asked another Connecticut man then living in New York to make inquiries about expenses. The friend replied that a house and stable could be had for $200 annual rental, food came to about 25 per cent more than in Hartford, and $1,000 a year would support him and his family very well. In fact Wolcott found that if he was careful he could save from his salary of $1,500 "more than he could expect to in Connecticut."

The best place to hire help was William Cavenaugh's "Intelligence Office" at No. 22 Great Dock Street. Wages were about $8.00 to $10 a month for menservants in the city, and about half as much out on a country estate. A maid was to be had for $25 annually.

In addition to the duties expected of her today, a maidservant performed many tasks which either our machines have supplanted or our habits no longer require. She did up ruffs, spun flax, greased the master's leather boots, and polished the long rows of brass and copper bowls and plates in the kitchen. If the family possessed a cow—pastured off Broadway—she did the milking and made the butter and cheese. She took the place of the telephone and ran errands from one end of the town to the other. The passing street cries were not always music to her ears. "Totoot-totoot-tootoo! East—here's East!" reminded her, when she bought a cent's worth of yeast in a tin measure, that she was part of a home bakery. "Straw! Straw!" at six cents a sheaf meant that the mattresses must be washed and stuffed anew. "Here's white sand; choice white sand; here's your lily-white s-a-n-d; here's your Rock-a-way Beach s-a-n-d!" served notice that the basement floor, tracked with mud, again needed sanding. As the autumn came on and the street vendors cried their fruit, she was, with the help of the cook, a canning factory. In the winter she was a heating plant, fetching the wood and laying the fires floor after floor. She brightened the nights by the daily chore of trimming candles and wicks, cleaning the candlesticks, and filling the oil lamps. Dr. Benjamin Franklin estimated (in 1780) that an average household burned fifteen pounds or $4.50 worth of candles a month; for reasons other than economy our maidservant might wish that the world had adopted the Doctor's scheme for daylight-saving time. Finally, throughout the year she was the plumbing system; she lugged the water from the well, cistern, or water butt; she filled the wash pitchers and bathtub with hot or cold as needed; and then she emptied the slops. She earned her $25 a year.

Unless she was very elegant or delicate indeed, the mistress too had her hands full. Her day began with the family marketing. Few self-respecting housewives permitted anyone but themselves to do the buying for the table, but the rich indulged in the luxury of having a servant carry home the purchases.

Early-morning hours were therefore lively and crowded in the six principal markets of the city. Besides Old Swago, already remarked, on Broadway, there were the Bear Market on Greenwich Street near Vesey, the Peck Slip Market at the foot of Ferry Street, the newly built Catherine Market a few blocks farther north on the East River, the Exchange Market on lower Broad Street, and the Fly Market, oldest of all, at the bottom of Maiden Lane. The latter was famous for its fish. "Black Sam" Fraunces, in his capacity of steward to the President's household, paid two dollars for an early shad. But Washington could not stomach the high price and refused to eat it.

Naturally no housewife of today, if transported to the old Fly Market, would complain at the prices. White bread sold for six cents a 2-pound-$1\frac{1}{2}$-ounce loaf; rye bread for three cents a $1\frac{1}{2}$-pound loaf. Butter cost seven to eight cents a pound—and on a warm day you rushed it home to the cellar. Beef varied from $3\frac{1}{2}$ cents to $6\frac{1}{2}$ cents a pound, depending on cut and quality. Ham brought seven cents a pound, and lard eight cents. White loaf sugar could be had for $15\frac{1}{2}$ cents, brown sugar for six to nine cents a pound, and molasses for fifteen cents a gallon.

Many vegetables and fruits common today could not be found

in the market stalls. Cauliflower, egg plant, rhubarb, head lettuce, artichokes, and okra were not raised on a commercial scale; tomatoes were unknown to America. Raspberries and strawberries were limited to the wild variety. The "wretched" fox grape was the only one of its species seen on the market; and, like oranges, bananas, and pineapples, it was a luxury of the rich —to be bought at Peter Deschent's or Cato Railmore's fruit shops, both on Broadway.

On the other hand, peaches and pears abounded in variety. Apples were profuse in kind and enticing in name: Raritan Sweet, Golden Pippin, Maiden's Blush, and Seek-no-Further. Brissot, who loved to haunt the markets, speaks of the "superb quinces," although he finds that "fruit generally is not so good or handsome as in Europe." Washington's expense accounts, kept for three months of his sojourn in New York, testify to the range of food that well-to-do housewives could procure in the markets. Among the fare that appeared on the President's table were butcher's meat, bacon, tongue, geese, ducks, turkeys, chicken, game, fresh and cured fish, lobsters, crabs, oysters, ice cream, watermelons, nuts, citrons, and honey.

Beverages were procured, not from the markets, but from the merchants. Tea was the general favorite—bohea for "wives of inferior degree" and souchong "as our matrons are richer." Bohea could be had for thirty cents a pound, and for the like amount of souchong a rich matron might part with as much as $2.40. Coffee cost twenty-two cents a pound and chocolate $13\frac{1}{2}$ cents. Washington spent more money on coffee than on tea. Stronger drinks cost him most of all. In three months the presidential mansion spent nearly £168 ($420) on wines, spirits, beer, and hard cider—over one fifth of the total expenses for the table. Madeira topped the list with $110, and $86.75 worth of beer came next. Common sweet wines such as Fayal retailed for forty cents a gallon, Teneriffe for fifty cents, and Lisbon for $62\frac{1}{2}$ cents. When bought by the pipe—a mighty barrel containing 126 gallons—good wines such as port came to ninety cents a gallon and Madeira anywhere from $1.30 to $1.80. Pure water, also a beverage, cost one cent a gallon if it came from the Tea-Water pump.

Madame's marketing would not be complete without a thought for the children and for her husband's sweet tooth. Joseph Corre on Wall Street and Adam Pryor on Broadway were the leading confectioners. Something of the dainties they offered may be gleaned from an advertisement of Pryor who, calling himself the Federal Confectioner, moved in May to Wall Street nearer his rival and the seat of government. Candies included burnt almonds, barley sugar, and peppermint, orange, lemon, cinnamon, and hartshorn drops. There were likewise coriander, caraway, almond, and cinnamon comfits. Desserts comprised pastries, jellies, blancmange, whip syllabub, floating island, rocky island, pound cake, and brandy preserves. We may be sure the children's favorites were not omitted: strings of rock candy from China, cakes of maple sugar, raisins, sugared almonds, and, as specialties of New York, crullers and Dutch cookies. Perhaps the crullers were bigger, fatter, and yet lighter at John Nixon's cookshop or George Walker's bakeshop on Broadway.

Children, in fact, occupied much more of a woman's time than they do at present. Kindergartens, radios, and movies have taken over many of the cares of motherhood. Moreover a child in 1789 had to be prepared for an industrious life. (Today a child perforce should be prepared for an even more industrious and difficult life, but most parents do not know this.) A girl was taught to sew, knit, embroider—"samplers" first—play at a pianoforte, launder, clean house, and cook. A boy, unless his father was very rich, was expected to go to work as soon as he outgrew his toys. All children were trained to do innumerable household chores, or the maid would never have got through her day.

But, outside school hours, the boys and girls of 1789 probably had as good a time as childhood ever enjoyed. Swimming and fishing were close to every doorstep. The streets, vacant lots, and near-by fields resounded with the immemorial games of old cat, rounders, hopscotch, I spy, chuck farthing, and prisoner's base. Hoops, marbles, tops, stilts, kites, sleds, and skates were seasonally epidemic. The more sedentary though hardly quieter games played with plants, string, pegs, and buttons—everything from cat's cradle to ticktack—filled the spare moments. A blade of grass from the back yard, a cattail from Collect Pond, or a whittled whistle could make the air hideous with the noise of joy. On the whole, toys were limited to dolls and simple devices; most of childhood's energy went into games. The Dutch influence made especially popular ticktack, coasting, and outdoor bowling. Anyone who believes that these rounds of amusements left a mother carefree has never settled a child's dispute, umpired a game, tidied up a nursery, or on a rainy day had to tell "another story" when there were no more to be told.

Unless the lady of the house possessed a steward or house-keeper, the superintendence of meals was no small part of her work. Four meals were the daily routine for families that could afford it. As a rule breakfast was at a ghastly hour, for the middle-class man kept his business going from shortly after dawn to dark. Dinner was served at midday, and it was a substantial affair. Lunch counters were unknown and sandwiches scorned: the businessmen went home and devoted two hours to eating—and napping. Tea came along about three in the afternoon. The day closed with supper. (Formal dinners were generally scheduled for four o'clock.) Finally, "baiting" was in order before going to bed—bacon and beef in the pantry or oysters from the cellar.

In contrast to all this was another New York, the New York of the poor who numbered about one quarter of the city. Here were no four meals a day nor mahogany four-posters. The one or two rooms of a poor man's home—he seldom has more in modern New York—were low and dingy. A garret, a cellar, a shanty in a back yard, a hovel in a sunken lot, a ruined hulk in Topsail Town or the Out Ward was his abode.

The floors were either dirt or bare boards. The best were

sanded, and it was a sign of gentility to etch intricate designs and scallops around the borders of the white sand. Rude benches, table, and bed summed up the furniture; traditionally the bed was painted green. The mattresses were often stuffed with cattails. Plaster and pictures were not to be found on the walls, nor glassware and china on the table. The food was coarse or badly wilted or decaying remnants from the markets. Meat was eaten possibly once a week. Light and fuel were scanty and used sparingly.

Clothing was equally coarse and simple. A workingman wore a checked linsey-woolsey shirt, a red flannel jacket, leather knee breeches, oxhide shoes, and an old cocked hat. His wife wore a striped linsey-woolsey dress and a kerchief or mobcap. Whenever possible these articles were bought secondhand, and when they wore out they were cut down to fit the children. Indentured servants inherited the garments of their predecessors. Slaves were clothed in a material which has been described as "bull's wool."

Altogether the squalor was enough to account for the city's 330 dramshops. "Said Tatum's death," ran a coroner's verdict in the winter of 1786, "was occasioned by the freezing of a large quantity of water in his body, that had been mixed with the rum he drank." Tatum's death is often ascribed to fanciful causes. Perhaps it is not fanciful to observe that Tatum died poor.

CHAPTER IX

The Social Whirl

For Queen Street is a fashionable place,
And folks live there in plenty with some grace.
—*The Milkiad* (1789)

THE anonymous writer of these lines was a bit out of date.
Fashionable families were abandoning Queen (now Pearl) Street
for Wall and Broadway; however, they continued to live in
plenty and with punctilious grace—a type of life which may be
accepted as a satisfactory definition of "society." In a city and
land without a patent nobility, without hereditary rank or hide-
bound castes, without an authoritative test to distinguish blue
blood from red, property and manners and public office were
the chief prerequisites to get a man and his wife into society or
among those whom the rest of the people called "topping folks."
John Adams' phrase, "the rich, the well-born, and the able,"
might do to describe the ruling class; but society was more concerned with enjoyment than government, and its chosen few were
likely as not more accomplished than able, and well dressed
rather than well born. It remained essential to be rich—or at
least rich enough to pay the fiddler. Writes the Duke de la
Rochefoucauld-Liancourt, an early visitor to the republic:

> Although there are no distinctions acknowledged by law in the
> United States, wealth and professional standing determine the
> different classes. The merchants, lawyers, great landowners,
> physicians, and clergy comprise the superior class. The shopkeep-
> ers, farmers, and artisans may be said to make up the second
> class; and the third class is composed of the hired workmen. At

balls, concerts, and public amusements these classes do not mingle; and yet, except for longshoremen and sailors, everyone calls himself a *gentleman* and is so called by everyone else. Modest means are enough for the assumption of this title, which enables a man to pass easily from one class to another.

Much in the same strain, another French tourist, M. Ferdinand Bayard, divided the population socially into those who drove in coaches, those who rode horseback or walked, and, lowest of all, those who neither drove nor rode and who worked with their hands.

However defined, the distinctions were sharp enough to be scrupulously observed. During the Revolution John Jay and his wife had once taken refuge in the home of a village clergyman. In 1787 the parson sent Jay some news of himself and in the course of his letter remarked: "Sir, we are prone to think that a Gentleman of your Rank would not be so free to converse with a Lower." It so happened that Jay was not only a Gentleman of Rank but a person of piety, and he invited the clergyman to his New York home—"We have a chamber at your Service, and your Horse shall be with mine." But the point remains that the "poor Clergyman and Family" knew their place.

Typical of their cosmopolitan character New Yorkers were not so quick to draw these lines as more homogeneous and hard-shelled communities. Noah Webster notes in 1788 that the city's "principal families by associating in their public amusements with the middle class of well-bred citizens render their rank subservient to the happiness of society"; whereas, by way of contrast, "an affectation of superiority in certain families in Philadelphia has produced in that city a spirit . . . which has given the citizens, too generally perhaps, the reputation of being inhospitable." In January of 1789 John Webb, who was visiting in Savannah, writes to his brother: "I must confess I would rather live in New York with 100 pounds than live here with as many thousands." Savannah, he continues, "is a heavenly Winter country . . . but the circle you have in New York—But—But!

Tomorrow I shall spend the evening with all the Belles and Beaux of this place. But it will not be to be mentioned at the same hour with your parties."

Nor was any past season which young Webb enjoyed in New York to be mentioned with the parties of 1789. The presence of the new Congress and the new administration with Washington at its head and the country's most brilliant statesmen at his side, as well as the determination of the "principal families" of the city to show that New York knew how to dazzle as the nation's capital, led to a burst of splendor which has never been surpassed. Like the ladies who wore their hats à l'espagnole at the Inauguration Ball, New York society paraded its plumes.

A "Republican" protested against this magnificence and in a blistering letter to the *Daily Advertiser* (June 19) proposed that "we leave to the sons and daughters of corrupted Europe their levees, Drawing-Rooms, Routs, Drums, and Tornedos." Certain other citizens perhaps more entitled by rank to enjoy these festivities held aloof. Governor Clinton was noticeable for his absence—out of democratic principles, parsimony, or mere distaste. Senator Maclay expressed the scorn of the backwoodsman when he feared "we shall follow on nor cease till we have reached the summit of court etiquette and all the frivolities, fopperies, and expense practiced in European governments." Mr. Jefferson, while he attended the dinner parties after his return from Paris, was as a matter of his philosophy filled with "wonder and mortification" that the dinner guests showed "a preference of kingly over republican government . . . evidently a favorite sentiment." M. Brissot had already been shocked at the décolleté of the ladies, which he considered "an indecency among republicans." Mrs. Washington confessed, "I lead a very dull life here and know nothing that passes in the town." She was in fact a victim of this new court etiquette—"a state prisoner" she calls herself and adds, "as I cannot do as I like, I am obstinate and stay at home a great deal." Although aware that she was not young and gay enough to ride the social whirlwind as the President's wife should, she determined in her obstinacy "to be cheerful and happy."

Mrs. Washington's situation was unique. Most of the participants had no need of "resigning" themselves to be cheerful and happy. They were joyously busy as they reveled in the routs and drums, the teas and tornedos, the dinners and the levees. A single worry plagued them. Mrs. Iredell, wife of the Supreme Court justice, phrased it neatly: "When shall I get spirit to pay all the social debts I owe?"

No detailed ledger of the social credits and debts of 1789 has survived, or any accurate estimate on the revolutions per week of the social whirl. Those who were in it were too giddy and happy to analyze it objectively; those who were out of it were either unaware of it or dismissed the matter with an acrid republican grunt.

The social gyrations were rather bewildering. Abigail Adams Smith remarked of New York in 1787—the relatively quiet days of the Continental Congress—that "public dinners, public days, and private parties may take up a person's whole attention if they attend to them all." Two years later the number of activities was better than doubled.

A typical week might begin on a Sunday with a visit to any of the twenty-one churches of the city. Trinity was not yet rebuilt; the fashionable thronged St. Paul's. There you might see and be seen by the best people. Some went to commune with God; others were more interested in the Washingtons, the Hamiltons, and the Jays. Some of the young chits, like Charlotte in *The Contrast,* knew that church was something melancholy, but appreciated that it was a fine place to "ogle the beaux." A promenade on the Battery and a cup of tea with friends might end the social obligations of the first day of the week.

Monday was a day quite empty of any official functions—a good time for private dinners or for simple relaxation.

On Tuesday, from three to four, came the President's levee

to which all ladies and gentlemen of rank and fashion were frequent visitors.

On Wednesday evening Colonel and Mrs. Hamilton either gave a dinner or held open house. There the gentlemen might survey the feminine beauty of the capital and discuss the policies that were going into the making of the new nation. The ladies might exercise their varied wiles upon the numerous gentlemen or discuss the latest fashions with Mrs. Church, who had recently returned from London.

Mr. and Mrs. Jay often gave their dinners on Thursday. They still retained the enormous social prestige they had acquired during the period of the Confederation when Secretary Jay was the outstanding character in the government. The Jays were acquainted with the fashions of Madrid, Paris, and London— and their graces were such that no person willingly declined the coveted invitation to their home.

On Friday evening came a more ceremonious event: Mrs. Washington's reception. The receptions were somewhat stodgy and stuffy, but there you met all the right people. If you were fortunate you might persuade the luscious Mrs. William Bingham to relate one of her risqué stories or you might be simply but heartily amused by the malapropisms of Mrs. Knox.

It was Mrs. Knox who sometimes put forth her best entertaining effort on a Saturday night with a grand dinner. She made a great effort, for she was laboriously climbing her way up the social ladder. She was the daughter of a plebeian family named Fluckner; she had married an enterprising Boston bookseller who finally became Secretary of War under Washington. It was her humble origins which provoked her to remark, upon her return to Boston after the Revolution, that "the scum of society has now risen to the top." In New York she had sufficiently insinuated herself into the best circles that Abigail Adams Smith could describe her as "a lively and meddlesome but amiable leader of society, without whose co-operation it was believed, by many besides herself, that nothing could be properly done, in the drawing-room or ball-room, or any place indeed where fashionable men and women sought enjoyment." Mrs. Knox was so eager to shine among the *ton* of New York society that General Knox, without recorded protest, spent a ninth of his salary on wines alone and incurred an annual deficit of one third of his income.

In addition to all these regular affairs were many special events. Governor Clinton gave an occasional dinner, the foreign diplomats frequently entertained, and there were holidays to be celebrated. Then President Washington gave many special dinners. His diary records some of the guests and the dates: October 1—8, November 16—25, December 3—4, December 5—10, December 17—26, December 31—(?). The last was a grand New Year's Eve party. In addition to all this were the festive meetings of the Dancing Assembly and the performances of the John Street theater (three evenings a week, with a different play almost every time).

Who was who in this scintillating galaxy? Mrs. Washington certainly did her duty, although she was resigned if not dour about the entire social scene. Mrs. Clinton did not often participate, whether because of her poor health or her husband's disinclination we cannot definitely say. Mrs. John Adams seems to have led an unusually quiet life in New York. The real leadership fell to others.

Mrs. Jay and Mrs. Hamilton were dominating figures. There were others, but they were lesser lights at the moment: Mrs. Ralph Izard was later to arbitrate over if not direct the social fortunes of Charleston; Mrs. William Bingham was to become the central figure of the republican court when, in 1790, the capital was moved to Philadelphia. Kitty Duer and Mrs. Robert Morris might have held their own in any society; they were resplendent in that of 1789. If you won the favor of any of them you might readily find your way to the elegant affairs of the nation's capital.

The most accessible of these social functions was the President's levee. "The highest qualifications necessary," Maclay sarcastically informs us, "are to be clean shaved, shirted, and powdered, to make your bows with grace, and to be master of small chat on the weather, play, or newspaper anecdote of the day." As the gouty senator dressed and prepared "to do the needful," he was wont to soliloquize on the subject with dour eloquence:

> The practice is certainly anti-republican. This certainly escapes nobody. The royalists glory in it as a point gained. Republicans are borne down by fashion and a fear of being charged with want of respect to General Washington. If there is treason in the wish I retract it, but would to God this same General Washington were in heaven! We would not then have him brought forward as a constant cover to every irrepublican act!

We can almost see the hair powder fly.

Barbered and tailored, you might well follow Maclay to the presidential mansion, though he admitted he was "no great thing of a pattern," being "but a poor courtier." Between three and four o'clock you presented yourself at the door of No. 3 Cherry Street. One of the secretaries, Mr. Tobias Lear or Major William Jackson, introduced you—taking care to pronounce your name distinctly. You observed that the President was clad in a black velvet coat and breeches. His powdered hair was caught behind in a silk bag. One hand held a cocked hat adorned with a feather and a cockade, and the other rested on the polished steel hilt of his long sword. When a sufficient circle of callers was gathered, he began at his right and passed from one guest to another, addressing each by name and chatting with him for a moment. This was the time to display your mastery of small talk. Thus (reports Maclay):

The President: "How will this weather suit your farming?"

Senator Maclay: "Poorly, sir; the season is the most backward I have ever known."

The President: "Fruit will be safe; backward seasons are in favor of it. But in Virginia it was lost before I left."

Senator Maclay: "Much depends on the exposure of the orchard. We Pennsylvanians find that a northern aspect is most certain in producing fruit."

The President: "Yes, that is a good observation and should be attended to."

And then, like Maclay, you made your bow and retired.

Unsuspicious minds found no smack of royalism in these simple gatherings. To be sure, the levees were confined to the "fashionable, elegant, and refined," and they were free from "the intrusion of the rabble . . . with boots, roundabouts, patched knees, or holes at the elbow." And a Revolutionary War veteran, stung at the sight of repentant Tories back in favor, took quill in hand to demand in the New York *Journal* (July 2) "from what authority the most inveterate enemies to the Independence of this country attend at every Levee of our Illustrious Chief . . . and come into the presence of the father of his country, attired in Garments stained with the blood of departed prisoners."

The illustrious chief himself saw the whole matter in a common-sense light. "Gentlemen, often in great numbers," wrote Washington, "come and go; chat with each other and act as they please. A porter shows them into the room, and they retire from it when they choose, without ceremony. At their first entrance they salute me, and I them, and as many as I can, I talk to. What 'pomp' there is in all this I am unable to discover." Nights, when the President sat down to write his diary, he took pains to record how well the levee was attended; whether (as on December 29) "being very snowy, not a single person appeared"; and if on occasion "the visitors were not very numerous, though respectable." The word "respectable" appears frequently enough to suggest that the writer put some weight by it.

Mrs. Washington's Friday-evening receptions were open to ladies as well as gentlemen, and they were rather more formal than the levees. The first lady stood at the President's side as the visitors arrived and were presented. Full dress was obligatory.

Washington generally wore a fancy-colored coat and waistcoat with black smallclothes; but he banished hat and sword and mingled with the guests on the easy terms of a private gentleman. Plum cakes, tea, and coffee were served. When the clock struck nine, Mrs. Washington advanced and said with a smile, "The General always retires at nine and I usually precede him." Whereupon the guests withdrew; and the general went to his library, read a while, took a nightcap, and noted in his diary, "The visitors of Gent'n and ladies to Mrs. Washington this evening were numerous and respectable" or whatever the facts warranted.

Formal dinners are by nature bores and, if the company has any spirit, never follow the ordained etiquette to the end. Still the essence of social behavior is to know the laws so that they may at least be broken with proper discrimination.

Etiquette decreed that the dinners to which you received a written invitation—it was fashionable to scribble them on the backs of playing cards—should begin àt three or four in the afternoon. At a "great dinner" of this character, "the candles are ready to be brought in with the going out of the last dishes."

The courses were usually two. The first comprised the entrées, roasts, and warm side dishes, which were simultaneously laid on the table in imposing abundance. Unless the acme of ceremony prevailed, toasts were in order at any moment. They were a sort of trial by combat. The Marquis de Chastellux, who fought in America during the Revolution, often wrote of things about which he knew little. But in discussing toasts he was traveling over familiar territory:

I find it an absurd and truly barbarous practice, the first time you drink, and at the beginning of the dinner, to call out successively to each individual to let him know you drink his health. The actor in this comedy is sometimes ready to die of thirst while he is obliged to ask the names or catch the eyes of twenty-five or thirty persons. The others are no less unhappy, for they cannot pay attention to what they are eating or listen to what their partner is saying to them, being incessantly called to, as they are, on the right and the left or pulled by the sleeve to acquaint them with the honor they are receiving.

Frequently four or five guests were thus toasted—or annoyed— at a time. The marquis complains:

> Another custom completes the despair of the stranger. . . . They call to you from one end of the table to the other, "Sir, will you permit me to drink a glass of wine with you?" The proposal must always be accepted. The bottle is passed to you and you must look your enemy in the face. You wait until he has likewise poured out his wine and taken his glass. You then drink mournfully with him, as the recruit imitates the corporal in his drill.

To the uninitiate there was no end to the helpings of food. A hostess who stopped offering another portion was ungracious; a guest who refused to accept it was rude. But when a diner reached his capacity he could, if he knew the trick, halt the flow by crossing knife and fork on his plate in a prescribed manner.

The second course consisted of pies, pastries, cakes, candies, and ices. After they were consumed the cloth was removed, and fruits and nuts were brought to the mahogany board. This was the signal for set toasts. "They serve to prolong the conversation," observes the marquis, "which is always more animated at the end of the repast." A ceremonious dinner required thirteen of these formal toasts, one for each state in the Union. Thereafter "volunteers" were in order to any number, so that even the present Union could have been accommodated. When the host felt that the safety limit had been reached, coffee was served—a hint for the guests to rise from the table.

Next day the town, or those in the know, could enjoy the bouquets of gossip gleaned the night before. There was that piquant episode on Richmond Hill. Vice-President Adams was entertaining a distinguished company—Baron Steuben, the Dutch minister Van Berckel, the deaf and eloquent Chancellor Livingston, and, seated next to Mrs. Adams, the French minister,

Count de Moustier, in his earrings and red-heeled shoes. After the soup De Moustier kept his plate empty, declining everything from the roast beef to the lobsters. "At length," so later rumor tells, "his own body-cook came bustling through the crowd of waiters and placed a warm pie of truffles and game before the Count who, reserving a moderate portion himself, distributed the rest among his neighbors." The Count's explanation was that he had had experience with New York dinners.

Mrs. Robert Morris, a vivacious gossip, passed along her experience with spoiled cream at the President's board. Maclay reports her tale:

> A large fine-looking trifle was brought to the table and appeared exceedingly well indeed. She was helped by the President, but on taking some of it she had to pass her handkerchief to her mouth and rid herself of the morsel; on which she whispered to the President. The cream of which it is made had been unusually stale and rancid; on which the General changed his plate immediately. "But," she added with a titter, "Mrs. Washington ate a whole heap of it."

No one excels Maclay for these candid shots. Next to him the memoir writers of the period appear as oily, somber, and pompous as the portrait painters on whom they apparently modeled their prose. The Pennsylvanian's account of his first dinner at the President's—which was the ultimate in social dining for the season of 1789—cannot be abridged.

> At a little after four [related Maclay], we went to the President's for dinner. The company were: President and Mrs. Washington, Vice-President and Mrs. Adams, the Governor and his wife, Mr. Jay and wife, Mr. Langdon and wife, Mr. Dalton and a Lady (perhaps his wife), and a Mr. Smith, Mr. Bassett, myself, Lear, Lewis, the President's two secretaries. The President and Mrs. Washington sat opposite each other in the middle of the table; the two secretaries, one at each end.
> It was a great dinner, and the best of the kind I ever was at.

The room, however, was disagreeably warm [in a New York August].

First was the soup; fish roasted and boiled; meats, gammon, fowls, etc. This was the dinner. The middle of the table was garnished in the usual tasty way, with small images, flowers (artificial), etc. The dessert was, first apple-pies, pudding, etc.; then iced creams, jellies, etc.; then water-melons, musk-melons, apples, peaches, nuts.

It was the most solemn dinner ever I sat at. Not a health drank; scarce a word said until the cloth was taken away. Then the President, filling a glass of wine, with great formality drank to the health of every individual by name round the table. Everybody imitated him, charged glasses, and such a buzz of "health, sir" and "health, madam" and "thank you, sir" and "thank you, madam" never had I heard before.

Indeed, I had liked to have been thrown out in the hurry; but I got a little wine in my glass, and passed the ceremony. The ladies sat a good while, and the bottles passed about; but there was dead silence almost. Mrs. Washington at last withdrew with the ladies.

I expected the men would now begin, but the same stillness remained. [Then] the President told of a New England clergyman who had lost a hat and wig in passing a river called the Brunks [Bronx]. He smiled—and everybody else laughed. He now and then said a sentence or two on some common subject, and what he said was not amiss.

Mr. Jay tried to make a laugh by mentioning the circumstances of the Duchess of Devonshire leaving no stone unturned to carry Fox's election. There was that Mr. Smith, who mentioned how *Homer* described Aeneas leaving his wife and carrying his father out of flaming Troy. He had heard somebody (I suppose) witty on the occasion; but if he had ever read it he would have said *Virgil*.

The President kept a fork in his hand, when the cloth was taken away, I thought for the purpose of picking nuts. He ate no nuts, however, but played with the fork, striking on the edge of the table with it. We did not sit long after the ladies retired. The President rose, went up-stairs to drink coffee; the company followed.

I took my hat and came home.

Fashionable teas, held in the middle of the afternoon, had their punctilios. Unwritten law required the hostess to refill the cups as quickly as they were emptied. As a result the Prince de Broglie on one occasion was nearly drowned. He was attending a tea at Mrs. Robert Morris'—it was back in 1782—and he held out bravely till the twelfth cup. Just as he was sinking, a neighbor whispered in his ear and told him that when he felt he had enough of the water cure he should place his spoon across the top of his cup. "It is rude," said his rescuer, "to refuse a cup of tea when it is tendered, but once you give the signal with your spoon, it would be indiscreet for the hostess to renew the offer." Another Frenchman, ignorant of this device, saved himself by hiding his cup in his pocket.

Tea and cards almost inevitably went together. "In New York," writes Rebecca Franks, a visiting Philadelphia belle, "you enter the room with a formal set curtsy, and after the how-dos, things are finished. All's a dead calm till the cards are introduced, when you see pleasure dancing in the eyes of all the matrons and they seem to gain new life." Some of them were known to gain— or lose—three or four hundred dollars, as well, at whist, omber, or quadrille.

In Miss Franks's opinion New York women turned to cards because they didn't know how to talk. "I don't know a woman or a girl who can chat above half an hour, and that only on the form of a cap, the color of a ribbon, or the set of a hoop." Philadelphia ladies were different. "They have more cleverness in the turn of an eye than those of New York have in their whole composition." This is all plainly libelous, for New Yorkers knew how to talk their own lingo at least to the extent of annoying the purists, who wrote protests in the *Gazette,* the *Packet,* and the *Columbian Magazine* against the fopperies, slang, and fashionable mispronunciations current in the drawing rooms.

New Yorkers, so the protests ran, said they were "bored" at tea without cards; one afternoon was "infinitely" better than another; disasters were called "unpleasant." A young chit "swam" in a minuet; or, "dangling over" the Battery, she "flirted" her hoop—all part of the art of "pulling caps for a man." If the man was a beau, his buckles were "tonish," and when he left the room he "minced out." If he was quite the opposite of a beau, he was "a Wabash"—a savage who didn't "know *Buffon* from *Soufflée*." To be thoroughly in style, belles and beaux, between sips of tea, spoke of their good *fortchune* at the last round of whist, or, seeking *quietchude,* cast their eyes toward a corner sofa where they hoped they would not be *distchurbed*. Once there—in a "snug party"—they could remain indifferent to the *virtchues* of the harpsichord.

Miss Franks says nothing of the popular songs she heard during 1783 at the tea routs of New York. In 1789 someone would surely be found at the newfangled pianoforte, singing "Roslin Castle," "Old Maid of the Mill," and that two-year-old hit from *The Contrast,* entitled "Alknomook, the Death Song of the Cherokee Indians." The words of the latter may be described as infinitely distchurbing.

The rout of all routs was a ball or dancing assembly. Two stand out red-lettered in the calendar of the season. One was the Inauguration Ball—although no one called it that until it had passed into history. Legend, assisted by the imagination of Mr. Jefferson who was still in France, has transformed it into a regal affair—with a dais for Washington, on it a sofa in place of a throne, and, as "favors" for the ladies, ivory-handled fans painted with a medallion portrait of the President and presented to them by a page at the entry.

Two days afterwards, however, the New York *Packet* (of May 9) soberly reports that the subscribers of the Dancing Assembly, society's pet dancing club, gave "an elegant Ball and Entertainment to his Excellency, the President of the United States," who "was pleased to honor the company with his presence." The ball was held in the City Assembly Room on Broadway and was attended by about three hundred persons. They included the Vice-President, most of the members of Congress and cabinet officers, Governor Clinton, Chancellor Livingston, Mayor Duane, Ex-president (of Congress) Griffin, Baron Steuben, the Count de Moustier, the French envoy, and other foreigners of distinction.

A "numerous and brilliant collection" of ladies graced the room. Washington danced a minuet with Mrs. James Maxwell, a cotillion with Mrs. Peter Van Brugh Livingston, and another cotillion with Mrs. Alexander Hamilton. "The Company retired about two o'clock, after having spent a most agreeable evening. Joy, satisfaction, and vivacity were expressive in every countenance—and every pleasure seemed to be heightened by the presence of a Washington."

A week later, Count de Moustier gave an official ball in honor of the President. His sister-in-law, odd Madame de Bréhan,* declared she had "exhausted every resource" to produce a showing worthy of France. Again the "three hundred" of society turned out in plumed and satined array, and next day an enthusiastic congressman from New Jersey wrote all about it to his wife. Boudinot relates:

> After the President came, a company of eight couples formed in the other room and entered two by two, and began a most curious dance called *En Ballet*. Four of the gentlemen were dressed in French regimentals and four in American uniforms; four of the ladies with blue ribbons round their heads and American flowers, and four with red roses and flowers of France. These danced in a very curious manner, sometimes two and two, sometimes four couple and four couple, and then in a moment all

* This strange woman has confused writers almost as much as she did her contemporaries. This, too, would have given her pleasure, but certainly she would have preferred it to be about more than a name. Madame de Bréhan came to the United States with her brother-in-law, the Count de Moustier, so that her son might get a good education as well as "be safer from seduction than in France" (so Jefferson explained about "Madame la Marquise de Bréhan" to Jay). Lafayette called her the "Countess de Bréhan." Her neighbors in New York gave her a variety of titles never listed in the *Almanach de Gotha*, for in the blunt language of the day, they thought that "she was sleeping with the French minister." Jay, then Secretary for Foreign Affairs, explained that while this might be proper in France it created a bad impression in America. This was the cause of Moustier's recall at the request of the American government—the first in our diplomatic history.

together, which formed great entertainment for the spectators, to show the happy union between the two nations.

Three rooms were filled, and the fourth was most elegantly set off as a place for refreshment. A long table crossed this room in the middle. . . . The whole wall, inside, was covered with shelves filled with cakes, oranges, apples, wines of all sorts, ice creams, etc., and highly lighted up. A number of servants from behind the table supplied the guests with everything they wanted as they came in to refresh themselves, which they did as often as a party had done dancing, and made way for another. We retired about ten o'clock at the height of the jollity.

Among the good-fellowship and fraternal organizations—the Masons, St. George's, St. Andrew's, St. Patrick's, and the like—only one was distinguished for its social pretensions. It did its best to compensate for the country's lack of an aristocracy by creating a hereditary membership, and its name was the Order of the Cincinnati. Through it some of the fathers of the Revolution, without waiting for their sons and daughters to take up the task, sought to form a self-anointed peerage. With Washington at their head, Louis XVI as their patron, the Counts de Rochambeau and de Grasse, the Marquis de Lafayette and Baron Steuben among their members, with gold eagles in their lapels, with chairs of state, silk standards, and diplomas, with membership guaranteed to their eldest sons in the remotest generation, the Cincinnati managed to earn their own unmitigated esteem. But other people—too many of them—laughed.

New Yorkers in particular could laugh every time they went to the theater and saw *The Contrast*. "Why," explains Jonathan, the Yankee hayseed, "the colonel is one of those folks called the Shin—Shin—dang it all, I can't speak them *lignum vitae* words —you know who I mean—there is a company of them—they wear a china goose at their button-hole—a kind of gilt thing." Senator Maclay noted their "arrogant airs" and told himself, " 'Tis probable the whole body of them will soon be demanding pensions to support their titles and dignity." When Baron Steuben asked John Jay to accept an honorary membership, the Secretary for Foreign Affairs replied, with his own proficient sarcasm, that he was "neither young enough nor old enough to desire that great *honor*." When the baron persisted, Jay waxed eloquent against a society which, so far as he could see, existed for the chief purpose of "conferring honors upon themselves."

No doubt unperturbed by all this—though Jay's shot must have struck home to a baron who had once conferred upon himself the title of general—the Cincinnati held their annual meeting on the Fourth of July at the City Tavern. They marched to the President's home, made him a speech, and received a reply. Then they "proceeded in procession, attended by Col. Bauman's regiment of artillery and band of music (whose appearance was truly martial) to St. Paul's church." They entered flag foremost, eagles on their breasts, and occupied seats "alloted for themselves." Colonel Alexander Hamilton delivered a eulogy on the late Major General Nathaniel Greene. And at four o'clock those members who qualified sat down in Fraunces' Tavern with the officers of General Malcolm's brigade and drank their thirteen toasts. Perhaps Colonel Hamilton favored the company with the song that, years hence, he was to sing for the last time to the Cincinnati before he went to his fatal meeting with Burr: "How Stands the Glass Around?"

A somewhat different organization has since become famous as New York's very own. On May 6 the *Daily Advertiser* carried the announcement that "The Sons of St. Tammany intend celebrating their Anniversary Festival, the 1st of May, Old Stile (corresponding to the 12th inst.) at the place appointed. . . . Dinner on the table at 3 o'clock." St. Tammany's Society had led a feeble existence since its appearance in several colonies before the Revolution and its rebirth three or four years after. But in 1789 it took on a fresh, vigorous life—unimpaired if not altogether untarnished to this day.

Its new founders came from a wide diversity of background. William Mooney, the grand sachem in 1789 and eminent in the society for more than thirty years thereafter, was an upholsterer. The guiding spirit was John Pintard, scholar, philanthropist, and wealthy merchant. Among the officers were Thomas Greenleaf and John Loudon, printers and publishers, Dr. William Smith, physician, and White Matlack, the city's big brewer; and on the roster of members appear the familiar names of Roosevelt and Livingston. The wiskinkie, "eyes" and doorkeeper of the society, was in a class by himself: little Gardiner Baker.

According to its announcements the following year, the society proposed to foster "whatever may tend to perpetuate the love of freedom . . . to promote intercourse between the States, and to remove local and class prejudices." Pintard revealed its social tendency when, in writing to a friend, he foretold that "its democratic principles will serve in some measure to correct the aristocracy of our city." But in 1789 and until the impact of the French Revolution penetrated New York, the sachems and braves were more interested in their tribal feasts than in political powwows.

The "old stile" May Day celebration had less elegance but more hilarity than the balls which graced the City Tavern. Tents were set up on the banks of the Hudson about two miles out of town. The braves smoked the pipe of peace, ravished the victuals, drank to brotherly love, bellowed in chorus; and little Gardiner sang his favorite "Battle of the Kegs."

Little Gardiner Baker—"little" he was and "little" was he called—was soon to bear the great standard of St. Tammany down Broadway when the tribe paraded in feathers and war paint. He was an amateur antiquarian, "himself a greater curiosity than any he collected," and liked to dwell on the good old days and their crumbling survivals with the ardor "of a monk in exhibiting an undoubted relic."

Regular meetings of Tammany were held in Sam Fraunces' tavern on Cortlandt Street. The high spot of these occasions came when the members resolved themselves into a "Committee of Amusement." As the surviving manuscript minutes of two and three years later record for posterity, the first feature was the recital of "American Anecdotes." No one will ever know the vintage of these stories or their nub, but something time-honored and familiar may be sensed in the "anecdote of a Sailor and his Girl . . . a Connecticutt Man and his Daughter . . . a Traveller and Hog . . . a Connecticutt Girl and her Mare . . . a Country Girl and Spark." There were stories of a Dutchman, an English sailor, a Boston Negro; and it may be wondered whether it was too early in the nation's cultural history for the wiskinkie to rise and begin his anecdote with the words, "Once there were two Irishmen . . ."

Debates followed next in the order of amusement. There was thrusting of pros and cons on the abolition of capital punishment except in cases of murder; on whether married or unmarried life is happier; on whether innate affection is planted in the human breast; and whether the abolition of the slave trade would damage the West Indies.

At formal celebrations—Washington's Birthday, the Fourth of July, the society's anniversary—the Committee of Amusement commanded the ritual thirteen toasts. Copious draughts were sacrificed to the sentiments Tammany men held dear: "May the Sons of Liberty be ever superior to the love of Property. . . . May the Eagle of Liberty hover over the World and Tyrants be its prey. . . . May the oppressed Sons of Liberty in foreign climes ever find a peaceful Asylum in this our Land of Freedom. . . . May the Genius of Freedom accompany the American Stars to the Uttermost Regions of the earth and under their Influence proclaim the *Rights of Man*."

Singing, for those who survived, invariably ended the program of amusement. Through the smoke of the calumets and the fumes of the toasts rang hunting songs, love songs, patriotic and moral songs, and a curious ditty entitled "Nothing at All." While Colonel Hamilton, gathered with the Cincinnati in a neighboring tavern, may have been rendering "How Stands the

Glass Around?" Brother Hawes of Tammany sang "One Bottle More."

In conclusion the assembled braves, sachems, grand sachem, father of the council, scribe of the council, sagamore, and wiskinkie intoned the twelve verses of the "Etho Song," official anthem of the Great Wigwam. The first couplet was sung in harmonious strains:

> Brothers, our council fire shines Bright,
> We feel its heat, we see its Light.

But the thunder of voices and stamping of feet were enough to raise the watch on Cortlandt Street when, reaching the last verse, they roared:

> Then pass the bottle with the Sun
> To Tammany and Washington!

CHAPTER X

Diversions and the Arts

THE theatrical district of the city was sharply defined. It lay on the north side of John Street, halfway between Broadway and Nassau; and it consisted of one playhouse. This was a wooden building, painted red, set about sixty feet back from the street and approached through a roofed passageway.

Almost any issue of the daily newspaper, the *Daily Advertiser,* carried a notice after this pattern of May 6:

THEATRE
By the Old American Company,
THIS EVENING, will be presented, a Comedy, called
THE SCHOOL FOR SCANDAL,
To which will be added a Comic Opera, called
THE POOR SOLDIER
With the original Overtures and Accompanyments.
Places in the Boxes may be had of Mr. Philips, at the
Office of the Theatre, who will attend from Ten to
Twelve o'clock, A.M. and on the days of the performance
from Three to Five P.M. where also Tickets may be
had, and at Mr. Gaine's, in Hanover Square.
The doors will be opened at Six, and the curtain drawn
up precisely at Seven o'clock.
Box 8s. Pit 6s. Gallery 4s.
Ladies and Gentlemen are requested to order their
Servants to take up and let down with their horses
heads to the East River, to avoid confusion.
VIVAT RESPUBLICA.

A full house—when the President attended and the line of horses and sedan chairs extended back into Broadway—brought $800 to the box office. The management did its best to secure this happy result by suitable publicity. Two days before the performance the *Daily Advertiser* was induced to report: "It is whispered that *The School for Scandal* and *The Poor Soldier* will be acted on Monday night for the entertainment of the President." Admonishing the leading lady—every journalist imagines he is born a dramatic critic—the newspaper continued: "Mrs. Henry ought on this occasion condescend to give passion and tenderness to Maria."

Washington's advertised presence drew to the theater "topping folks"—the pink of society, the governmental and diplomatic world, and even avowed enemies of the stage and all its immoral works. A humble spectator who paid his four shillings (50¢) for admission to the gallery enjoyed quite a show before he entered the playhouse. Not least would be the sight of the star, John Henry, who had the gout and who always arrived in a one-horse carriage upon which were painted two crutches with the motto: "This or These." There is social history, something for a Hollywood star to read, in his remark, "I put this motto and device on my carriage to prevent any impertinent observations on an actor keeping a coach." The leading lady, Mrs. Henry, likewise provided a thrill. "A perfect fairy in person," she wore such enormous hoops that her husband was obliged to slide her out of the coach sideways and then carry her in his arms to the stage door.

The same humble spectator could describe his first visit to the John Street theater in the words of a country bumpkin in Royall Tyler's play, *The Contrast:* "I saw a great crowd of folks going into a long entry that had lanterns over the door. They showed me clean up to the garret, just like a meeting-house gallery. And so I saw a power of topping folks all sitting around in little cabins, just like father's corn-cribs—such a squeaking with fiddles and such a tarnel blaze with the lights, my head was near turned."

The lights may have turned the yokel's head, but their dripping wax did worse to the heads of those below. On cold nights the discomfort was increased by lack of stoves, and what the actors may have taken for applause was only the audience stamping its feet to keep warm. Other inconveniences arose from the absence of programs, ushers, or reserved seats. Servants sent on ahead held places for their masters. The orchestra consisted of fiddles and drums; even so, the audience complained when it was deprived of its full half-hour of overture. A further annoyance may be read in the newspaper notice: "Gentlemen crowd the stage and very much interrupt the performance."

But there was much to enjoy. When the President entered his box, which was painted with the arms of the United States, the fiddles and drums struck up the "President's March," a tune written by the orchestra leader, Philip Fyles (or Phila), and later developed into our familiar "Hail, Columbia." There were cheers for Vice-President Adams when he entered another box painted with the national coat of arms, and for Governor Clinton, too, when he sat behind the arms of the state—"the genuine effusion of Freemen." Opera glasses came into style this year, and the gallery had an extra treat making fun of these "spy-glasses." On occasion the scenery was ambitious. A performance of *The Shipwreck* was enlivened by a "real balloon" on the stage. The pantomime of Robinson Crusoe furnished, so the advertisement claimed, "the most brilliant display of Scenery ever exhibited in the Western World." This brilliant display included landscapes described in Captain Cook's voyages to Tahiti and New Zealand—except, that is, a view of the Falls of the Passaic. In describing the latter, the *Daily Advertiser* pictures a darkened stage; then the Genius of Columbia, gradually lighted, rose from the waterfalls; at a motion of his wand, the new Federal Hall appeared in the background; and, still rising, the Genius ascended to a cloudbank surmounting a Temple of Concord, a "superb transparency" with columns symbolic of Wisdom, Fortitude, Virtue, and Justice. Even when the drops were crude and stale, there were always nonsense choruses—that "double talk" common to popular songs throughout the ages—to be bellowed back from gallery and pit; choruses such as:

> Ditherum doodle, adgety,
> Nadgety, tragedy rum,
> Gooseterum foodle, fidgety,
> Nidgety, nadgety mum,
>   Goosterum foodle!

Finally the playwrights could be counted on to exercise their liberty "to make a smutty joke, throw the ladies into confusion, and give the jessamies [fops] a chance of tittering to show their teeth."

These same jessamies and pretty chits enjoyed "snug parties" in the sideboxes. They could hear their own behavior described by a lively young belle in *The Contrast*:

> The curtain rises, then, by mere force of apprehension, we torture some harmless expression into a double meaning which the poor author never dreamed of, and then we have recourse to our fans, and then we blush, and then the gentlemen jog one another, peep under the fan, and make the prettiest remarks; and then we giggle and they simper, and they giggle and we simper, and then the curtain drops, and then for nuts and oranges, and then we bow, and it's pray, Ma'am, take it, and pray, Sir, keep it, and oh! not for the world, Sir; and then the curtain rises again, and then we blush and giggle and simper and bow all over again. Oh! the charms of a sidebox conversation!

As for the performance at which the President first appeared, Senator Maclay, who sat in the presidential box, did not approve. "The play," he wrote, "was *The School for Scandal*. I never liked it; indeed I think it an indecent representation before ladies of character and virtue. . . . The house," he added, "was greatly crowded, and I thought the players acted well."

The Poor Soldier, a favorite comic opera which Maclay dismissed with the one word "farce," was played four times in '89.

The season opened April 14 and closed December 15; but the house was dark throughout August and on several other dates because of illness, building repairs, or the weather. Altogether 118 performances were given—usually two and sometimes three plays an evening. The double-headers were mostly comedies followed by a farce, comic opera, or pantomime. During the intermission between the comedy and farce, Mr. Durang and Mrs. (or Miss) Durang favored the audience with a hornpipe dance.

The year's repertoire included thirty-one comedies, twenty-six farces, nine comic operas, six tragedies, and two pantomimes—the work of more than three dozen authors. The most popular playwright was O'Keefe, whose farces, which included *The Poor Soldier,* were given on twelve nights. Sheridan was played eight nights—*The Critic, The Duenna, The Rivals,* besides *The School for Scandal.* Shakespeare's *Merry Wives of Windsor, The Tempest,* and *Richard III* each had one performance. Otway, Goldsmith, Garrick, Fielding, and Cumberland were among the authors ever heard of before or since. As a whole the program, if not the actors, did well by English drama.

Of native playwrights there were but two. Royall Tyler's *The Contrast,* which was revived on June 10, was in fact the first American play to be acted by professional comedians; its initial performance was at the John Street theater in 1787. The second of America's professional playwrights was William Dunlap—"dramatist, theatrical manager, painter, critic, novelist, and historian," eventually the author of forty-nine plays and, among other major works, a *History of the American Theater,* a *History of the Rise and Progress of the Arts of Design in the United States,* a *History of the New Netherlands,* and a lively diary. Dunlap's maiden effort, *The Father—or American Shandyism,* opened on September 7. On November 24 he had another first night with his farce, *Darby's Return,* which had the distinction of making Washington laugh. Or, as the *Daily Advertiser* reported, "Our beloved Ruler seemed to unbend." Read today, neither *The Contrast* nor *The Father* is intolerably dull. What they lack in plot and character study, they make up in slang, "wit," and local "cracks," though hardly enough to raise a laugh one hundred and fifty years too late.

The nearest thing to a circus was a collection of wild animals to be seen at No. 28 Wall Street, opposite the Coffee House. Here Dr. King, lately from South America, exhibited "a Male and Female of the surprising species of the Ourang Outang or Wild Man of the Woods; the Sloth, which from its sluggish disposition will grow poor from travelling from one tree to another; the Baboon of different species and of a most singular nature; Monkey, Porcupine, Ant-Bear, Crocodile, Lizard, and Sword Fish; Snakes of various kinds and very extraordinary; Tame Tyger and Buffalo: Also a Variety of Birds"—all for 5s. an adult and 2s. 6d. a child.

But there were cheaper shows. For two shillings (and one for a child) you could see Joseph Decker's wax figures, burglar and fire alarm, and a "small paradox" at No. 14 William Street. The feature of the collection was "a Speaking Figure, suspended by a ribbon from the centre of a beautiful Temple, which asked questions itself, and answered with delicacy and propriety questions addressed to it either in a whisper or a more audible tone."

This was only a sample of what you saw at Bowen's wax works, No. 74 Water Street, for 2s. 6d. for adults and 1s. for children. Besides a number of edifying Biblical scenes, and figures that moved their heads, winked, and performed other feats "to the admiration of the spectators," there were effigies of "the President of the United States sitting under a canopy in military dress . . . the King, Queen, Prince of Wales of Great Britain habited in cloaths which were presented by the King" and three leading clergymen of New York. Among the admiring spectators on September 17 were "the President and his Lady and family and several other persons of distinction."

During the summer Mr. Decker was amusing the populace gratis by flying balloons up the Harlem River. Then he raised a hundred guineas, by subscription, to build a balloon one hundred feet round, in which he himself proposed to ascend. When the day came—it was September 23—two thirds of the city turned out for the show. Just how or why, no one knew, but a minute before Decker was to take off, the balloon went up in flames. Next day the New York *Journal* published a notice no doubt inspired by one of the unlucky investors: "Yesterday at four o'clock departed in a blaze the much Celebrated Balloon, constructed under the admired abilities of Mr. Decker . . . which perfectly accorded with his *Nota Bene* that he should leave the city after his descent—into the purses of the generous spectators."

We have already learned of Christopher Colles and his scientific exhibits.

Other spectacles cost nothing—unless you bet and lost. Considerable money was placed on a shooting match, August 8, in a field off Greenwich Road. One-armed Captain McPherson of Philadelphia won the match, his competitor, Captain Stakes, having failed to hit the barn door on which the target was fixed. A week later there was a boat race off Sandy Hook between a local pilot boat and a Virginia-built schooner from Curaçao for a purse of fifty half-joes ($400). The pilot boat beat her rival by about seven minutes covering a course of forty-two nautical miles in five hours. Thirty boatloads of spectators watched the race, and $5,000 "exchanged their owners." There were only two horse races during the season of '89: one on Greenwich Lane and the other at Jamaica.

Hessian bandmasters—so a traveler reports—helped elevate musical taste after the Revolutionary War was over and they had settled in America rather than face the music back home. In any case the music lovers of New York, who must have been fairly numerous, possessed many opportunities to indulge themselves. A musical society was organized in 1788, and its members were required to perform as well as listen. To this end instruments could be bought from the president of the society, George Gilfert, who ran a music store and published current compositions. John Jacob Astor, at No. 81 Queen Street, imported pianofortes from England. His rival and neighbor, Thomas Dodd, manufactured a variety of instruments. Dodd's own make of pianofortes—the "most fashionable instrument"—cost 25 per cent less than Astor's importations. Benjamin Carr, music dealer and publisher of Philadelphia, maintained a branch store in New York. If pianofortes were most fashionable, the popular instrument for men was the German flute and for ladies the four-stringed guitar. Other favorites were the violin, harpsichord, 'cello, hautboy, clarinet, and bassoon.

There was no dearth of teachers. Mr. Gilfert gave lessons in the instruments he sold. John Rudberg, of No. 4 Great Dock Street, taught the guitar, violin, and clarinet. Henri Capron and Alexander Reinagle, players in the Old American Company's orchestra and concert managers on their own hook, both taught music. Reinagle was a prolific composer and a friend of J. C. Bach.

Time passed quickest for those who studied under William Hofmeister, better known as Billy the Fiddler. Billy was a dwarf, about four and a half feet tall, who wore seven-league boots and an oversized cocked hat. In his studio at Broadway and Fulton he regaled the students with anecdotes of his old friend Mozart, and played for them a Mozart sonata which he claimed he himself had written. When he announced in the newspapers his proposal to teach, he was candid enough to say that he was incapable of doing anything else.

The best instruction was given by Peter A. Van Hagen, "organist, klokkenist, and componist," formerly concert master at Zutphen and now resident at 23 Ferry Street. Mynheer Van Hagen was a Dutch refugee whom political troubles at home and a desire to taste republican freedom abroad had driven to American shores. He came to New York in October of '89; and he brought with him a son eight years of age, the inevitable prodigy, who fiddled for the public at the Van Hagen concerts. On the day of his last concert an admirer announced in the

Gazette that he would undertake to prove "before any judge who had taste enough to take the matter into consideration" that Mr. Van Hagen, senior, was the first master of music who had ever visited America. Twelve lessons from the master, together with the entrance fee, cost $8.50. He taught any number of instruments, including the "violino harmonika," a contrivance which enabled the player to extract a melody out of iron nails. He likewise gave instruction in "shaking" a trill and the other elements of singing. His companion, Mr. Frobel, tuned pianos for five shillings each.

Eight concerts were given in the course of the year. In the spring the Musical Society offered two concerts, one at the Lutheran church and the other a benefit performance for jailed debtors. The fall season provided six subscription concerts. Messers Reinagle and Capron managed three of them; Mrs. Anna Maria Sewell, who had retired from the Old American Company to run a young ladies' school, managed the fourth; and Peter Van Hagen, assisted by Frobel and the Van Hagen prodigy, gave the last two.

The taste of the day, elevated by Hessian bandmasters, may be judged, perhaps wrongly, by sampling the programs of these concerts. There were overtures by Giordani, Guglielmi, Vanhal, Ditters, J. Stamitz and C. Stamitz; a symphony by Goffec, and a piano and violin duet by Billy the Fiddler's friend, Mozart.

Even before the rush of French masters who were soon to take refuge in America from the carmagnole, dancing was a serious, precise, and complicated pleasure. The cotillion, allemande, and rigadoon demanded the use of the head as well as the feet. No one dared substitute energy for art and "swing" a minuet. The Marquis de Chastellux had long before remarked (in 1781) that dancing in American society worked more by grace of law than by the law of grace. "Places are marked out," he said, "the contré dances are named, and every proceeding provided for, calculated and submitted to regulation." He told of a young lady in Philadelphia who was so busy chatting that

she forgot her turn in a contré dance. "Come, come!" shouted
the master of ceremonies. "Have a care, miss, what you are
doing! Do you think you are here for your own pleasure?" But
such crimes were apparently common in Philadelphia. When
Congress and its "court society" moved there in 1790, Mrs. John
Adams complained that etiquette in its dancing assemblies "was
not to be found"; and she remembered that "it was not so in
New York."

New Yorkers learned their steps and etiquette from a trio of
dancing masters. Like his father before him and his son after
him, John H. Hulett ran a school (at No. 15 Little Queen Street)
for the newest dances "according to the present taste both in
Paris and London." Mr. J. Robardet came from Albany in the
fall and opened another school at Fraunces' Tavern on Cortlandt
Street. Andrew Picken, "lately from Britain," conducted classes
in the City Assembly Room on Broadway a little above Wall
Street. He gave frequent exhibitions at which his pupils showed
off their skill from half past five till eight o'clock, when the
public could join in—for six shillings a gentleman, or with a
lady eight shillings. Naturally an ordinary citizen didn't need
a school or an assembly hall—Bowling Green or any tavern
would serve—to do a jig, a hornpipe, or a reel.

John Trumbull, the artist, once advised a young beginner that
"it would be better for him to learn how to make shoes or dig
potatoes than to paint pictures in America." The absence of the
country's best painters—Gilbert Stuart, Benjamin West, John
Copley—who found Europe more congenial and profitable, gave
point to Trumbull's advice. Still something was to be gained
in portraiture and in the decorative arts—painting fans, china,
and coach panels. The trade, for it was hardly more than that,
could be learned from Mr. James Cox (at 52 Beekman Street),
who gave lessons for five dollars a quarter-year in painting
gowns, flounces and coats of arms. Besides coach and sign painting Mr. Ignatius Shnydore (of 28 John Street) taught the art of
representing landscapes, figures, and flowers in oil and water color.

The most appreciated artist was John Ramage, an Irishman who came to New York via Boston in 1777. People considered him the best miniature painter of the day—although he was also skilled at making life-size portraits in crayon and pastel; and everybody who was somebody, including Washington, got Ramage to record him for posterity. William Dunlap, in his history of American art, records for us Ramage himself, at least sartorially; and it is a pleasure to know that one artist in 1789 could afford to saunter along Broadway clad in "a scarlet coat with mother-of-pearl buttons, a white silk waistcoat embroidered with colored flowers, black satin breeches with paste knee-buckles, white silk stockings, large silver buckles on his shoes, a small cocked hat on the upper part of his powdered hair"—the whole set off by a gold-headed cane and a gold snuffbox. Whatever Trumbull might say, this was better than digging potatoes.

Trumbull, who was a native of Connecticut, sought his own fortune in New York this same year, after studying under West in London. He did not fare badly, either. The Common Council of the city paid him $466.66 to make a portrait of Washington and a like sum for one of Governor Clinton; and the taxpayers growled their disapproval, not at the portraits but at the expense. Shortly after his portrait was completed, Washington entertained a number of Creek Indian chiefs with whom the government was negotiating a treaty. After dinner he led them suddenly up to this counterfeit of himself, dressed in battle array and standing by his war horse. They stared in mute astonishment, and then one by one touched the picture and said "Ugh!" If this was Early American art criticism, it must be considered as unfavorable; for, despite urging, the chieftains refused to sit for Trumbull.

More compliant, Washington yielded to everyone who thought himself an artist. He wrote a friend:

> I am so hackneyed to the touches of the painter's pencil that I am now altogether at their beck and sit "Like Patience on a monument." At first . . . I was as restive under the operation as

a colt is under the saddle; the next time I submitted very reluctantly, but with less flouncing; now no dray-horse moves more readily to his thill than I to the painter's chair.

He sat four times in Edward Savage's chair for a portrait commissioned by Harvard College. He sat for Madame la Marquise de Bréhan, sister-in-law of the French minister, who did two profiles of him—"exceedingly like the original," or so he said.

The names of others who plied the brush that year—such as Ralph Earle and Joseph Wright—have remained hardly more than names and may be read about in Dunlap's history. Dunlap, as we know, had abandoned painting for the stage; and he did not return to his easel until 1816.

New York discouraged sculpture and its one practitioner, John Dixey, of Dublin and the Royal Academy, who arrived in the city—and languished there—in 1789. Two years later the arrival of the Italian sculptor Giuseppe Ceracchi made more of a stir. He did busts of Hamilton, Jay, and George Clinton; he proposed to make for the Federal government a marble Statue of Liberty one hundred feet high at a cost of but $30,000 and displayed a model of it at Tammany headquarters; then, rebuffed in turn, he went back to Italy. True to his love for liberty, he was eventually shot for trying to assassinate Napoleon.

While it is true that individuals cut silhouettes, painted, chiseled, and etched, art in any profound sense was non-existent. Of local color or character there was no trace. Neither was there a corporate body of artists or a communal appreciation of the pleasures that art could give. The first quasi-successful academy of art in the United States had to await the efforts of New Yorkers in 1802, and it is worth noting that its moving spirits were not artists but laymen. The first creative association of artists themselves, the National Academy of Design, had to wait till 1826. Its founder was the versatile William Dunlap, and its first president a man who, typical of America itself, was to win immortality in the practical arts—Samuel F. B. Morse.

CHAPTER XI

News and Reviews

IT WAS a Monday morning in October. A breeze whipped across Manhattan and set the day's wash flapping on the lines. Blue Monday. Lazy autumn weather. But blue?—proverbially so.

The President of the United States sent a messenger from his Cherry Street home down to the New York Society Library in Federal Hall. He wanted a book. Events were in the loom, a tapestry of intricate pattern was weaving, and even in the infant days of the Republic the problem of isolation pressed for solution. What to do? how to act? were not abstract rhetorical questions. They were to be answered promptly and with all the consequences implicit in formal statements by the responsible Executive of a sovereign state—the first President of the United States of America to face the difficult duties of that office. It was Monday morning, the news from abroad was perplexing, and His Excellency in this circumstance sent for Vattel's treatise on the *Law of Nations,* a solid statement of the prevalent conventions as accepted between states, tenuous agreements then, as now, hinging on the dubious interests of the parties involved. It was the President's intention to consolidate the position of the United States of America in that company, to look after its welfare, and to save it, a child of the new humanism, from premature and unwise commitments. What he found in Vattel is not now in question, but no doubt he pondered its contents with care.

Apart from what he learned from his old friend Mr. Jay and from the files of the office of the Secretary for Foreign Affairs, the President, like every other wide-awake resident of New York, learned of the world's events from the morning newspapers. There were neither newsstands nor newsboys,* but carriers delivered the *Daily Advertiser* and the *Daily Gazette* to the leading taverns and coffeehouses and to the private subscribers—at the cost of six dollars a year. Single copies could be bought for four cents at the booksellers' or the publishers' offices.

Let us glance, as Washington did, at that Monday morning's *Daily Gazette*. Though it numbered only four pages, it was about as high and wide if not as handsome as our contemporary dailies. It contained much the same proportion of advertising to reading matter, and it gave the current news. To be sure, the news was exasperatingly slow in arriving, but when it came it was new— a topic for the day.

The front page—which the President turned as rapidly as we do—tells little not already known. A ship is about to sail for London, another for Saint-François, a third for Glasgow. Someone advertises for sale a likely Negro wench, a mulatto, aged about fourteen. Two sailors have run away from a ship, and a reward is offered for their apprehension. The page is entirely devoted to running advertisements, most of them an old story. It corresponds to the want-ad section of the twentieth-century press.

Page two is solid reading matter. A letter from France summarizes the happenings of two eventful days in Paris, the progress of the initial stages of the French Revolution. We had news of the event two or three weeks ago; but this article, carefully written, throws greater light on the subject. Excitement, we learn, has

---

*The history of the humble newsboy has not yet received adequate attention from either historians or Ph.D. candidates. Certainly the newsboy which we know did not exist. It is possible that the printer's devil was sometimes sent into the streets to garner a few coppers. We know that a printer-editor himself sometimes sallied forth to peddle his wares on public corners. Over in Philadelphia Ben Towne, the one-man staff of the *Pennsylvania Evening Post*, himself hawked his daily publication with the street cry of, "All the news for two coppers!" Sidewalk customers were few; they had only to drop into the nearest tavern to read the news "on the house."

died down in the countryside—a traveler from Paris to London has come through unmolested. Order is restored. Turn to page three.

Page three contains a concise summary of the doings in Congress (lately adjourned); a London letter dated 29 July 1789; a news item or two from Philadelphia (not complimentary to that city); the assize of bread; tides for the day; ship arrivals; ships spoken; number of ships in the harbor. The theater management announces its doors to open at 6:15 of the clock and the curtain to go up promptly at a quarter past seven. The play is *Merry Wives of Windsor,* the afterpiece *Barataria,* a farce, in which will appear the famous horse, Dapple. Mr. Durang dances the hornpipe between play and farce, and the editor, in a news item, bespeaks for the company a goodly audience. The Spanish minister, about to sail, requests that all bills against him be presented forthwith at the residence of His Excellency, No. 1 Broadway. The post office is moving today into temporary quarters at Crown and Broadway. The German society meets at seven P.M. at the Lutheran Schoolhouse. One of the bookshops announces a new dictionary, an improvement on Johnson. Four dollars reward is offered for the return of a runaway slave. France is congratulated on the abolition of serfdom. The Moors and Arabs are at war. Russia and Sweden are at war. Turkey and Austria are at war. The Spanish fleet is scouting for Barbary pirates.

The date is 5 October 1789. It is Monday. On that day the Paris mob was marching on Versailles. It was raining, the mob was hungry, and things began to look dark for Louis XVI. No longer absolute monarch of France, he was about to become a prisoner in the Tuileries. Meanwhile there was a President in America.

In this welter of anarchy and discontent how does a President of the United States of America act? He falls back on precedent. Or if he makes precedent he makes it warily. He consults his advisers. He borrows a book and reads up on the rights and duties of neutral states, determined if possible to keep clear of this European mess. The pages of Vattel, *Law of Nations,* lay open to the President's scrutiny, but it is not to be hastily assumed that he found in them an answer to his problem. He was learning to be President, and at long last the Republic was a going concern.

The *Daily Gazette,* published by John and Alexander McLean at the sign of Franklin's Head, No. 41 Hanover Square, could lay a slight claim to fame. Two years previously, when it was called the *Independent Journal,* its pages carried the first batch of *Federalist* letters in which were explained for the American people the nature and constitution of the new government then in the making. In 1789 nothing more noteworthy can be told of it than its serial publication of the life of Baron Trenck, the death of its editor, John McLean, and the similar fate which overtook its carrier, John Quirk, who in the exercise of his duties fell down in a fit and rose no more.

Its more formidable and successful rival, the *Daily Advertiser,* was published by Francis Childs, a protégé of John Jay, at 190 Water Street. Jay had first set him up in the printing trade; and it was through Jay that Dr. Franklin assisted Childs in securing a press, type, and paper. His newspaper has often been described as the first daily in New York City. Childs's publication was the first to be launched as a daily. His first number appeared on March 1, 1785, but during the previous week William Morton and Samuel Horner had transformed their old paper into a daily, the *Morning Post.* Two daily newspapers were already appearing in Philadelphia, so that the *New-York Daily Advertiser* was the fourth daily in the nation, but the first to be founded as a daily paper. In typography and in contents it was a credit to its eminent sponsors. The growth of sea-borne commerce more than an appetite for learning what was going on in the world led to the creation of these dailies; a goodly portion of their printed matter, and the most scrutinized, was devoted to the arrival and departure of vessels, the ships spoken en route across the oceans, and other maritime news. On this October fifth we learn that the vessels in New York harbor numbered 19 ships, 36 brigs, 4 snows, 21 schooners, and 37 sloops—a total of 117, which meant about twelve hundred sailors in port.

Three other newspapers led a straitened existence. The *Packet,* appearing thrice weekly, was edited by Samuel Loudon, an Irishman, a fervent patriot, and Presbyterian, who appealed to the working classes for support and who delighted in opening his columns to acrid religious and sectarian disputes. The *Journal* came out weekly; its editor, Thomas Greenleaf, was an ardent opponent of Federalism, a sachem of Tammany Society, and a printer for the state of New York. The leaders of New York society and government officials in the public eye could enjoy seeing their names in print in the *Gazette of the United States,* a paper which first appeared on April 15, 1789, and then twice a week, and which bid for a nation-wide audience. Alexander Hamilton backed the paper, John Fenno edited it; and its columns read like a fulsome and arrogant court gazette in a third-class German principality. Its rivals, almost needless to say, lashed out against its monarchist tone, its passion for ceremonies and titles, and its truckling to the leaders of Federalism as though they were American blue-bloods; republican editors scorned "such a contemptible creature as Johnny Fenno"—all of which was not calculated to fulfill the announced purpose of the paper, that is, "to endear the General Government to the people." The people were so little endeared to the gazette that by October Mr. Fenno complained that he had attracted only 650 subscribers, not enough to butter his bread.

But no New York paper promised to be on the road to fortune. It was a red-letter day when one of them sold two thousand copies; a high average was around sixteen hundred. On the other hand, when a paper failed, the crash could not have been resounding. A comparatively new press, cases, and four fonts of type represented an investment of about $200. The standard wage for journeyman printers was six dollars a week. The press and printers working under full pressure turned out two hundred copies an hour.

A newspaper, in fact, was liable to be as laggard in getting delivered as it was slow in being printed. Sometimes it never got delivered at all. The *Daily Gazette* was dispatched for three years to Richard Henry Lee in Virginia. In all that time it failed to arrive. However, the bill did—which was a victory for the post. Lee, in a letter to one of his clan, explained that he didn't mind paying and hoped that someone in the family received the sheet.

Historians such as McMaster and Henry Adams have charged that the press said little or nothing about significant events. They forget that the press was local; that even if it wanted to, it had no facilities for getting very far beyond its own doorstep; and as to significance—if it means significance for a historian— it all depends on the school to which the historian belongs.

Certainly there was no dearth of news. Hardly a day passed without its event—a fire, a runaway team, a man overboard off Peck Slip, to say nothing of dog fights, tavern brawls, riots in the Fields, and the parade of fashion on Wall Street. Much of this never got into the papers, and what did often failed to accord with our contemporary notion of a good news story. The January 1 number of the *Daily Advertiser* may serve to show how fashions in news change as they do in clothes. All the news of local origin in this issue was contained in less than half a column. In that half-column thirty-one lines were devoted to a fire which burnt out one story of a house and scared the apprentices living in the attic. Yet in that same half-column, only ten lines were given to the following drama:

> On the 29th ult. Capt. Darrel, of the sloop *Cato,* spoke a brigantine from Jamaica, bound to this port, off Egg-Harbour, which had lost all her masts, sails, and rigging on the 21st. A sloop from Rhode Island had her in tow the day before; but was obliged to part with her in the night, as it blew fresh. The brig in distress has lost all her people, except the Captain and four hands.

Eight days adrift without masts, sails, or rigging; all the crew lost save four and the captain; the rescuing sloop forced to give up towing in the night gale—total coverage in the *Daily Advertiser,* ten lines.

Yet New York kept in touch with its neighbors and also foreign affairs (retailed, by means of a pair of scissors, from the London press). The neighborly attitude comes to light in a news item or two from Philadelphia. That city, it appears, had recently gone through a moral crisis; bawdy houses were raided right and left; and it had been compelled to clean up its markets —spoiled meat. New Yorkers chuckled. The French ship of state, launched in troubled waters, had their wholehearted sympathy. They were or had recently been revolutionaries themselves, and they congratulated the French people on its release from bondage. The press gave tongue to this sentiment without stuttering.

More than forty display advertisements of leading merchants offered wares for sale—books, mathematical instruments, charts, silverware, salt, nails, window glass, Bath porter, Jamaica spirits, Liverpool coals, tea, Bordeaux, claret, cheese, sweet oil, aniseed, sherry, Malaga, Irish linens, hides, gin, Swedish iron, German steel, gunpowder, paint, paper, sugar, hats, opium, carpets, leather, fruit trees, earthenware, looking glasses (some with thirteen stars in the medallions), waffle irons, white lead, woolens, and at No. 6 Fly Market a healthy, active Negro wench with child of twelve months—by no means an exhaustive list of available commodities, but illuminating. Mr. Van Hagen, organist, offered music lessons; M. Robardet offered the quaver, the pigeon-wing, and other dance steps, for gentlemen; and the editor himself offered an oblation to Thespia:

It is to be expected that the friends of the drama will be highly gratified with the entertainments of the evening at the theatre. The Merry Wives of Windsor is perhaps one of the first comedies of the world (not played here these sixteen years); and there is reason to believe that in the representation it will produce as pleasing effects as any play yet attempted by the American company.

—gunning no doubt for a few free tickets. All of the above from a single issue of the *Daily Gazette*. Even Adams and Mc-Master would be surprised at the mass of material, recently collected, covering at least one significant event of 1789 and reported at length in the press of every sizable town between Alexandria and New York—the inaugural journey of Washington from Mount Vernon to No. 3 Cherry Street, New York City. The coverage on that story was just about 100 per cent.

If New Yorkers tired of the daily, semiweekly, triweekly, or weekly press, they could always turn to another periodical, the almanac, read about the stars in their courses, interrogate the zodiac, and as a last resort make a will.

The almanac was at once a calendar, a nautical guide, weather forecast, compendium of literary gems, guide to the moon and to all the roads of the Western world. It was a popular little book, handy to have around, and widely consulted by our fathers. It got them up at sunrise, a shifty event and hard to pin down; helped them catch the tide if they were putting out to sea; and pointed the way to the wilderness or to Canada if the local constables became pressing. *Moore* confined himself largely to the waters of New York Harbor, tides not in the affairs of men about town. *Hutchins* was more urbane. He indulged in poetry and prose of a nature designed to meet their needs. *Beers* and *Judd* were a little more rustic, but with any of them as a guide the New Yorker could plant potatoes, find his way to the magistrate's court, or to the Philadelphia stage house—which is the last thing in the world he would think of doing if it were not located at Fraunces' tavern. With *Hutchins* in hand, he possessed other information. An approaching comet is mentioned, but for its appearance he had to watch the sky—it was given the nod but not precisely dated. If the New Yorker was financially embarrassed, *Hutchins* told the way out: plant sunflowers. A bushel of seed at so much per quart nets you a fortune per acre. It seems rather involved at this reading, but some unrecorded genius may actually have worked it out. He was most helpful, this Mr. Hutchins. His opus is not limited to material affairs, but includes pertinent data on a cure for love and notes on the way to felicity in the other world. It also has a word to say on the uses of castor oil, the wane of "Belly-Ache in Jamaica," on avarice, ambition, political liberty, cheerfulness, the consequences of intemperance, together with rules for choosing real friends and maxims for promoting matrimonial happiness "addressed to all widowers, husbands and bachelors." If in one of those categories, the men could hardly do without *Hutchins,* for even on Manhattan's isle it is something to know your way around. And if he leaves the affair of the comet somewhat obscure, about the eclipses of the moon he is quite explicit, putting those events definitely on 9 May and 2 November—nights of wonder and wild surmise for the superstitious and for lovers a presage of happiness.

A useful dispenser of local information was the city directory, for it not only gave the exact location of some two hundred taverns but, in addition, printed in full, and with address attached, the name of its possessor. Thus he could always find his way both there and back. It had a map, helpful in an emergency of this sort. Of the 4,100 listed citizens, perhaps as many as five hundred were purchasers, the price being 3s. 6d. and rather steep, but a good investment if you considered its many uses. It gave the New Yorker a clue to his neighbors, and it gives us of today a splendid picture of the city, its streets and public buildings, its people and their government, their institutions and how they went about the business of getting a living. It is the real book of Manhattan, and, if no other source were available, the historian could still compose a pretty fair picture of the city. He would have to invent a few current happenings such as riots and soirees and lawsuits, but such things are all but universal and his task would be light. If in addition to the directory he had the minutes of a good rousing police court, his cup would overflow. Adams and McMaster and so many giants of other days have sighed for these things in vain.

With the directory in the pot, let us see what comes out of it. Let it be said at once that it lists in alphabetical order the names, occupations, and residences of the citizens; and its title, if printed in full, would discourage the restless reader of our day. It was done for Hodge, Allen, and Campbell and sold at their respective stores—144 pages of current information. Its alphabetical arrangement was somewhat erratic in spots, and its spelling was not always consistent, and by its own admission it could not vouch for every house number, since the system itself was somewhat vague. But despite these idiosyncrasies (and perhaps because of them) it turns out to be a lively affair. It does not say that Elizabeth Carr ran a disorderly house, or that John Henry was knocked cold in a street brawl and confined to his bed for seven days, or that a man crying "Murder!" rushed into Mooney's and hid under a table. Its readers knew all these things —why bring them up again? Nor does it mention that old story about Marinus Willett being haled up before the Committee and the Board of Governors for stealing a large quantity of wine out of the President's garret—in his college days of course, at King's—everyone knows it. It does not say a word about the trial of Alderman John Wylley for extortion, so recently aired in the General Sessions.

What it does say is enough to recall these lapses and many like them; it mentions names, and memory was never known to fail in affairs of this nature. In that sense the directory was something to chuckle over, a nudge in the ribs. "Who's Elizabeth Carr? Oh yes, that drab!" The directory reads: Elizabeth Carr, 4 Old Slip; John Henry, comedian, 5 Fair street; widow Barham, porterhouse, 16, Broad-way; Frederick Bassett, pewterer, 4 Burlingslip; Elizabeth Anderson, bird-seller, corner of Greenwich and Chambers streets; Margaret Le Brun, fruit shop, 118 Queen street; John Graham, merchant, 20 Little Queen street; Charles Cox, oyster and punch house, 33 John street; Graham and Johnston academy, Little Queen street; Hoysted Hacker, pilot through Hell gate, 72 Water street; Daniel Hawxhurst, glover and breeches maker, 27 Peck slip; widow Fleming, milliner, Smith street; Barnet Mooney, hatter, 43 Cortlandt street; Peter Ritter, iron mongery and jewelry store, 50 Broadway; Andrew Gray, slop shop, Front street near Fly market; Richard Haight, carpenter, Rope walk; Drew Hall, silversmith, 243 Queen street; J. Jadwin, packer of pork, 5 Gold street; widow Job, 10 Cliff street; Peter Lacour, drawing master, 17 Princess street; Henry Knox, Secretary at war, Broadway; William Dunlap, portrait painter, 13 Queen street; Mrs. Fortune, tavern, 30 John street; John Forsythe, taylor and habit maker, 88 Fair street; Charles Thompson, late secretary to Congress, 26 King street; William C. Thompson, vellum and parchment manufactory, 28 Dyes street; John Wood, vestry clerk of St. Paul's and master of the free school; Thomas Lloyd, short hand writer, 56 Water street; James Miers, tavern at the horse and harrow, Bowery lane; Richard Varrick, 52 Wall street; James Duane, 17 Nassau street; John Jay, 133 Broad way; Alexander Hamilton, 58 Wall street; Thomas Smith, sea captain, 1 Battery barracks. These are names taken at random from the directory for 1789.

Around 4,100 names listed there—and so many widows! For there had been a war, and war takes men by the throat. No bachelors or widowers are listed as such, and no spinsters are definitely given that status, although Eunice Jaenes or Dorcas Sketch might perhaps qualify, both of them being schoolmistresses. Mrs. Hazard, cake shop, 50 Chatham street; Thomas Phillips, lapidary, 20 New street; Thomas Barrow, coach-painter and print-seller, 38 Broad street; James Bramble, white smith, 49 King street. There is no end to the fascinating picture of New York in 1789. Adrian Dowe, rush bottom chair maker, Bowery, and of a different trade from Matthias Bloom, windsor chair maker, 105 Queen street. Obviously these items are not of interest to everybody, but it is nice to know where you can order a pewter bowl, or a bowl of punch, or a new spring bonnet. The directory included a register of the Congress of the United States; foreign ministers in residence; the governors of the several states; officers of the state of New York and of the city and county, of the Chamber of Commerce, the Marine Society, the Assurance Company; ministers of the gospel; a roll of attorneys licensed to practice in the Supreme Court; information concerning the New York Society Library and Columbia College; a roll of militia officers; a list of Masonic Lodges and their officers; post days, stage and coach rates; and extracts from sundry laws for the guidance of the unwary.

Turning from the light and airy reading of the directory to something more solid, we run afoul of the periodical magazines of the day. A new venture (its first issue dated January 1790), *The New York Magazine or Literary Repository,* follows closely the scheme of things laid down by other journals of the time. Each number contained sixty-four pages of reading matter largely filched from the New York press or from the British magazines or lifted bodily from any dog-eared book that was handy. It was not a great financial success, and although at the end of the first year it boasted a subscription list of about 360, it was unlikely that the circulation increased much in the following five years. Of the subscribers about three hundred were New Yorkers, the remainder either from near-by towns or living along the seaboard from Nova Scotia to Charleston. Its out-of-town list was augmented by several members of Congress and was probably depleted following the removal of the national capital to Philadelphia.

Each number included three or four short pieces of fiction heavy with the dew of moral fervor, and such fugitive pieces as the Sentiments of an Austrian Lady on Religion; the Benefits of Temperance; the Fatal effects of Seduction; Remarks on the manners (etc.) of Naples; the inclemency of Winter; On a Proud Young Lady who encouraged two Lovers; a cutting from Dr. Adams' *Defense of the Constitution;* the popular play, *Darby's Return;* and an Account of Trinity Church, New York. Its verse was native. It discussed in three or four pages congressional affairs, domestic intelligence, marriages, deaths, etc., and each number was embellished with an elegant representation of some notable public building or local scene. A recent commentator suggests that by including as they did short fiction pieces with their other miscellany the publishers promoted the reading of novels in America. Since a very large number of its readers were also members of the Society Library and were already avid for fiction, as the records of the Library disclose, it is much more likely that the publishers sensed the already existing demand and had a weather eye out for subscribers.

In the preceding year Noah Webster used similar bait but in vain. His *American Magazine,* which ran from December 1787 to the same month in 1788, was heavily laden with fiction. It devoted especial attention to the ladies and their interests, including their moral improvement. Moreover it strove, as the editor promised, "to collect as many original Essays as possible; and particularly such as relate to this country." No predecessor had freed itself to a like extent from English influence and the slavery of scissors and paste. Original American verse, articles on American commerce, agriculture, and travel covered numerous pages. The public, however, refused to bite. However emancipated in politics, it remained colonial in literature. "I will now leave writing," Webster declared, "and do more lucrative business." And he added, "I am happy to quit New York."

When, on October 5, the President sent for Emmerich de Vattel's *The Law of Nations,* he followed the practice of many other New York readers—to the detriment of authors' royalties and booksellers' profits. He borrowed the copy from a library. Borrowing or renting a book, however, had substantial justification in those days. American publishers as such did not exist: they were job printers and newspaper printers who turned an occasional book off the press; they were few in number and the variety and quantity of their output small. Bookstores selling nothing but books were likewise non-existent. A bookdealer, like a modern druggist, was a merchant who displayed a few books in what was otherwise a general store. An enterprising book-seller like Hugh Gaine, whose book business was a minor adjunct to a printing and stationery establishment, managed to import several hundred volumes from London twice a year, and their arrival became a duly advertised event.

Individuals possessed private libraries, naturally, but the gaps and wants could be filled only at the price of patience and long waits. Occasionally the newspapers announced the sale of such libraries in extensive advertisements, giving the titles which were classified by size (octavo, duodecimo, etc.) rather than by subject matter. A private collection of five hundred volumes was not uncommon, and many of the average books fetched prices at about our 1913 levels. Still, when a reader wanted a book in a hurry he usually had but one resort: a rental or a quasi-public library.

Three such libraries catered to the city's needs. King's College (now Columbia University) offered a choice of 1,500 volumes to the faculty, students, and clergy. Open to its paying members, the Union Library possessed 1,000 volumes. The most extensive and best patronized was the New York Society Library, with 3,500 volumes. It was housed in Federal Hall, and there the notables and intellectuals of the town stood before the rail, asked for a classic or a popular novel, and had their names entered in the big charge-out ledger.

On the day that Washington sent for Vattel as well as for twelve volumes of the *Commons Debates,* thirty-three subscribing members likewise drew out books. The members, who on May 1, 1790, numbered 242, made up a roster of names prominent in the annals of the city. The Livingstons repaired there, the De Peysters, the Roosevelts, and Hamilton, Jay, and Burr.

Founded in 1754 and rechartered by the state of New York in 1784, the society was democratic in principle and exclusive in practice. Its membership was open to anyone who paid an initial fee of five pounds and annual dues of ten shillings. The subscribers were privileged to draw one book at a time for each

ADVERTISEMENTS

From New York City newspapers, April 1789.

New York Magazine.

View of Columbia College in the City of New York.

Anderson Del.

Tiebout Sculp.

COLUMBIA COLLEGE

A view of Columbia College in 1790 from the engraving by Tiebout.

"membership" or share they possessed, although regardless of the number of shares he might own a member received only one vote. Borrowers who kept books overtime were fined. The library was open from twelve to two on Mondays, Wednesdays, and Fridays; and the members were required to apply for the books in person. On rare occasions this rule was broken, a servant appeared instead and his name was noted parenthetically in the big ledger. Washington—who sent a servant—was a member only by courtesy; and while no fine lay against him, legend charges him with keeping the books a long, long time.

Many historians of the period have the curious notion that the men of 1789 read only or largely theology. They picture our fathers with their eyes glued to a denominational tract and their minds fixed on the other world. Nothing could be further from the truth, though the mistake no doubt arose from the dearth of reliable information or from "facts" which, while true in themselves, belie the reality.

A glance at the eighteenth century itself, without examining a publisher's catalogue, should dispel the illusion that the men of that age, whether in the Old World or the New, lived extensively in or for the kingdom of heaven. It was the century of great wits—Pope, Swift, Fielding, Voltaire, Johnson, Sterne, and Goldsmith. Gibbon was doing a modern history of ancient Rome. Locke, Montesquieu, and others were asking pertinent questions. Richardson begat *Pamela*. There was a great stirring of mind. It was polite to be learned. Johnson did his dictionary in English, the Academy did theirs in French, and Voltaire did his in a tongue everyone could understand. It was the century of Burke, Fox, and Pitt, of Lord Chesterfield, Thomas Gray, and *Peregrine Pickle,* of Rousseau, Catherine the Great, Frederick the Second, George the Third, Louis the Sixteenth (among others), of Diderot and Helvetius—a mixed lot, writers, professors, statesmen, kings, and rogues. It was the day of the diplomat, of intrigue, of colonial enterprise and expanding markets, of chartered companies, boudoir politics, and potentates

—all the nabobs of the world, each convinced of his (or her) own particular rendezvous with destiny. And into this whirlpool of conventional piracy a new polity was born. There was a revolution in America, and one in France. And along toward the end of the century a king lost his head in Paris and a president was inaugurated in New York City.

Neglecting this broad unmistakable background, American historians have allowed themselves to be misled by the statistics of our native publishing business. The impression created, for example, by a study like Evans' *American Bibliography* is one of a people whose reading habits ran pretty much to devotional subjects, and although it is true that the reading of New Yorkers is not necessarily an index of the country at large, at least for that particular city a glance at Evans throws us completely off the track. Fully 25 per cent of the imprints there listed for the years 1789 and 1790 dealt with theology, and only 4 per cent of them were fiction. But New Yorkers were not reading theology in that proportion. Far from it. Almost the reverse, in fact. Fortunately there is a source of exact information on this point, if not watertight at any rate indicative—the charge-out ledger of the New York Society Library for the years 1789 and 1790, and perhaps a word about the nature of this unique document is pertinent to the subject in hand.

The ledger is a book of some three hundred pages, 14 × 20 inches, strongly bound in its day. It has come down through the years in splendid shape. It is replete with unconscious error, odd abbreviations, and one or two lapses of memory. It is, however, perfectly legible. Indeed the handwriting of its first custodian is almost oriental in its delicacy and precision. The ledger is a key to the reading habits of 242 prominent New Yorkers, members of the Society Library. What they read a hundred and fifty odd years ago is a matter of record. It is, so to speak, down in the book.

The first entry in the ledger was made 24 July 1789. On that date the Rev. Dr. Linn (chaplain of Congress) borrowed Goldsmith's *Animated Nature* and had his name inscribed on the first line. He was fined 7d. for keeping it more than a week. The librarian was faithful, a scholar and a gentleman. The work was too heavy for him, however, and on November 20 he charged the novel *Chrysal* to Major Pratt and laid down his pen. Later librarians were indifferent penmen, but they made marks and the marks have been interpreted, reducing an old and fascinating manuscript to dull statistics.

Animated Nature and *Chrysal* are pretty fair samples of what was being read in the late eighteenth century. The men of the time were primarily interested in foreign lands, in the strange, the exotic, and inevitably in problems of the heart. They were curious, and they were in love or somehow caught in love's meshes. They read poems and plays of passion, novels and story-books of history, just as we ourselves do, for escape, for comfort, and for the joy of it.

All but a scant dozen of the society's members used the library. They read on an average a book every fortnight. Great readers like John Jay and Patrick Murdoch and John Pearss read three books a week. Following is a rough classification of titles circulating in 1789–90 together with figures showing the total circulation of each class:

Class	Titles	Circulation
Biography and letters	76	712
Classics	20	74
Essays	99	615
Fiction	138	3,133
History	151	1,550
Poetry and drama	66	351
Reference and periodicals	51	872
Religion and philosophy	69	282
Science	66	264
Travel and discovery	82	1,172
Totals	818	9,025

Contrast this table with the impression to be gained from the output of American publishers (or printers) in the same years of 1789 and 1790. According to Evans' *American Bibliography*, the American presses issued a total of 1,493 items, classified as follows:

Class	Imprints	Percentage
Theology	370	25
History	82	6
Travel and geography	62	4
Fiction	55	4

The printers, in other words, devoted only 14 per cent of their products to history, travel, and fiction, whereas the readers (of the Society Library at least) were devoting 65 per cent of their reading to books in these categories, fiction alone accounting for 35 per cent.

The printers, it should be observed, did not misjudge their public in turning out only 4 per cent of fiction and flooding the booksellers with 25 per cent of theology. No reader of Fielding can forget that, however great the surprise of Abraham Adams to learn the sad fact, ministers and doctors of divinity *paid* to get their tracts and sermons into print. And no printer forgot that novelists, historians, and other mundane writers expected, on the contrary, to be remunerated for their labor.

The ledger of the Society Library records, to be sure, the reading habits of only a few select New Yorkers—representing about 4 per cent of the total number of households. But its members were the leaders of the community and of the state, and presumably they were readers of at least average taste. Sentiment was in the air, and they read the sentimental novels of the day. They absorbed the realistic fiction of Voltaire and Swift and Fielding. They read the memoirs of Baron de Tott and the confessions—she called it an apology for herself—of the noted actress George Anne Bellamy. They also read the *Lives of the Poets* wherein Doctor Johnson exhibits his remarkable critical decency and insight.

And it is safe to say that other literate New Yorkers read much the same thing, or would have if they had possessed the leisure and opportunity.

The tastes of the Society Library's borrowers did not differ greatly. They varied in the choice of titles but not in the character of their reading. Out of the sixty-two books borrowed (and presumably read) by the Rev. Dr. Linn, thirty-seven were fiction. Frederick Rhinelander, a layman and merchant, consumed in ten months the same number of novels out of a total of fifty-eight borrowings. Both read *The Fair Syrian* and *The Platonic Guardian, the History of an Orphan;* and while the clergyman read Fielding and Smollett, the merchant read Dryden's plays and Voltaire's *Henriade.* Elizabeth De Peyster borrowed fifteen works; ten were novels or plays—Richardson of course and *Betsy Thoughtless* in four volumes; but the remaining five included Mitford's *Greece,* Hawkesworth's *Voyages,* Henry Swinburne's *Travels,* and Chastellux's popular reporting of America. The Vice-President, John Adams, stepped in one day and borrowed Kames's *Elements of Criticism.* Aaron Burr was an assiduous reader of history; month after month he plowed through eighteen volumes of the *Modern Universal History;* he read Gibbon's *Decline and Fall* and eight selected volumes of Voltaire; but even he relaxed with Lyttelton's *Dialogues of the Dead* and *L'Isle Inconnue, or the Memoirs of the Chevalier des Gastines.* His mortal rival, Hamilton, found time for the two widely read novels, *Edward Mortimer* (By a Lady) and *The Amours of Count Palviano and Eleanora.*

On the other hand John Jay's reading tells little of typical tastes. As chief justice of the Supreme Court in the first years of that august body he apparently had ample leisure, and when it came to books he was omnivorous. Everything was grist for his mill, from *The Children's Friend* and *Candide* to Henry Swinburne's *Travels in the Two Sicilies.* In eighteen months he devoured sixty-eight volumes. Did he suffer from insomnia?

The most popular books of the year—the "best sellers"—may

perhaps be judged those most frequently borrowed. In analyzing the society's ledger for this purpose, it must be assumed that Shakespeare, the Bible, and many classics and standard reference works reposed at home on the bookshelves of the borrowers.

The six books of non-fiction with the largest circulation carry the explanation of their contents and popularity in their titles:

NON-FICTION

Author and Title	Circulation
Cook: *Voyages Round the World*	154
Gibbon: *Decline and Fall of the Roman Empire*	110
Johnson: *Lives of the Poets*	106
Hooke: *Roman History*	68
Gordon: *History of the American War*	67
Baron de Tott: *Memoirs of the Turks and Tartars*	66

Captain Cook, whose voyages were sealed with his comparatively recent death, saw the South Seas for the whole world that was housebound but itching to travel. His description of coral reefs and the ravages of the venereal disease and the fauna of the islands, which was largely female, awakened grave interest. Although only runners-up for the popularity prize, Wilson's *Account of the Pelew Islands* (circulated 42 times), Grosier's *Description of China* (19 times), Grose's *Voyage to the East Indies* (19 times), Jones's *Life of Cook* (17 times), Osbeck's *Journey to China and the East Indies* (3 times), an anonymous *Chinese Traveller* (12 times), Duhalde's *History of China,* in seven volumes (15 times), and Dow's *Hindoostan* (3 times) foreshadow the age of the China clippers. As our reader has already learned, in May 1789 the first vessel to display the American flag in the Ganges River had returned very profitably to New York.

New Yorkers were on the make, and the world was their oyster. They read for the delight of opening their eyes. So much to know. It was, they learned, a custom in the port of Hamburg to pay seamen upon signing articles two months' wages in advance. Splendid idea. That money never left the town. With Russia and Sweden at war, they read Bruce's memoirs on his *Travels in Germany, Russia, etc.* (circulated 41 times), Bell's *Travels from Petersburgh in Russia to Asia* (7 times), Coxe's *Travels in Poland, Russia, Sweden and Denmark* (41 times), Richard's *Tour from London to Petersburgh and Moscow* (5 times), Harte's *History of Gustavus Adolphus* (13 times), and Sheridan's *Revolution in Sweden* (3 times). They also read an item in the newspapers about shipping in the Baltic: taking advantage of Swedish and Russian preoccupation with mutual destruction, England was engaged in monopolizing the northern trade: a commentary on the advantages of neutrality. Shrewd traders themselves, they planned, while reading Bruce and Coxe, a raid on British shipping. They proposed to build a fleet.

Still another class of books, though it fed the craving for vicarious adventure and travel, was not without its practical bearing. The wide circulation of Baron de Tott's account of the Turks and the Tartars pointed to an interest in the Moslem world that soon was to reach close to home. Chenier's *Empire of Morocco* (circulated 18 times), Vertot's *Knights of Malta* (18 times), Mathew's *Voyage to the Coast of Africa in 1785–1787* (14 times), Addison's *The State of the Jews in Morocco, etc.* (once), a *History of the Herculean Straits* (3 times), and *Revolution in Fez and Morocco* (once) informed New Yorkers of the shores where the United States and the marines were to fight their first foreign war.

The interest in Gibbon, who heads the list, should excite no wonder. The author was still extant, and his masterpiece in the first flush of its immortality. Hooke was probably read in order to learn what happened before Gibbon took up the tale. Classical history, besides, was the requisite of a gentleman and the ammunition dump of a patriot with a gift for oratory.

Despite the meager supply of printed material, recent American history aroused the inquisitive. Dr. Gordon's *History of the American War of Independence* (fifth on our "best-seller" list) was, we are told, the most sought-after book of the year. Lan-

guishing in the Debtors' Jail, General Samuel Webb's brother
begged for a copy of it and criticized it at length on his creditor's
time. Society Library borrowers for the year learned about themselves as best they could from Chastellux's *Travels through the
United States of America* (circulated 53 times), J. Smyth's *Tour
in the United States* (23 times), David Humphreys' *Life of Putnam* (16 times), John Adams' *Defence of the American Constitution* (11 times), Jefferson's *Notes on Virginia* (10 times), Mante's
War in America (7 times), Smith's *History of New York* (7
times), Bossu's *Travels in Louisiana* (6 times), and Hitchcock's
Domestic Memoirs of a Pennsylvanian Family (once). Obedient
to a universal trait in human nature, New Yorkers slaked their
thirst for romances in the waters of the South Seas and along the
shores of Tripoli, oblivious of the drama and adventure to be
found anywhere west of Pittsburgh. But the romance of pioneering
and the Red Indians was probably too realistic. They contented
themselves by looking from afar at the Iroquois across the northern boundary—eight of them borrowing Colden's *History of the
Five Nations of Canada.*

An Universal History, "from the earliest account of Time, com-
piled from original authors," was an ambitious work designed to
make further inquiry into history both unnecessary and impertinent. Divided into two parts, Ancient and Modern, it ran to
forty-three volumes. Both Goldsmith and Johnson were reputed
to have had a hand in its compilation. The Ancient part attracted
forty-one borrowers and the Modern part forty-nine. Among the
latter was, as we have noted, Aaron Burr who, at the end of it,
picked up the *Dialogues of the Dead* and buried himself. Cor-
nelius Roosevelt and twenty-six other borrowers chose a wiser
course; they took a short cut and read the one-volume *Beauties
of History* with its lessons in virtue and vice. Still others, among
the fifty borrowers of Voltaire, may have selected the *Essai sur les
mœurs* which accomplished what Goldsmith and Johnson intended and which no one achieved again till H. G. Wells wrote
his well-known *Outline.*

Another outline, entitled *Animated Nature,* served the eighteenth century much as J. Arthur Thomson's *Outline of Science* and Wells and Huxley's *The Science of Life* have served the twentieth. Its four animated volumes enlisted fifty-eight borrowers—an inadequate measure of its wide appeal. The President of the United States was thoroughly familiar with its contents. Some of its statements may seem startling, and many are intentionally amusing. As a compendium of scientific lore, no living thing from man to flea is neglected. We can learn from it much useful and entertaining information, as the following:

Queen Elizabeth erred when she decreed a fast day; a discussion of final causes is as barren as a virgin dedicated to the Deity; the dodo bird makes a meal for twenty-five men; the prevailing wind off Cape of Good Hope in September is northwesterly; the kings of the Cherokee take longer to perform their toilets than do the ladies of London; the Greeks preferred red-headed women; at Ispahan the king's messenger runs 36 leagues (108 miles) in 14 hours; in Africa the natives outrun the lion; there is a race of ants that sallies forth periodically in search of adventure; the buck goat grows old before his time.

The book discusses the human species at length. Man is given a proud air, a conquering tread, a glance heavenward, and buttocks unlike those of any other work of God. The writer investigates the hidden, mysterious process of procreation, the rôle of male and of female, the embryo in its various stages, the difficult drama of birth. All is not dark. The microscope reveals a fascinating series of developments. But of conception itself there is still great argument. Indeed it is touch and go whether or not the male is an essential factor. Happily our writer inclines to the comfortable theory that he is.

To descend from man to brute is something of a comedown, and to make the way less hazardous is the writer's concern. He does it neatly. You are not plunged headlong into a pool of infusoria as it is prescribed by the doctrinaires. On the contrary. You are led to the paddock, take a look at the colts, and recall the remarkable performance of Flying Childers who did the New-market course in 6:40. The horse kind, which includes the ass and the zebra, is carefully limned. No detail is wanting. The zebra barks like a dog. The wild ass is even more asinine than his brother in chains. The mule—Aristotle vouches it—is sterile. The three breeds of Arabians are explained, their elaborately attested pedigrees discussed. The ass not infrequently lies down and dies after covering his mate.

The work begins with a consideration of the universe, the phenomena of night and day, and the phases of the moon. It runs on through twelve hundred pages of lucid prose and imparts to commonplace facts a charm all its own, and at the end of it the inquisitive reader is possessed of valuable data respecting the entire animal world. He knows that the seed of the cottonwood tree intoxicates parrots as wine does man; that the male and female wall bee are of a size, the former without a sting; that the breath of the lion is very offensive. The author of this work is Oliver Goldsmith. "Poor fellow!" Cumberland said of him, "he hardly knew a turkey from a goose but when he saw it on the table." This may be true, but discerning men have suspected that poor Oliver, poor Poll, was the slyest leg-puller of his generation.

The society members may have read *Animated Nature* for entertainment, but their curiosity in the realm of science was strong and their judgment sound. An equal number of borrowers—fifty-eight—read Buffon's *Natural History,* and learned how, with the proper gifts, style can make a man out of a scientist. Thanks to Fontenelle and Voltaire, astronomy and physics had reached the multitude; and Count Algarotti's *Newtonian Philosophies explained for the ladies* attracted twenty readers who, like our own nibblers of Einsteinian philosophies, probably stood as much in need of explanation when they finished the survey of the universe as when they began it. Twenty-three bold spirits tackled Priestley *On Air,* as much a matter of puzzlement then as the quantum jump today. A new science, if such it may be called, dismal but only too pertinent, won fourteen readers to Adam Smith's *Wealth of Nations.* In such works modern biology, physics, and economics came of age; the most advanced of our contemporaries can re-read them with profit. Only Freud, his particular *Fach* still un-dreamed-of, would read Hayley's *Essay on Old Maids* (27 bor-rowers) with a superior smile.

The divine science, theology, had but few students among the members of the Society Library and they were chiefly clergymen. Top place among the borrowers went to the works of Gregory (16 withdrawals), followed by Helvetius' *Essay on Man* (13 with-drawals), a deistic work smelling powerfully of heresy, and by a similar number of withdrawals for Prideaux's *Connections.* New-ton's musings *On the Prophecies* came next (10 withdrawals), and the remainder of the sixty titles on religion and philosophy dwindled to seven or three withdrawals or less. Rousseau drew a substantial clientele—sixty readers—but whether it was for his political writings, his novels, or his deism, there was nothing in the record to cheer a theologian.

At this late date it is probably impossible to fathom why the most frequently borrowed work in the field of biography was Sully's memoirs—claiming sixty readers. And what could have been the *Interesting Letters of Pope Clement XIV* which in-terested fifty-five borrowers? Johnson's *Lives of the Poets,* which indeed leads the list, was the 54-volume edition containing the poetry under consideration; and the poems were no doubt read in preference to the Doctor's prefaces—if so, this was in many cases the reader's loss.

George Anne Bellamy's memoirs are something else. No popu-lar actress can write a book about herself or get one written for her without attracting an audience. George Anne, a star of the Lon-don stage, published a sheaf of revelations which, as have many since of her profession, set New Yorkers agog. The sales of her book are not properly represented by the forty-seven calls for it at the Society Library. It was entitled *An Apology for the Life of George Anne Bellamy, late of Covent Garden Theatre, written by her-self;* it appeared in 1785; the ghost was reputed to be Alexander

Brickwell (who likewise edited Carver's *Travels in Africa*). Mistress Bellamy had nothing to apologize for, at least to the theater-loving readers, but there was much to explain. To begin with—her arrival in the world. It surprised her father, a sea captain; and since the lying-in did not tally chronologically with his marriage log, Captain Bellamy sailed away in a huff and never returned. The baby was deposited on the doorstep of Lord Tyrawley (a whilom friend of General Braddock); and His Lordship did the handsome thing—acknowledged the child and had it tucked away with sundry offspring of other loves. She grew up to follow the stage and made a name for herself that her father might have envied—or not. She met the best people in the greenroom of Drury Lane, she heard and retailed the choicest tattle of London, and she had the good fortune to be kidnaped by a gentleman (just before the fifth act of *The Provoked Wife,* in which she was playing the role of Lady Fanciful) and spirited away to a cottage in the country. She had temperament; she fell into a dither when she moved across the way from Drury Lane to Covent Garden. Nevertheless she pulled herself together in time to bring down the house and become the toast of the town. Eventually she fell on evil times, likewise retailed in detail, but to the end she never forgot the thrill of that abduction. *He* was the only man she really loved; and *she,* in the long line of mimics, the only genuine Juliet. There must have been something to George Anne, for hers is a robust book sharply in contrast to the sentimental truck of the day. Only an ungracious skeptic would classify the *Apology* as fiction.

In the field of acknowledged fiction, the "best-seller" list provokes comment for both the good judgment it reflects and the bad.

The two poles of late eighteenth-century fiction—labeled realism and sentimentalism—are represented by their masters, Fielding and Sterne. The romantic horror story had not yet come to flower; and the romantic variant of sentimentalism, intended

FICTION

Titles	Circulation
Female Stability, by Charlotte Palmer	116
Fielding's Works	115
Emmeline, or the Orphan of the Castle, by Charlotte Smith	96
Arundel, a novel from real life, by Richard Cumberland	88
Sterne's Works	87
Arpasia, or the Wanderer, by the author of *The Nabob* [Mrs. Monkland]	76

not to moisten but flood the eyes and lead the reader to wild dreams of suicide, was barely on the threshold of success. Only eighteen New Yorkers borrowed *The Sorrows of Werther,* written by a young German named Goethe.

The common run of popular novels—four of which made our list—were incredibly weak dilutions of Richardson. His *Pamela* drooped with nineteen readers. *Grandison,* however, held its ground with fifty-seven. And with such superior products at hand or still fresh in mind—pap though they were—it would be hard to conceive why *Female Stability* conquered the public if we did not observe the same indiscrimination prevalent today.

The full title of this most-sought-out novel of the year is *Female Stability, or the History of Miss Belville, in a series of letters; by the late Miss Palmer.* It had appeared, London 1780, in five volumes. Only one copy of this former best seller is known to be now extant in America; and the Library of Congress, its happy possessor, need not fear it will ever be read to tatters.

Light fiction in all periods is designed, like millinery, to give a transient bit of pleasure; and it is as absurd to poke fun at a past century's popular novel as at a last year's hat.

Adeline Belville, the heroine of the tale, is a model of chastity and lofty sentiments and remains so throughout the five volumes.

"I often think when I am going to do anything material," she says, "would Augustus have acted thus?"

Augustus? Mr. Augustus Grenville is the hero. He is Miss Belville's ideal. He is dead. Indeed she was never actually wooed by him; but things were shaping in that direction when, by a lack of attention to detail, he was run through the body in an affair of honor. Between groans he managed to discover his love to Miss Belville and breathed his last in an early chapter, bequeathing to some twelve hundred succeeding pages an air of moral rectitude almost thick enough to slice.

The story builds itself around these two pure souls. Miss Belville is widely loved, deservedly, for she is very beautiful, very good, and very rich. Obviously an orphan. She never weds. Augustus lives on in Miss Belville, and they go down the book together.

Shortly after the story opens, Miss Belville is newly taken in charge by Mr. Evelin, one of her guardians. Mr. Evelin's household is not altogether without blot, but Miss Belville runs no danger. She is too good for that. Despite her great wealth and great expectations she escapes all entanglements. Her true love is dead, and though she does not mourn she still remembers. Who can compare with her Augustus?

One after another, or in pairs, males fall in love with the heroine. She rejects them kindly. Her stance is infallibly correct. She never takes a misstep or utters a thoughtless word. She scatters sweetness and light, and in an emergency quotes Milton—his homilies on moral earnestness. Strangely enough no one, not even bad Sir Harry Evelin, seems constrained to do murder.

Sir Harry (Mr. Evelin's brother) is a rake. He is a seducer of innocence and one of those whose protestations of love precede but do not necessarily follow seduction. As a result of one of his careless and carefree betrayals he wrecks a home, causes the death of one parent and the withdrawal of the other from all intercourse with the world.

Miss Belville is so sweet and universally beloved that she quickly

becomes one of Mr. Evelin's family. Mrs. Evelin, it is true, does
not at first understand the business of so much stress on morals.
She herself is used to compromise, but like all who meet Miss
Belville she rapidly grows earnest. It is a kind of epidemic. Sir
Harry Evelin comes and goes. He meets the heroine and in spite
of his wide experience is no more immune than the others. He too
falls in love—in his fashion—and thereafter he does not wander
far. He lingers, but to no avail.

One after another Miss Belville slays her suitors. They fall in
sheaves, and she contemplates them tidily bound and stacked—
like Sir Harry protected from future and penitent for past trans-
gressions. In despair some of them marry into the circle of her
friends, whom she distributes as consolation prizes.

Not that Miss Belville is hardhearted or cold-blooded. She is
merely faithful to the memory of Augustus. Once or twice, it is
true, she is tempted—but for a moment. Toward the end, in a
dream, she sees herself led by Augustus into a beautiful sunlit
garden, filled with bird song and fragrant with flowers. There,
with the approval of Augustus, she finds herself betrothed simultaneously to the Right Honorable Earl of Arundel and Sir Edward
Wilmot, a delicate situation—her one lapse from strict morality—
but in the circumstances excusable.

No one in Miss Belville's world forgoes a possible inheritance
even on pain of separation from a beloved. This apparently is the
higher morality. Most of the men are tethered to aged aunts and
the women to decayed uncles. Miss Belville herself is compelled
to remain in England in order to inherit a further fortune, consolidate her position, and be prepared for sundry estates that
might otherwise go begging. Everywhere she turns, another
benefactor shows up. Admiral Harrison leaves her a pretty penny,
and so do others. Because of her fidelity to Augustus it appears
that better men are drawn from a happy life, bask in the sun of
her moral earnestness till they are like to wither, and finally escape into prosaic matrimony.

So ends the history of Miss Belville—a pattern of female stability. She remains to the last page "a sweet, grave, demure little Venus," apparently not a day over sixteen and fixed indefinitely at that charming age.

In *Arundel* it is the hero who incarnates the seven virtues. He is curiously intact, and his goodness was no doubt a consolation to many of the readers in certain phases of the moon. In any case it was as much read as *Emmeline,* that lovely orphan of the castle. Such tales always have a castle. It is in ruins, one wing habitable. When His Lordship pays a visit, the other wing gets a going over. Give the castle an orphan, a desolate moor, and an unscrupulous housekeeper. Give the orphan Diana's shapely limbs, Juno's eyes, and a casket—her sole inheritance. Give the casket a letter which lies unread. Give the letter a break and you have the story. Not so very different from a good movie and possibly as edifying. Besides, Bunyan started it. Or Rabelais.

Most of the popular novels were debased copies of originals that we now call classics. John Shebbeare's *The Marriage Act* (41 borrowers) was a debased *Moll Flanders.* The *Platonic Guardian* by a Lady (45 borrowers) was debased Fielding. Charles Johnstone's *Chrysal, the Adventures of a Guinea* (34 borrowers) was debased Smollett. But even the alloy of hack writing didn't rob it of liveliness. We can understand the pleasure which John Jay, Major Pratt, the Honorable John Lawrence, and its other readers took in its company. The hero, Chrysal, was, as the title indicates, not a man but a gold coin. As it passed from hand to hand, rough and dainty, grimy and gloved, the readers were introduced to "a dispassionate account of quite remarkable transactions" in every corner of Europe. No one can accuse the generation of 1789 of being stuffy, after a glance through *Chrysal.* That coin went everywhere. The heading of the second chapter of Book Two is typical: "Chrysal Comes into the Possession of a Celebrated Female." The paramour who relinquished the coin is described as "in the prime of life" but "remarkable for the coolness of his constitution," whereat the philosophic guinea piece is set to wondering whether "he kept my mistress to hide his inability, as a failing tradesman sets up a coach." On the whole, the book is Turkish blend—largely seraglio.

But its betters were not neglected. Fifty-three members of the Society Library borrowed the *Arabian Nights,* forty-four *Don Quixote,* forty-one *Peregrine Pickle* and Marmontel's *Tales,* thirty-nine *Gil Blas,* and nineteen Rabelais.

Meanwhile, on the fourth of February, Robert Hodge the printer announced the publication of *The Power of Sympathy, or the Triumph of Nature,* which the blurb claimed to be the first American novel. The story was based on the suicide of a lovesick young woman in Boston during the summer of 1788, an untimely event fully described in the press; and it was dedicated to the young ladies of America. Since the 1789–90 ledger of the Society Library contains no mention of it, we cannot learn its fate.

Noah Webster had given up writing for more lucrative business. He remembered well those capricious females who had not subscribed to and salvaged his *American Magazine* from disaster. So in 1790 he declared he was alarmed by the "newfangled tastes for fiction." He rightly continued, "A hundred volumes of modern novels may be read without acquiring a new idea. . . . At best novels may be considered the toys of youth, the rattle-boxes of sixteen." He merely forgot that new ideas in sex, passions, and human character are hard to come by, and that most of the world loves to remain sixteen years old or less.

In his edifying *Memoirs of the Bloomsgrove Family,* published in Boston in 1790, the Reverend Enos Hitchcock said that "nothing can have a worse effect . . . than the free use of those writings which are the offspring of modern novelists. Their only tendency is to excite romantic notions while they keep the mind devoid of ideas and the heart destitute of sentiment." A moralist, writing in the *Monthly Mirror* of 1797, made graver charges as novels gained wider audiences. Under the alarming title of "Novel Reading, A Cause of Female Depravity," he bemoaned the disappearance of "moderately stiff stays, covered elbows and concealed bosoms" and declared that "those who first made *novel-*

reading an indispensable branch in forming the minds of young women, have a great deal to answer for."

Thomas Jefferson saw in the "inordinate passion prevalent for novels" almost a national menace. To Nathaniel Burwell he wrote: "When this poison infects the mind it destroys its tone and revolts it against wholesome reading. . . . The result is a bloated imagination, sickly judgment, and disgust towards all the real business of life."

But *Chrysal* and *Female Stability* continued to circulate.

In a city which had but one theater, plays were read extensively. Besides miscellanies, the works of nineteen dramatists were drawn from the Society Library shelves. Molière had twenty-one readers and Dryden eleven. But the most popular playwright was a woman then in her grave almost seventy years. Twenty-eight borrowers still delighted to read the comedies and dramas of Mrs. Susannah Centlivre, an Englishwoman who married an ex-chef of Louis XIV and wrote a score of successful plays. Two of them, *The Wonder: A Woman Kept a Secret* and *The Busybody,* were produced at the John Street theater during the season of 1789. They were in the Restoration tradition and light enough to be enjoyed when Congreve and Farquhar went begging for borrowers. A few lines will give a taste of her vein. The prologue of *A Bold Stroke for a Wife* promises that

> Our plot is new and regularly clear
> And not one single tittle from Molière

and the epilogue concludes:

> But yet I hope for all that I have said
> To find my spouse a Man of War in bed.

Mrs. Centlivre had a talent for the epigrammatic flick of a phrase. Says a character in the *Bold Stroke,* "Marriage is reducing a man's taste to a kind of half pleasure; but then it carries the blessing of peace along with it—one goes to sleep without fear and wakes without pain."

Among the modern poets, Ossian—or Macpherson—was understandably the most popular, with seventeen borrowers. The day was shortly coming when an Adeline Belville would be christened Minona or Malvina if she was to be considered a stable female, and Augustus can remain a hero only upon condition of changing his name to Oscar. But what local passion gave Pindar twenty readers? It is a long drop to the five customers of Robert Burns. Meanwhile three hardy souls read *The Vision of Columbus,* an epic poem by Joel Barlow; five read *The Conquest of Canaan,* a poem by Timothy Dwight; and only one read *McFingal,* a satire by John Trumbull. So fared the Connecticut literati, the Hartford Wits.

Concerning the reading of the late eighteenth-century New Yorkers, the gist of the matter is this: they read a great deal of fiction in proportion to their other reading; they read widely of history and travel; they read the newspapers certainly, otherwise five newspapers would not compete in a city of thirty thousand; they read the magazines, and particularly the British magazines; they found a useful and perhaps interesting guide in the city directory; they read law and medicine, and we know from the results with what distinguished success; and, it goes without saying, they consulted the almanac on every important occasion— pinning their faith on the answer of the stars. In all the amenities of a machine civilization we are far ahead of our fathers. In matters of the heart, and of the mind, and of taste (if it is not dangerous to use that word), we are very like them.

CHAPTER XII

To School?

TO SCHOOL. For generations of American youth these two
simple words have evoked a prospect or a promise that has
brought pleasure or dismay. To the average child of 1789 these
two words would have had no great meaning—certainly nothing
to provoke either anticipation or alarm. The New Yorker of the
twentieth century takes just pride in the extent and the quality of
the free public school system. The New Yorker of 1789 could
have pointed to only one example of a free, non-sectarian school.
This had been founded in 1787 for Negro boys by the Society for
the Manumission of Slaves. During its first several years it never
had more than a dozen pupils. By 1792 it had added a small department for Negro girls and had changed its name to the Free
African School. And by this time there was another publicly supported primary school in operation—in the Almshouse where one
schoolmaster and one schoolmistress presided over some sixty-five
children, mostly under the age of eight.

This was typical of the attitude of the eighteenth century. Elementary education and secondary education were not problems
of the government. The men of the period were property-minded
—and at the same time they were influenced by the rising spirit
of philanthropy. The rich sent their sons and daughters to private
tutors and private academies; and for the poorest of the poor
they opened their purses to provide a meager elementary education. And this bit of charity was not unmixed with self-interest,
for these tiny waifs of society might thus become equipped to earn
their own livings and would not remain a charge to the taxpayers.

Several of the churches of the city conducted free schools for the children of their parishioners. But if one had no connection with a church which boasted a school and if that person could not afford private tuition—then there was no "education" to be had. The Regents of the University of New York had recommended as early as 1785 that elementary education was of such importance that it ought not to be left in the hands of private individuals. But the taxpayers had prevailed—and nothing was done.

In this chapter we are treating what is usually called "formal" education. Elsewhere we discuss libraries, bookstores, the newspapers, the clubs, and debating societies which spread knowledge and provoked the contemplation of ideas. We have already discussed a category of persons who called themselves schoolmasters and institutions that termed themselves academies. In New York in 1789 it was possible to secure instruction in singing, dancing, fencing, music (including the bassoon, guitar, violin, clarinet, and the harpsichord), drawing, painting, embroidery, cloth work, filigree work, and japanning. Some of these academies pretended to teach almost any or the greater part of these subjects. William Hofmeister, better known as "Little Billy the Fiddler," candidly advertised that "being incapable of other employment, he would teach music of almost any kind."

It is possible to find in the city Directory the names of some fifty-five schoolteachers—and there were some who were not listed. Not a few of them were like "Billy the Fiddler." Incapable of other employment they took to teaching: widows, old Revolutionary veterans, French soldiers who remained in America after the peace, and simple incompetents. A writer in the *American Magazine* declared that many who pretended to run academies were low, ignorant persons and that time spent under their so-called instruction was worse than wasted. Some of the schools consisted merely of a teacher who conducted classes in the parlor of his lodgings. James Robins, who came from Philadelphia in October 1785, conducted an evening school in French "at his Lodgings, No. 77, Fair-street," from six to nine except Sundays.

There were some good schools for boys. James Hardie at 9 Gold Street conducted a school from which thirteen scholars were admitted to Columbia College in June 1789. Malcolm Campbell's was located at 85 Broadway, almost opposite Trinity Church. Superior instruction was provided in each of them. Hardie was the author of a Latin grammar and Campbell, who had taken an M.A. at the University of Aberdeen, edited several volumes of the classics. Messrs. Graham and Johnson ran a school at 19 Little Queen (Cedar) Street that met with generous approbation. The Columbia Grammar School was the best in the city.

There were three principal schools for young ladies. Mrs. Sewall opened her academy at 5 Crown (Liberty) Street in June 1788; Mrs. Carter, "late of London and Philadelphia," received her first pupils in January 1789 at 76 Broadway, opposite the City Tavern; and Mrs. Graham began her teaching late in 1789 and the following year occupied the house at 1 Broadway. In all of them the young ladies were taught "the polite arts," which ranged from reading, writing, and spelling through deportment and dancing to embroidery and painting. The fees varied from $80 a year for full boarders to $6 a quarter for day scholars. Beyond a few polite and useful accomplishments the American woman was not expected to have much learning. La Rochefoucauld-Liancourt observed that American women were primarily good wives and good mothers and that "household affairs occupy all their time and cares; destined by the manners of their country to this domestic life, their education is in other respects too much neglected." A picture of what a cultivated young lady was expected to study is presented by Thomas Jefferson's admonition to his daughter Martha:

> With respect to the distribution of your time, the following is what I should approve: from 8 to 10, practise music. From 10 to 1, dance one day and draw another. From 1 to 2, draw on the day you dance and write a letter the next day. From 3 to 4, read French. From 4 to 5, exercise yourself in music. From 5 till bedtime read English, write, &c. . . . Inform me what books you

read, what tunes you learn, and inclose me your best copy of every lesson in drawing. . . . Take care that you never spell a word wrong. . . . It produces great praise to a lady to spell well.

Gouverneur Morris, who was something of a *bon vivant*, looked at the education provided for women and noted one great lack which he proposed to remedy by establishing a school of cooking for women. Noah Webster looked at the whole field of education and saw nothing very admirable in it. He advocated a greater study of modern languages and grammar and urged that schools should specifically train their students for later careers in the occupations, professions, government, and the social duties.

But schoolmasters were by nature and by self-interest conservative. Changes were slow to come. The state was only beginning to recognize its responsibilities in the field of education. Democracy, in education as in politics, was only slowly becoming articulate and effective. The revolution in American education was still a matter of the future.

While the government assumed but slight interest in elementary and secondary education it was actively concerned with the fate of the greatest educational institution in the city: Columbia College.

The picture presented by Columbia College, reorganized under the new charter and name in 1787, was not an encouraging one. The institution had had an interesting, honorable past and was destined to a future beyond the most fertile imagination of the time, but in the year 1789 its prospects were a matter of great concern to its friends.

King's College (as it was formerly known) had suffered gravely from the events of the Revolution. Classes had been suspended, the faculty had been widely scattered, and the building itself had been taken over by the British and used as a military hospital. Soldiers had found that the library books could be bartered for drinks at the local pubs; consequently they did a very thorough job of spreading learning throughout the city. Even before the physical plant of the college had been commandeered by the Committee of Safety and then seized by the British, the morale of the faculty and of the students had been shattered by political divisions. Latin essays, experiments in physics, the variegated pursuit of truth had all been forgotten in arguments between loyalty and opposition to measures of the British government. With the eventual expulsion of the British military forces came the exile of many of the wealthy and cultured Loyalists and the weakening of a good tradition. The dislocations of war and the economic crisis which followed the peace were blows from which the college did not recover for almost half a century.

The college had been established by royal charter thirty-five years before—October 31, 1754—as the College of the Province of New York. Known always as King's College, it began with an enrollment of eight students and one instructor, the Reverend President Samuel Johnson, D.D., one of that little Yale group who, a generation before, had stirred Connecticut to its foundation by going over to the Church of England. For six years King's College held its sessions in the schoolhouse in the rear of Trinity Church; in 1760 its new building, on the outskirts of the town, overlooking the river on what is now Park Place, was occupied. Three years later Dr. Johnson was succeeded by the Reverend Myles Cooper, D.C.L., Fellow of Queen's College, Oxford, who proceeded to reshape the institution in the likeness of his alma mater. By 1775 his Tory sentiments had become so obnoxious to certain groups of the citizens and students that one night the portly president, clad in his nightshirt, made an undignified but successful flight over a fence and to a British war vessel at anchor in the Hudson while the youthful Alexander Hamilton had meanwhile harangued an eager mob outside the college building. He never returned. The following spring the college gave up its building for military use at the request of the Committee of Safety, and because of the disturbed state of public affairs and the divided loyalties of its constituency, ceased all but its corporate existence during the remaining years of the war. During its twenty-two years King's College had had in all 232 students on its rolls, of whom 107 were graduated in the liberal arts and 12 in medicine. Some thirty-six undergraduates were left academic orphans upon the closing of the college, one of whom was its most distinguished alumnus, Alexander Hamilton.

At the time of the British evacuation in 1783, the college had a building which was in a sad state of disrepair, some remaining invested funds, and a few devoted alumni. There was no faculty, and not even a sufficient number of its corporation remained to form a quorum. These remaining trustees petitioned the new state legislature for a revival of the charter, but instead the legislature in 1784 created the University of the State of New York, a state-wide public educational system with a large board of regents, and the college, renamed Columbia, was incorporated into the system. This form of government proved quite unsatisfactory for the college, and, on April 13, 1787, the legislature finally passed another act giving Columbia its independence and a new charter, under which it has continued to operate.

Columbia had no president under the regents, chiefly because of insufficient income, and the professors administered the college, in rotation. A month after the new charter had been passed, William Samuel Johnson, D.C.L., son of the first president and, strictly speaking, the first layman to hold the presidency of any American college, was chosen president of Columbia. Educated at Yale, Johnson had quickly become one of the most distinguished members of the Connecticut bar, had been that colony's agent in London for a decade, had served on the governor's council and as judge of the superior court. He came to Columbia fresh from service in the Constitutional Convention, where he had been chairman of the committee on literary style, and from 1789 until the Federal government moved to Philadelphia, Johnson was senator from Connecticut. The college had made a good selection; he was a distinguished, kindly, and able gentleman whose scholarship and talents were highly respected by his contemporaries, and his relations with the faculty and students were notably harmonious. His salary was £400, and a portion of the college building was fitted up for his residence; the trustees also built him a stable and set aside a portion of the college garden for his use. Some critics charged that his duties as a United States senator caused him to neglect his academic obligations; and his colleague, Senator Maclay of Pennsylvania, declared that the academic gentleman "padded" his expense accounts by claiming traveling expenses from Connecticut when he actually lived in New York City. Thus the senator-doctor-president may have the dubious honor of having first established what later generations have regarded as a hoary and venerable tradition. In any event, the evidence indicates that Dr. Johnson did well by the college.

At the end of 1787 Johnson assumed the professorship of logic, rhetoric, and belles-lettres, and £50 was added to his salary. Three other professors completed the active faculty in 1789: the Reverend John Daniel Gross, D.D., professor of geography, moral philosophy, and German; John Kemp, LL.D., F.R.S. (Edin.), professor of mathematics and natural philosophy; and Peter Wilson, A.M., professor of Greek and Latin.

The faculty was an interesting, cosmopolitan group. Dr. Gross was a native of Germany who had been educated at Marburg and Heidelberg, and had been pastor of German Reformed congregations on the American frontier; as chaplain of regiments of New York militia he had taken part in the battle of Oriskany and other engagements before coming to Columbia. Unlike most professors he managed to acquire considerable wealth (through the purchase of soldiers' land warrants) and spent the latter years of his life in philosophic retirement on a farm near Fort Plain, New York. His course in geography and chronology, which he delivered to the sophomores twice a week, was a broad historical orientation course, which Herbert Baxter Adams of Johns Hopkins University characterized a century later as "a highly creditable course, the best that the writer has found in the annals of any American college at that period." His lectures on moral philosophy, published in 1795 as *Natural Principles of Rectitude,* were thorough and laborious. But when delivered in person under the ornamental buttonwoods of the tiny campus, generations of Columbia students found the professor's disquisitions on moral philosophy both relevant and inspiring.

Dr. John Kemp was a precocious Scotsman, a graduate of the University of Aberdeen, who, after a year's trial appointment at the college, was made a professor at the age of twenty-three. One of his students, after many mellowing years, declared that "Dr. Kemp, a strong mathematician, ably filled several departments of science; impulsive and domineering in his nature, there were moments with him when a latent benevolence towards the student quickened itself, and he may be pronounced to have been an effective teacher." Although he was seemingly "devoid of genius and lacked enterprise," his course in natural philosophy, which included some six hundred experiments, was so popular that it drew the attendance of the general public.

Peter Wilson, the lovable eccentric of the faculty, was also a native of Scotland and an alumnus of the University of Aberdeen. He had been principal of the Hackensack Academy, had served in the New Jersey legislature, and had made a codification of the laws of the state. He wrote or edited several treatises and texts and was known to some as a pioneer American classical scholar. But Professor Wilson, although by far the most earnest member of the faculty and despite his wide reading, lacked any penetrating scholarship. He was the complete pedagogue but not a profound scholar. He was "cramped with dactyls and spondees" and was usually harassed in his classical exegesis to the point where his derivative theory and verbal criticism provoked gales of unrestrained laughter among his students. Professor Wilson was remarkable, not for his knowledge, but for his generous nature and his kindly attitude toward his students. His enthusiasm, unlike his knowledge, never faltered; he constantly reminded his students that "without the classics you can neither roast a potato nor fly a kite." The professor of Latin and Greek became so infatuated with Josephus and the history of the Jews that he resolved to bring them "the proper spiritual salvation." He joined a Society for the Conversion of the Israelites, and after years of personal effort it is alleged that he finally persuaded one of the lost sheep to embrace the stern beauties of Calvinism.

The course of study in Columbia College in 1789 was very little different from the traditional curriculum introduced into America at Harvard from the English universities a century and a half earlier. Before entrance the student was examined orally on Caesar's *Gallic Wars,* Cicero against Catiline, the first four books of Vergil's *Aeneid,* the Gospels in Greek, some Greek and Latin syntax, Latin composition, and "the first four Rules of Arithmetic, with the Rule of Three, and Vulgar and Decimal Fractions." After he had paid the president (for the use of the library and philosophical apparatus) the sum of one pound sterling, written his name in the Matriculation Book, and been handed a copy of the *Statutes,* he was a member of the college. As a freshman he attended the professor of languages twice a day for Latin and Greek, the professor of mathematics three times a week, and the professor of logic and rhetoric once a week, with whom he studied "English grammar, together with the Art of Reading and Speaking English with propriety and elegance." He was also obliged to turn in every day a written Latin exercise; once a week a translation from Latin. As a sophomore he attended the professors of languages and mathematics once a day and the professor of geography three times a week; there was a written Latin exercise every day, and an English composition on a designated subject once a week. As a junior the student took logic once a week, languages twice a week (consisting mainly of the professor's remarks "upon the peculiar beauties" of the Greek and Latin authors, which the student took down in his notebook and gave back on the quarterly examinations), and natural philosophy three times a week—his only taste of science—with lectures and experiments performed by the professor. The weekly assigned composition in English or Latin was continued. In his senior year the student took ethics three times a week, Latin once, and logic and rhetoric twice; he was at last permitted to choose the subject of his weekly composition. There were weekly exercises in public speaking, public exercises at every monthly Visitation (of the trustees), and public examinations at every quarterly Visitation. If the student bore up under this for four years and behaved himself moderately well, he was given the Bachelor of Arts degree; at the commencement three years after his graduation, if he had turned in a written exercise to the president and paid another degree fee, he was given a Master of Arts degree, completing what survived of the medieval seven-year course in the liberal arts.

The average age of entering students at Columbia was between fifteen and sixteen. The undergraduates were often in high spirits and required much disciplining. This was the duty of the president. There had long been an elaborate system of rules and regulations. From the early days of the college the attendance at chapel was so irksome that a special prohibition of "Talking, Laughing, Justling, Winking, etc." was established. There were other curious regulations concerning "Drunkenness, Fornication, Lying, Theft, Swearing, Cursing, or any other scandalous immorality." Further statutes forbade the frequenting of the numerous houses of ill-fame near the college, cockfighting, cardplaying, dice, and "Dilapidations of the College." For detected violations there was an elaborate system of penalties, from a fine of sixpence for absence from a lecture or the required morning and evening prayers to five shillings for "profane cursing, or swearing; or being intoxicated with liquor; or . . . telling a wilful falsehood"; for repeated offenses the student was publicly admonished before the entire college and finally rusticated or expelled. Beginning in 1788, the students were permitted to wear gowns, reviving the King's College custom; after April 1789 they were required to wear them. The weekly holiday was Saturday, and Saturday mornings the Columbia College Society held regular meetings, at which the students read original compositions or engaged in "Disputations."

The undergraduate body numbered between thirty and fifty,

most of whom lived at home or at other lodgings in the city, although there were a few chambers, with studies, available in the college at a quarterly rental of one dollar; John Randolph of Roanoke and his brother lived there in baronial style with a colored serving man. Life was not so easy for the average student, like John Barent Johnson of the Class of 1792, whose diary has survived; he had to furnish his own wood, candles, etc., make his own fire, and fetch his water from the College Pump. John, the barber, dressed his long hair Saturdays when he could afford it. His weekly ablutions on Saturday are duly recorded, his whitening of his breeches and the brushing of his shoes and boots, as well as his lament at once being aroused by the chimney sweep at five-thirty in the morning.

Thursday the thirtieth of April 1789 was a gala day for the nation and for Columbia. Young Barent Johnson was up at quarter past six—"A fine Day"—and attended prayers in one of the churches at nine. At one he saw the oath administered to "his Excellency" George Washington by the chancellor of the state, Robert R. Livingston of the Class of 1765; afterwards he attended the services for the president at St. Paul's Chapel, conducted by the Bishop of New York, Samuel Provoost of the Class of 1758.

Commencement Day, May sixth, was another proud day for the college. The exercises were held at St. Paul's Chapel after the academic procession had marched over from the college building, and were attended by President Washington, making his first public appearance since his inauguration, Vice-President Adams, the members of the Senate and House of Representatives, Governor George Clinton, and the principal state officials. Ten students, who were about to receive the degree of Bachelor of Arts, gave orations. Matthew Mesier spoke "On the Passions," John Bainbridge simply "On Happiness," but the other subjects ranged from "The Rising Glory of America" through "The Progress and Causes of Civilization" and "Government,—its Progress from East to West" to "The Utility and Study of History" and the valedictory. Dr. Johnson then conferred the degrees upon the successful candidates and the degree of Master of Arts upon DeWitt Clinton and three of his classmates of 1786. Washington's presence was a graceful tribute to the labors of the graduates of King's College who had been so active in establishing the nation's independence and the new government.

A critic railed against the college because of its small number of graduates: ten for Columbia as against thirty for Yale and forty-nine for Harvard. Time has adjusted that, and today the graduates of any one year at Columbia will approach the total enrollment of either of the more ancient institutions. Another critic, Dr. Hugh Williamson, suggested that less attention be paid to the classics and more to natural philosophy and natural history. But the same suggestion might well have been made to any American college of the period.

No other American college, however, had the eminent Peter Wilson as the professor of Latin and Greek. When he began his celebrated explanation of the English noun "stranger," from the Latin preposition "E" ("Thus, young gentlemen," the Doctor would say, "E—ex—extra—extraneus—gallice *étranger,* anglice, *stranger*"), many a student thought of the fine fish waiting to be caught in the Hudson, and some braved the risk of a college fine and snared them; others merely wished the good professor were back in Hackensack or even in the Scotland whence he came— a stranger in a promising land.

In spite of all the crudities and all the difficulties of early American education, the eminent Dr. Benjamin Rush could declare, ten years after Washington's inauguration: "I am satisfied that the ratio of intellect is as twenty to one and of knowledge one hundred to one with what they were before the American Revolution."

But the revolution in American education was still a matter of the future.

CHAPTER XIII

The City at Prayer

TO ANY foreigner possessed of a sense of history, the most astonishing spectacle in New York was its churches. There were twenty-two of them, representing thirteen denominations: Reformed Dutch, Jewish, Protestant Episcopal, French Huguenot, Quaker, Lutheran, Presbyterian, Baptist, Moravian, German Reformed, Methodist, Roman Catholic, and Independent Congregational. And, unrepresented by a visible organization or edifice, there were Deists and citizens of no religion at all. It was not, however, the number and variety of these faiths that would make a foreigner's hair stand on end, but the curious fact that not one of them was subsidized, controlled, or "established" by the government, that all of them were voluntary and self-supporting, and, finally and incredibly, that no member of them suffered a single disability as a citizen of the Federal union because of his religious views.

"Here, no particular modes of faith or worship are established," said the Rev. Dr. William Linn in his Fourth of July sermon (1791) on the blessings of America. "No undue preference is given to one denomination above another. Every one stands upon equal footing, and can prove successful only by the piety, virtue, learning, and liberality of its professors."

Nothing like this had ever been known in human history. The nearest approach to such freedom must be sought for in the palmy days of the Roman Empire or in the vanished Dutch Republic; but even in these and few similar instances a privileged state-paid cult held a superior position. Before 1789 had run little more than half its course, a second nation in the history of man, the French, was to free the conscience of its citizens from dictation, discrimination, and tithes. The ideal, if not the reality, of this liberty—first effected in America—was to become a commonplace of the nineteenth century. Yet so unaccustomed is mankind to religious freedom, so low it reckons the dignity and value of the individual, that any day now, if the totalitarian forces of the world prevail, the worth of man—which is another name for the rights of man —will again be lost. Most of humanity will relapse to its habitual level of primitive savage intolerance. The American experiment may once more be unique as it was in 1789.

Even then the experiment was not yet complete. The sixth article of the Federal Constitution guaranteed that "no religious test shall ever be required as a qualification to any office or public trust under the United States"; and the first of the amendments which Congress passed in September of 1789 ordained that "Congress shall make no law respecting an establishment of religion or prohibiting the free exercise thereof." But several of the states still carried on their statute books, as a hang-over from colonial days, enactments which lagged behind these enlightened views. After the adoption of its constitution of 1777 and the enabling acts of 1784, New York, unlike the laggards, was a free state in matters of religion—with one exception. Catholics were barred from holding public office until 1806, when the first practical test—the election of Francis Cooper as assemblyman from New York City—led to the removal of this last disability.

The liberty enjoyed by church, synagogue, and freethinkers of New York, as elsewhere in America, was deeply grounded. It did not spring from a ready-made body of doctrines loudly trumpeted and suddenly enacted by a rush of enthusiasm. On the contrary its development as a principle was long, slow, and obscure. Over more than a century the colonists debated religion in meetinghouses and general stores and absorbed the ideas of Erasmus, Montaigne, Milton, and Locke probably without a mention or even a knowledge of their names. Nor was the principle gained at a stroke in bloody warfare, to be won on one battlefield and perhaps lost on the next. Religious liberty lay implicit in the emptiness of the American wilderness and in that give-and-take between man and man which alone could tame it, turning forests into meadows and towns. If the new world was to be conquered, the need for healthy men—unfettered if not fully rounded individuals—was supreme; and an instinct of self-preservation prevented any one group of Americans from crippling another for more than a passing spell. Obedient to that instinct, clergymen of all faiths played a powerful part in creating a sense of American unity and laying the foundations of American independence.

In the eighteenth century it was the traveler's fashion to tour the churches. Little of antiquity and less of art could be seen in the churches of New York or any other American town; but a round of Sunday visits enabled a stranger to estimate the character of the natives, appraise the choirs, and sample the pulpit oratory. He inspected no Sunday schools, for they did not exist.

For antiquity of structure, such as it was, the oldest example in New York was the Garden Street Church of the Reformed Dutch. It was built in 1693—that is to say, it was less than a century old; it stood on what is now Exchange Place between Broad and William; and its only concessions to art were the coats of arms painted on its small leaded panes. Here you could enjoy the Rev. Gerardus Arense Kuypers, lately of Hackensack and Paramus, reading the prayers and preaching the sermons in Dutch. There must have been pathos in the last Dutch sermon as a regular feature of the service—which he gave before a handful of die-hards in 1803.

Organized in 1628, the Collegiate Reformed Protestant Dutch Church, to which the Garden Street edifice belonged, was naturally the oldest religious body in the city. Even in 1789 it boasted the largest membership—so large that two additional buildings were normally in use: the Middle Dutch Church on Nassau Street, which was closed for repair of the damages done by the British occupation, and the North Dutch Church on William

Street between Fulton and Ann. The latter was erected in 1767–69 to accommodate the many members who desired services conducted in English.

The stranger had plenty to gape at in the North Dutch Church. Clad in a black silk gown with large flowing sleeves, the dominie was perched in a high cagelike pulpit. Above him a huge sounding board gave to the sermons an appropriate roll of thunder. After pronouncing the text it was customary for the dominie to exclaim: "Thus far!" An hourglass stood at his side; and when the sand ran out, the sexton gave three raps with a cane, warning the dominie that he had gone far enough and that it was time to bring the sermon to a close. On one never-to-be-forgotten mid-summer Sunday the heat put the sexton to sleep; twice the sand ran out, and each time the dominie glanced at the dozing sexton, drew a long breath and a fresh text, turned the glass, and preached an additional hour. Before the sermon the sexton employed a long pole to hoist announcements and notices up to the pulpit; and after the services the deacons collected alms by means of long rods hung with bells and velvet bags.

Two distinguished divines occupied this aerial pulpit in 1789. Dominie John Henry Livingston, a graduate of Yale and Utrecht, was the son-in-law of Philip Livingston, a signer of the Declaration of Independence. He was professor of theology in the Dutch Church and ended his days as president of Rutgers College. His commanding appearance, deep voice, eccentric gesticulation, enormous wig, and copious notes all added weight to his sermons. As for his colleague, Dominie William Linn, no sexton ever went to sleep under his trumpetlike voice, which "could be heard for a mile." Nor Congress either, after he was chosen chaplain of the House (at a salary of $500). He memorized his sermons, dramatized them with vehement gestures, and won the reputation of being the most eloquent preacher in the city. A stranger who heard him deliver a charity sermon was moved to write in the *Daily Advertiser* (October 30): "Would ministers always preach thus, I venture to say that it would soon become fashionable to go to church and perform Christian duties in general." Unquestionably Dr. Linn merited his $1,000 salary and rent-free house on Cortlandt Street.

The Jews represented the second-oldest faith in the city. A shipload of them, coming from Curaçao, settled in New Amsterdam in 1654; and from the outset private services must have been held in one of their homes. Two years later their religious life was organized at least to the extent of possessing a burial ground; a fragment of it remains intact to this day off Chatham Square, where the oldest decipherable stone, commemorating one Benjamin Bueno de Mesquita, is dated 1683. A map of New York in 1695 locates their synagogue on Beaver Street near Mill. Their congregation, called "Shearith Israel," or the Remnant of Israel, drew up a constitution in 1706.

But the Jewish house of prayer to be seen on Mill Street in 1789 was only sixty-one years old. It was a small, simple structure of stone and brick, with wooden beams imported from Curaçao. A visitor needed to be a linguist in order to follow the entire service, which was mainly in Hebrew, with a sprinkling of Spanish and English. However, the occasional sermons of Rabbi Gershom Mendez Seixas were in admirable English. His Thanksgiving Day sermon was published in pamphlet form, to be purchased for one shilling; and the *Daily Gazette* (Dec. 23, 1789) informed the public that "this excellent discourse, the first of the kind ever preached in English in this State, is highly deserving the attention of every pious reader, whether Jew or Christian, as it breathes nothing but pure morality and devotion." On another occasion he preached in St. Paul's Chapel. Rabbi Seixas was a trustee of Columbia College, he participated with thirteen other clergymen in the inauguration of Washington, and he served for fifty years (1766–1816) as leader of the Jewish community. His congregation, "Shearith Israel," the oldest in American Jewry, still flourishes; and today the same liturgy may be heard on Central Park West, with no doubt something new in sermons, as on Mill Street a century and a half ago.

Then as now the fashionable church was the Protestant Episcopal. The members of this offshoot from the High Church of England had a hard time looking down on the Dutch, who were on the spot first; but they succeeded, even to the point of recruiting society-minded Knickerbockers. However, they found it no trouble at all to look down upon Presbyterians, Baptists, Congregationalists, and other dissenters. One stranger touring the churches in 1784 did not relish this attitude. He wrote in the New York *Packet:*

> A foreigner presents his most respectful compliments to the congregation of St. Paul's, and begs leave to observe to them that he must think they are devoid of any manner of humanity or common politeness, when they can see genteel strangers come into their Church, and not endeavor to procure them a seat, but sit with a mortifying indifference upon their countenance. . . . He is persuaded such unfriendly inattention cannot proceed from influence of climate, as their neighboring city is possessed of good breeding and politeness.

Still it might have been the climate, for the stranger's letter was written on a New York fifteenth of July.

It must likewise be considered that the Episcopal Church, alone among the New York denominations, was the proprietor of many goodly acres of land. By royal grant it possessed what was once known as the Church Farm, which extended northward from Fulton Street to Greenwich Village and westward roughly from Broadway to the Hudson River. Its holdings, however, were as unremunerative as they were extensive. In May of '89 the corporation advertised forty-six lots for sale in an effort to secure ready money for rebuilding Trinity Church, and it also announced its determination to collect back rents.

The original Trinity Church, built in 1696, had been destroyed by fire at the outbreak of the Revolution. Demolition of the ruins had begun in 1788, and the work of rebuilding occupied all of 1789 to the great fascination of the sidewalk superintendents.

Among them the editor of the New York *Journal* particularly approved of the spire which, if equipped with lightning rods, would he claimed, furnish excellent protection to Wall Street and the Federal Hall. The completed church, with a steeple which carried lightning rods two hundred feet into the sky, was consecrated on March 25, 1790. All the clergymen in the city and high government officials, including the President, participated in the solemn event. (Forty-nine years later—in 1839—Trinity was torn down and was replaced in 1846 by the present edifice.)

Meanwhile the visitor on tour had to be content with the two Episcopal chapels: St. George's on Beekman and Cliff streets, built in 1752; and St. Paul's on Broadway, which was opened in 1766. St. Paul's, now the oldest religious structure and, after Fraunces' Tavern, probably the oldest building extant in the city, looked much the same in 1789 as it does today—except for the steeple, which was added in 1794. It was here that Washington could be seen attending services in a canopied pew set apart for his use and listening to the discourses of Bishop Provoost.

The Right Reverend Samuel Provoost, D.D., Bishop of New York and Rector of Trinity Church, was a portly gentleman with a round full face and much dignity of bearing. What he lacked in intellectual power and oratorical fire he made up in classical learning, knowledge of languages, science, and botany, and, more to the purpose, in public spirit, hospitality, and charity. In 1789 he served as chaplain to the United States Senate as, in years gone by, he had served the Continental Congress. People who knew him said that he gave more liberally to the poor than his salary of $1,750 and rent-free house on Nassau Street should warrant.

His assistant, the Rev. Benjamin Moore, had been his predecessor as rector of Trinity. This strange mutation was an aftermath of the Revolutionary War. Trinity was rife with unreconstructed Tories, fearful of their fortunes and prestige. Upon the conclusion of peace in 1783 and before the refugee patriots could get back to their homes and vote, the Tories elected Moore to the rectorate. Next year the patriots, who had returned in force, ousted Moore and installed Provoost. As part of this struggle the New York State government changed Trinity Church by statute into a purely American institution. The episode was typical of a transformation that took place in a number of sects with English or Dutch affiliations.

Dr. Moore was a modest man whose sermons were marked by their simplicity. He lived to become rector again of Trinity, then bishop, and also president of Columbia College. His son, Clement C. Moore, built up Chelsea, endowed the Protestant Episcopal seminary with its land, and wrote " 'Twas the night before Christmas."

The Huguenots were the third congregation to build a church in the city. After using the Dutch church in the Fort for some years, they erected their own in 1688. But in 1789 their Church of the Saint-Esprit, a later structure on Pine Street, was an unusable wreck as the result of British depredations; and in 1803 the dwindling congregation merged with the Episcopalians.

The Quakers had two meetinghouses—one on Liberty Street, built at the beginning of the eighteenth century; and the "New Quaker Meeting" erected in 1775 on Pearl and Oak streets. The Friends were prominent in the formation of a society, in 1785, for the liberation of slaves; and the Quaker, Samuel Franklin, became its first president. Another Quaker, Robert Murray, contributed the funds to create a school for Negroes, the African Free School, in 1787.

The Lutherans built their first church in 1702, on the corner of Broadway and Rector Street. Its fate was told in the name, "Burnt Lutheran Church," which clung to the corner for many years. In 1789 they were to be found in their steepleless Swamp Church, built in 1767 at William and Frankfort streets. Their pastor was the Rev. Dr. John Christopher Kunze, lately of Philadelphia but born and educated in Saxony. He was not a man to listen to from a pew, for his sermons were learned, delivered in a weak voice with a thick German accent, and never less than one hour long. But in private he could discourse profitably on theology, numismatics, and astronomy. Except for his intimate friend Rabbi Seixas, no New Yorker was his peer in the mastery of Hebrew and other oriental tongues, which he taught at Columbia College. His brother-in-law was Frederick Augustus Conrad Muhlenberg, one-time pastor of the Swamp Church and now Speaker of the House of Representatives. The star boarder at his home on Chatham Street was Senator Maclay. Decidedly Dr. Kunze was worth cultivating.

A stranger not only found a ready welcome in the Brick Meeting of the Presbyterians on Beekman Street, but he was ushered directly to one of the two Governor's Pews. Reserved for visitors, these pews were installed opposite each other near the middle of the side walls; they were raised magisterially from the floor and were surmounted with imposing wooden canopies. Thus the visitor commanded a full view of the pulpit affixed to the top of a sturdy column. At its base a circular pew was occupied by the officers and the chorister. There were no choir, organ, long rods, or velvet bags with bells. The lines of a psalm were sung alternately by the chorister and the congregation. At the conclusion of the service tin plates were passed about, and each Presbyterian contributed one copper and no more.

If you liked the sermon you heard on any given Sunday morning in the Brick Meeting, you could hear it again the same afternoon in the other Presbyterian church on Wall Street. Or vice versa—for the ministers repeated their discourses twice on a Sabbath, switching from one church to the other. There was, however, a difference in background. The Wall Street Church, the first Presbyterian place of worship in the city, was an ancient structure dating from 1719. The Brick Meeting, which Noah Webster called "genteel" but Manasseh Cutler described as "elegant," was a bare twenty years old.

During 1789 the permanent pastor of these churches was a towering figure in American Presbyterian history—the Rev. Dr.

St. Pauls Church & New Presbyterian Meeting, New York.

ST. PAUL'S AND THE NEW PRESBYTERIAN MEETING

From a later water-color drawing by Robertson of a scene familiar to all New
Yorkers of 1789.

OLD FEDERAL HALL AND WALL STREET

This reproduction is an original drawing from Robertson.

John Rodgers. He was moderator of the first Presbyterian General Assembly in the United States, which was held this same year in Philadelphia; and he was likewise president of the New York Society for the Relief of Distressed Debtors and vice-president of the Society for Promoting Useful Knowledge. During the Revolution he was an ardent patriot and never relinquished his interest in public affairs. Senator Maclay tells of his lobbying in behalf of Hamilton's funding bill—a sort of relief for distressed creditors. "The Rev. Dr. Rodgers," he writes in his diary, "called on me and General Muhlenberg this evening. He owed me no visit, for that he paid a day or two ago. Directly he began to extol Hamilton's system, and argued with it as if he had been in the pulpit. I checked him; he made his visit short." Dr. Rodgers' salary and perquisites came to $2,250 a year.

Prospective colleagues of Dr. Rodgers came and went thoughout the year. Candidate James Muir, a young Scotsman, nearly won acceptance, for his sermons were rarely more than half an hour in length; but his strong burr and a defect in his speech made half an hour not short enough. The Rev. Jedediah Morse also offered himself as a candidate, with the result that the congregation disagreed so firmly on their respective merits and demerits that neither was chosen. Towards the end of the year John McKnight, a Pennsylvanian, secured the position and preached his first sermon on the text, "I ask therefore for what intent ye have sent for me."

The roll of Presbyterian churches would not be complete without mention of two offshoots of this sect. The Associate Reformed Church, popularly known as the Scotch Presbyterians, worshiped on Cedar Street near Broadway under the leadership of the Rev. Dr. John Mason. An Associate Presbyterian congregation, formed in 1785, occupied a frame church on Nassau Street, called the "Seceders' Church." For a part of the year 1789 its pulpit was occupied by the Rev. Dr. David Goodwillie, whose sermons were "intensely evangelical, and divided and sub-divided with most systematic exactness."

The first Baptist church was built in 1728, but within a few years the congregation dissolved. In 1762 a fresh start was made in a church which stood on Gold Street, between Fulton and John. Its membership numbered 196 in October of '89. The twelve preceding months may not have been typical, but during that period twenty-one new members were admitted and seventeen old members were dismissed or excommunicated. The Rev. Benjamin Foster, pastor of the Gold Street church, was a close rival to Seixas and Kunze in his knowledge of Hebrew and Chaldaic; and he was probably unrivaled for his output of sermons. Year in and out he delivered four to six discourses a week.

In 1752 the Moravians or United Brethren built a small wooden church on Fulton Street near William. The Rev. James Birkby was its pastor in 1789.

Another German group, the German Calvinist Reformed Church, began its New York history in 1758, and it remained affiliated with the classis of the Dutch Church in Amsterdam until the close of the century. Its church on Nassau Street, rebuilt in 1765, was commonly called the Baron's Church, because here on any Sunday of '89 the chances were good for meeting Baron Steuben among the worshipers. Although John Jacob Astor was the treasurer, it was too early in his career for him to be of much help to the Rev. Dr. John Daniel Gross. The members were on the whole humble folk, artisans and little shopkeepers. Dr. Gross's salary was £150 a year, but in 1789 he received only £107 of it. The total church expenses for the year, about $600, would probably not have been met if George Gilfert, music dealer and organist, had not contributed more than one tenth of the sum. Dr. Gross eventually resigned on account of ill health, went to Canajoharie, New York, and grew wealthy speculating in soldiers' land warrants.

From their various rungs on the social ladder, High-Churchmen and dissenters alike joined in looking down on the Methodists. The latter committed two unforgivable sins against the canons of respectability: they were audibly demonstrative in their worship and they were incorrigibly democratic in their member-ship. A considerable number of their New York congregation were Negroes. Moreover—such is the illogic of human nature—many Methodist ministers, despite their democracy, had been tainted with Tory sympathies; and it was not forgotten that during the British occupation of the city the congregation remained un-molested in its worship. The work of Francis Asbury in creating not only an independent American Methodism but the first na-tional church organization on straight American lines—a work crowned with his appointment as bishop in 1784—had not yet altogether penetrated the public mind. In the summer of 1789 attacks upon the patriotism of Methodist leaders appeared in the New York press.

The Methodist Society of New York, which was the oldest in America, was founded about 1760. Its Wesley Chapel on John Street, built in 1766, was America's first Methodist church—a long, low, rubble structure coated on the outside with blue plaster. About three hundred members united here to listen to the Rev. John Dickens or to Elder Thomas Morrel—the latter a powerful speaker who continued to preach until his ninetieth year. Negroes likewise preached in the John Street church; and the whites of America were astonished to discover, in an age as yet innocent of Zion churches and camp meetings, that the colored race is gifted with oratory.

Somewhat before the outbreak of the Revolution a small group of Roman Catholics worshiped privately under the direction of a Jesuit father. The first public congregation was formed in 1783; and two years later the cornerstone of its first church, St. Peter's, was laid by Don Diego de Gardoqui, minister of Spain. Conse-crated but still unfinished by 1789, St. Peter's was a brick build-ing on the corner of Barclay and Church streets. The Rev. Wil-liam O'Brien, a Dominican, officiated there until his death in 1816. Father O'Brien had studied in Bologna, and one of his fellow students eventually rose to an archbishopric in Mexico. The infant church in New York badly needed funds, and Father

O'Brien remembered his faraway friend. Accordingly in 1789 he made the arduous journey to Mexico and managed to bring back nearly $6,000 and several paintings for the completion and adornment of St. Peter's.

This same year a new church made its appearance in New York. The *Daily Advertiser* of November 6 announced that the Independent Congregational Church, under charge of the Rev. George Wall, would hold initial services on the following Sunday in their meetinghouse on Great George Street (Broadway). Presumably this was the first Congregational church building in the city.

More new churches were on the horizon, and other new faiths were already at work. In 1785 the synod of the Dutch Church of New York and New Jersey complained of the "mighty flood of errors, the free-thinking, with all the different kinds of irreligion" that were sweeping the country. By this extravagant language the synod meant that deism and kindred beliefs typical of the century of reason were noticeable in America. Whether error or not, a faith in the fatherhood of God and brotherhood of man independent of divine revelation and formal creeds—which was the essence of deism—was far from irreligious and hardly a mighty flood. Still it perceptibly influenced the temper of the times.

Few people, to be sure, had read *Reason the Only Oracle of Man,* published in 1784 by Ethan Allen, the hero of Ticonderoga —the first important deist work written in America. Acquaintance with Voltaire and Rousseau or Shaftesbury and Bolingbroke was limited to intellectual circles. Neither Franklin, Washington, Jefferson, Madison, nor other deists among the Founding Fathers cried their faith from the housetops. But the rationalist character of the Declaration of Independence, with its invocation of the "laws of Nature" and "Nature's God," and the very silence of the Federal Constitution, which avoided any implication of revealed religion, testified to the new spirit.

Around boardinghouse tables, in the taverns, and on the doorsteps of churches people were debating and questioning tradi-

tional creeds. From his own boardinghouse Senator Maclay
writes:

> Went down-stairs; found a large company; the subject was re-
> ligion and most unmercifully was it handled . . . it was at-
> tempted to be established that the whole was craft and imposi-
> tion; that all our objects were before us—believe what you see;
> observe the fraud and endless mischiefs of ecclesiastics in every
> age, etc. . . .
> Few of the historic facts which they adduced could be refuted.
> But by way of opposition Luther's Reformation was mentioned.
> It was easily answered that, had there been no abuse, they needed
> no reformation. But a further remark was suggested—that Luther
> was a mere political machine in the hands of those German
> princes who could no longer bear to see their subjects pillaged by
> Roman rapacity. The [old] doctrine was, pay for indulgences and
> purchase salvation with good works, *alias* money. The new doc-
> trine was, faith is better than cash; only believe, and save your
> money. It need not be doubted but the new doctrine was on this
> account more acceptable to both prince and people. Luther, how-
> ever, had the Scripture with him.

At this point the discussion switched from history to science—
to the kind of talk the backwoods of America still enjoys. Continues Maclay:

> Another position I thought still less tenable: that man was but
> the first animal in nature, that he became so by the feelings of his
> fingers and hence all his faculties. Give, said they, only a hand to
> a horse, he would rival all the human powers.

But Maclay had the answer:

> This I know to be groundless. The 'possum, from its feeble, harm-
> less and helpless faculties, is almost extinct in Pennsylvania, and
> yet one I killed on the island at Juniata had as complete a hand,
> with four fingers and a thumb, as one of the human species.

On another occasion Maclay tried to figure out the age of the
earth from the erosion of rocks by the Falls of Niagara. He con-

cluded that the Falls, to say nothing of the earth, was 55,000 years old. Despite the discrepancy between this estimate and Bishop Usher's calendar of creation, Maclay remained an observing Presbyterian. But his talk, his speculation, and his tolerant concessions showed which way the new wind was blowing.

In the 1790s it blew Elihu Palmer to New York, and this noted freethinker soon established a Deistical Society. It blew in John Butler, who argued against Trinitarianism in the Large Assembly Room on Cortlandt Street, created a Unitarian Society in 1794, and embarrassed the orthodox clergy by inviting them to public debate. Two years later the same wind brought to town the Rev. John Murray and other itinerant preachers of universal salvation, who launched the Universalist Church. Before the century had closed, the first two parts of Thomas Paine's *Age of Reason* released deism from its confinement to philosophers and highbrows and, till the age of Ingersoll and beyond, made it one of America's popular faiths.

CHAPTER XIV

Preserving the Peace

NEW YORK suffered from the War of the Revolution more than any other American city. It was the one important center held by the British throughout the Revolution—from September 1776 to November 1783. Within a brief span of years it had experienced two drastic and sudden changes in population. When the British easily seized the city in 1776, they estimated that 95 per cent of the people had already fled. But once the British were in control, many Tories and others drifted into and partially repopulated the stronghold abandoned by the patriots. The Tories, in turn, were rudely disturbed by the surrender of Lord Cornwallis at Yorktown and then thrown into confusion by the final peace of 1783. Before the victorious American forces reoccupied New York, more than ten thousand persons fled in search of a hasty refuge in other parts of the British Empire. During the British occupation there had been a vast and destructive fire, wholesale looting, and destruction of property. The normal life of the city almost vanished, and with its disappearance there came a general breakdown of law and order and morality. Every war means a relaxation of standards—even for those who win. And these are things far more easily destroyed than rebuilt.

Preserving order in colonial New York had never been simple; it was doubly difficult in the years which immediately followed the Revolution. There were numerous breaches of the peace, cases of assault and battery, gambling, dueling, larceny of many descriptions, swearing, drunkenness, and prostitution. The discreet and law-abiding New Yorker went home early of a night, bolted his doors, and placed his trust in the city watch. If he lived in one of the better sections of the city his slumbers might be undisturbed, but in less desirable precincts there were tavern brawls, street fights, lewd merriment, and occasional riots which taxed the full strength of all the officers of the law. The lanes and streets and the highways leading from the city were dark and twisting and infested by footpads, who were described by apologetic New Yorkers as "wheelbarrow men [i.e., prisoners and convicts] escaped from Philadelphia." Whatever the origins of these nocturnal disturbances, the prudent New Yorker of 1789 was ensconced in his home after dark, unless he wished to witness something of what the clergy termed "scandalous and heaven-provoking improprieties."

The most apprehensive citizens—especially the taxpayers—were well aware that the City Fathers were making valiant efforts to police the metropolis. It would be too much to expect that even the most prescient could have predicted that a time would ever come (within a century and a half) when the police force of the city would number fully two thirds of the total population of the first capital of the new nation. The well-informed New Yorker of 1789 understood the complicated structure of law enforcement; certainly visitors were impressed by the variety and efficiency of the officers who preserved the peace of the city.

These officers of the law included a high sheriff and his under-sheriffs, a high constable and sixteen elected constables, a chief marshal and his deputy marshals, the city watch, and, during great emergencies, the state militia.

The sheriff was appointed annually from among the "substantial freeholders," was permitted to hold no other office, and could not retain the post longer than four years. Robert Boyd was the sheriff of New York from 1787 to 1791. He had many duties connected with the holding of courts, choosing of juries, supervising of elections and the issuing of legal papers. He and his deputies were officially instructed to exert their vigilance to prevent the theft and destruction of personal property during fires. His was the custody of the prisoners in the Jail, whether awaiting trial or under sentence. That the sheriffs were often lackadaisical, if not negligent, in their duties is indicated by the great number of state laws providing penalties for accepting money for excusing jurors, corrupt conduct during elections, concealing or neglecting to arrest felons, taking illegal fees in court actions, allowing prisoners "to escape voluntarily," and taking prisoners to taverns and overcharging them for food and liquor. The sheriff had the power to appoint jailors, and, since the post of jailor was one of profit, he probably did not remain oblivious of this possibility of augmenting his income. Altogether the sheriff was an important, respected and busy official.

The high constable (the officer who nearest approximated the modern police commissioner) was appointed each year by the mayor and was eligible for any number of reappointments. James Culbertson served in this important post from 1789 until his death in December 1799—a decade of notable public service. His opportunity first came when, on the last day of December 1788, the Common Council formally charged Captain Frederick Wiessenfels, of the city watch, with irregularity of his command. The accused replied that "his advanced Age and Infirmity of Body" prevented his doing any better and asked to be permitted to resign or be discharged. The council discharged him and appointed Culbertson one of the captains of the watch. Within three months came a greater opportunity. The mayor removed James Burras from his office of high constable for total neglect of duty and then appointed Culbertson as a fitting reward for the capture of "a dangerous robber in the night." Culbertson continued to serve as one of the two captains of the watch, as superintendent of street cleaning from 1789 to 1794, and as deputy clerk of the market. It was his general responsibility to see that the peace of the city was kept, and, until the creation of a corporation attorney in 1801, the high constable brought suit against the violators of municipal ordinances to recover the stipulated penalties. The constables who served under the high constable were elected each year: two from each of the first six wards and four from the Seventh (or Out) Ward. Election as a constable was generally esteemed a misfortune, and the most ingenious pleas were invented to escape it—so ingenious that penalties of from five shillings to £10 were devised for those who refused to serve. The constables received no regular stipend but took fees for a variety of services: serving legal papers, apprehending prisoners and recalcitrant witnesses, and transporting prisoners to jail. These officers were also paid a reward of four shillings for each vagrant they seized and thrust into the toils of the law. In 1785 the city treasurer paid the constables £20 12s. for 103 vagrants taken to the Bridewell. The increasing number of vagrants made this too expensive, so that in November 1786 the reward was reduced to two shillings sixpence a head. But in January 1788 the city paid the police officers £45 18s. for apprehending vagrants. The high constable and his assistants were also charged with the grave responsibility of keeping the numerous hogs of New York off the streets of the city. Their efforts were not conspicuously successful, for in 1790 the Common Council ordained that any person might seize a stray pig for his own use. However, if the pig was turned in at the Almshouse the captor was given a reward of seventy-five cents—a dollar a head if delivered by a constable or marshal. Many a diligent constable augmented his income by snaring hogs.

It would appear that there were, in 1789, between twenty and twenty-five mayor's marshals under the supervision of a chief marshal. They held office by the appointment and at the pleasure of the mayor. Their general powers were similar to those of the constables—a broad jurisdiction over all breaches of the peace, murderers, robbers, "all idle Strollers," vagabonds, houses of prostitution, and gaming houses. In addition they were to attend diligently on the Mayor's Court and General Sessions to execute any orders. Despite their powers the marshals were not prominent in the policing of the city.

The city watch, however, was a famous institution dating from

the period of Dutch control. The watch was alone responsible
for the preservation of law and order during the night. In 1789
there were between forty-five and fifty men in active service under
the command of two captains, who were directly responsible to
the Common Council. The members of the watch carried sticks
and wore painted "leathern hats" and each evening at nine (later
moved forward to seven) began their duties by an ostentatious
little parade to their posts from the old watchhouse near City
Hall. Each member received three shillings a night for his
services; during the winter this was increased to four (approximately fifty cents). The captains were paid eight shillings a
night; in winter, a shilling extra. But the members of the watch
were sometimes voted special rewards for meritorious services:
forty shillings to a watchman who captured a robber single-
handed in May 1786; £15 to watchmen Culbertson, Schofield,
and Gobel for having seized dangerous robbers at night in
September 1789; and the same sum to three watchmen for a
similar feat during December. Despite their painted leather hats
they were not always easily recognized. A farmer once came to
the city and caused some excitement by declaring that he had
been stopped in the early hours of the morning by a gang of
thugs, who, after much questioning, permitted him to depart
unharmed. The next day, however, the high constable published
a notice saying that the alleged gang of thugs had consisted of
himself and several of his men, engaged upon very important
and secret service for the city. Culbertson was ever alert, whether
in protecting the safety of the metropolis or its good reputation.
The same, alas, cannot be said for the majority of the watch.
There were a few brave and impudent spirits among them, and
to them went the rewards; the others were prompt in giving the
fire alarm and in apprehending minor violations of the law, but
too many of them seem to have possessed an intuitive understanding that some culprits were too dangerous to molest. The
average member of the watch was not celebrated for courage or
rash exploits.

In grave emergencies threatening the public safety the mayor could request the governor to summon the militia, or the governor might do so of his own initiative. The militia was potentially a powerful force; it included every male citizen between sixteen and forty-five. Many inhabitants of that age had received considerable military experience in the Revolution, and, since the governor resided in New York City, which was the state capital as well as the Federal capital, these forces could be quickly summoned. The first important service rendered by the militia was in the so-called "Doctors' Riot" during April 1788.

Medical students had need of corpses for dissection. Since this was an item not easily come by, they had for some time been secretly removing bodies from the potter's field and from the Negro burial ground. This obnoxious practice was so prevalent that early in 1788 the free Negroes and slaves petitioned the Common Council to establish some restraints upon it. During the spring of that year the newspapers contained numerous complaints against the rifling of graves by medical students and by doctors. Several irate citizens charged that one body had been snatched from Trinity churchyard. These complaints were promptly ridiculed and described as an effort to interrupt "the students of physic and surgery in their pursuit of knowledge." On Sunday, April 13, a fun-loving medical student, wishing to frighten some boys playing near the hospital, threw some sections of a cadaver out of the window. The practical joke was successful beyond any student's calculation. The boys scampered off through the town and spread their weird tales. A crowd soon collected, broke into the building, and destroyed much equipment. The next morning a mob two thousand strong began to search the houses of the suspected doctors, who had already taken a prudent refuge in the City Jail. The infuriated throng then proceeded to the Jail as Governor George Clinton hastily called the militia.

The Secretary for Foreign Affairs, John Jay, and his wife were just leaving their house on Broadway to keep a tea engagement when General Matthew Clarkson panted down the street and up to their door:

"My God, Jay, the mob is surrounding the jail! They're going to break in and rip up the doctors. If they succeed we'll have murder and universal confusion. There's not a minute to lose. Can you let me have a sword?"

Jay was not accustomed to sudden, swift exertion, but he bolted up the stairs to return quickly with two swords. He thrust one at Clarkson and armed himself with the other. Both rushed off toward the jail. Governor Clinton was already there with a few of the militia. He was accompanied by General Steuben, who, somewhat out of breath, was remonstrating with the governor for having ordered the militia, if necessary, to fire upon the mob. In the midst of his expostulations a brick neatly flattened him to the ground. When he had recovered enough breath to announce his speedy conversion, he yelled: "Fire, Governor, fire!" Jay and Clarkson quickly approached the door of the jail. Jay was almost there when he was struck by a stone and fell to the ground. They carried him into the Almshouse, where he was attended by Dr. Charlton, who finally brought him home with "two large holes in his forehead." Within a few days he was out of danger, but two weeks later he still nursed two large black eyes. However, at the Jail, the militia did finally fire upon the mob, killing three of them. For several days the city was in a turmoil, but there was no further bloodshed. The medical profession had suffered in prestige. In January of the following year the state legislature passed an act to prevent "the odious practice of digging up and removing, for the purposes of dissection, dead bodies interred in cemeteries or burial places." By the same act, however, the legislature decreed that the bodies of persons who suffered the extreme penalty for murder, arson, or burglary might, by order of the judges, be delivered by the sheriff to such surgeons as the courts might name for the purposes of dissection.

There were not many riots which demanded the calling of the militia. But in 1791 "upwards of thirty foreign sailors, armed with Bludgeons" made an attack against the city watch which was repelled only with assistance. Two years later a mob attacked and destroyed two houses of prostitution and created a disturbance which only the militia was finally able to control; in 1799 a similar action brought forth the armed military force of the state to preserve its domestic peace.

These gentlemen—ranging from the constable through the discreet watchman with the painted leather hat to the assembled might of the state militia—preserved the peace and maintained the laws. They were the police of a great American metropolis of 1789, yet their abilities, their training, and their services were hardly greater than those of a spirited village constable in any hamlet of the twentieth century.

The twentieth-century sheriff of New York might recognize a certain kinship with the duties of Robert Boyd, but for some years sundry citizens have notably agitated (and without success) for the abolition of that part of the law-enforcement system which has long since become obsolete and unduly expensive.*

The modern commissioner of police would find very few familiar things in the activities of High Constable Culbertson. He would look in vain for a traffic bureau, a bomb squad, an alien squad, a detective force, a homicide bureau, or for any fingerprinting or other scientific aids in crime detection. He would certainly blush (before his certain removal from office) if the governor were called upon to summon the militia to deal with a disturbance centering around a house of ill fame.

If he wished to look back to the New York of 1789 to see an early picture of his own activities, he would search everywhere in vain. Only his remote and distant contemporary, the village constable, would feel at home.

*Despite popular impressions to the contrary, the sheriff still exists. Certain modifications were made in the office in 1942, the sheriffs of other boroughs were eliminated, and now the Sheriff of New York is selected by civil-service examinations.

CHAPTER XV

Be It Enacted by the People . . .

TO MR. BUMBLE, in *Oliver Twist,* and to the many thousands of others who have had contact with it, it might logically (and emotionally) appear that the "law is a ass." But that is hardly a satisfactory solution to a legal problem. Certainly it will never modify the actions of those charged with its enforcement. To all persons, whether wishing to abide by it or break it, there is ultimately posed one paramount question: what is the law?

In 1789 there were few Federal statutes that might be broken, for Congress had been too engrossed in the inauguration of the new national government and in the establishing of the various executive departments to pass many laws. However, there were many state laws. The state legislature had been enacting them since the Revolution, and by 1789 there were (when finally published several years later) some 753 closely printed pages of them—badly indexed, it is true, but still rather clear in their main provisions. Of the multitude of municipal ordinances there was no adequate compendium; the best way to avoid any possible entanglement was to consult one of the aldermen (the city fathers who legislated) or a good lawyer, of whom there were many.

When the constitution was hastily drafted for New York State in 1777, it was done in the midst of a great war, and the English penal code had been retained—with only one important modification: in important criminal cases the accused was permitted to have legal counsel to plead his defense. Otherwise the criminal code was barbarous and brutal—not yet touched by the slowly rising tide of humanitarian reform. In New York there were nineteen crimes for which the penalty of death by hanging was prescribed for the first offense: treason, murder, rape, buggery, burglary, robbing a church, six degrees of larceny, arson, malicious maiming and wounding, "the forcible taking of women" (even though marriage might eventually ensue), forgery and counterfeiting, stealing bills, bonds, or public securities, or assisting in any of these crimes or knowingly receiving stolen goods. In addition there were many felonies (excepting petty larceny, described as being under £5) which demanded the death penalty upon any second conviction. It is true that juries were more humane than the law and their verdicts tended to mitigate the harshness of the criminal code. Yet the Court of Oyer and Terminer pronounced ten sentences of death during 1789—all for burglary, robbery, and forgery. The visitor to the city on October 23 might have had the grim experience of witnessing five executions on the public gallows housed in the quaint Chinese pagoda near the Jail.

For less serious offenses other punishments were decreed: branding, confinement in the public stocks, whipping (either at the public whipping post or in designated spots around the city), imprisonment at hard labor, simple imprisonment in either the Bridewell or the Jail, and/or fines. Both fines and punishments were frequently left to the discretion of the judges. One Sarah Crowdy received twenty lashes on her bare back for petty larceny. John Carroll, who stole "one loaf of sugar to the value of Seven Shillings and 12 spades of the value of 80 shillings," received thirty-nine lashes. But William Glover, who robbed John Collins of a "Mettal Watch of the price of forty Shillings [$5.00]" was sentenced to hang. William Matthews, who stole seventeen gold rings, was given twenty lashes on his bare back on each of three successive Mondays, near the Exchange, the Fly Market, and the Peck Slip Market. James Shelvey, the public whipper, more than earned his annual salary of £25. How busy he was we shall better understand when we visit the sundry courts of law which held their jurisdiction and their sessions in New York.

Even those who agitated for an enlightened revision of the penal code could hardly object to the numerous laws which applied to slander, bigamy, assault and battery, fraud and perjury. Nor did they object to the laws regulating a variety of lesser matters.

Taverns were carefully regulated by a series of enactments designed to give protection and comfort to the public. No tavern licenses were to be granted unless it appeared to the commissioners that the inn or tavern was "necessary for the accomodation of travellers." The generous interpretation placed upon this clause is indicated by the fact that there were more than three hundred licensed taverns in New York—one for every ninety men, women, and children in the city. The tavernkeeper had to be a person of good character. He was bound not to keep "a disorderly inn or tavern, or suffer or permit any cock-fighting, gaming or playing with cards or dice, or keep any billiard-table, or other gaming-table, or shuffle-board, within the inn or tavern . . . or within any out-house, yard or garden belonging thereunto." All strong liquors were sold for consumption on the premises, but home-made metheglin, currant wine, cherry wine, and cider might be sold and taken home. Unless especially exempted by the commissioners (and most New York City taverns were exempt by statute), each tavern was forced to keep "at least two spare beds for guests" and sufficient stabling and provender for four horses or other cattle. It was not permitted knowingly to sell strong drink to any slave, servant or apprentice without express permission of the master. If any tavernkeeper permitted a person —other than a lodger or a traveler—to run up a bill of ten shillings or more for strong drink, he was legally disbarred from collecting it; he was also enjoined by statute from accepting from such persons anything but cash for all bills of ten shillings or more. Each proprietor of a tavern had to erect a proper sign containing his name on or near his tavern—else a penalty of ten shillings for each month's neglect would apply.

The prevalence of gambling and gaming in New York was attested by many statutes. All games of chance were prohibited in inns and taverns, but a special law "to prevent excessive and deceitful Gaming" was passed by the legislature in February 1788. It declared that all notes, bills, mortgages, and securities for money that were won by gaming or betting on games "shall be utterly void, frustrate and of none effect, to all intents and purposes whatsoever." In a word, gambling had to be for cash and cash alone. There was also a limit to one's cash losses. The law declared that if, at any one sitting, a player lost a total of £10 or more and paid his losses, he might, within three months of the event, go into any court of record in the state and sue the winner or winners for the total sum lost, together with the costs of the suit. Another provision of the statute was directed against "any fraud or shift, cousenage, circumvention, deceit, or unlawful device or ill practice whatsoever" in gaming; any player thus winning more than £10 at one sitting might be fined five times the amounts so cunningly won. Any person winning or losing £10 or more at any one sitting or £20 or more within twenty-four hours might be indicted within one year of the offense and, upon conviction, be fined five times the amounts won or lost. Since, under this provision, the loser might be fined as much as the winner, it is not surprising that the judicial records show no complaints on the part of those who lost—and the more fortunate were less likely to complain. The lawmakers provided for the problem of professional gamblers: "And whereas divers lewd and dissolute persons live at great expences, having no visible estate, profession or calling, to maintain themselves," any two justices of the peace were empowered to make such persons find sureties for their good behavior for a period of one year, during which period the person so bound was not permitted to win or lose more than twenty shillings at any one sitting. It is a safe wager that these laws were more honored in the breach than in the observance.

The august legislators of the state were determined to keep, if possible, Sunday as a day devoted to quiet relaxation and the contemplation of the Almighty (any persons observing a Sabbath day on Saturday were exempted from some of the Sunday provisions). On February 23, 1788, the legislature passed a broad "Act for suppressing Immorality." It stated that "there shall be no travelling, servile labouring, or working (works of necessity and charity excepted), shooting, fishing, sporting, playing, horse-racing, hunting or frequenting of tippling-houses, or any unlawful exercises or pasttimes, by any person or persons within this state, on the first day of the week, commonly called Sunday." It applied to all persons over fourteen years of age, and the penalty for each proved violation was six shillings—to be forfeited and paid for the use of the poor. No person could sell anything (excepting small meat, milk, and fish before nine o'clock in the morning) under penalty of forfeiting all the goods and chattels so offered for sale. If the fine was not paid, the culprit was to be put in the public stocks for the space of two hours for each offense. All persons breaking these regulations for the Sabbath were to be seized by a constable or any other citizen, detained until the next day, and then carried before a justice of the peace. Officers of the law were forbidden to serve any writs or processes (except for treason, felony, or breach of peace) on Sunday. Any person convicted of profane cursing or swearing was to be fined three shillings for each violation; if the offense was committed within the hearing of any justice of the peace or higher officer of the law, no trial or further evidence was necessary for a speedy and certain conviction. Persons guilty of drunkenness paid a fine of three shillings (for the succor of the poor) for each lapse; otherwise they were confined in the stocks for the space of two hours for each spree.

Of all those who came in contact or conflict with the law, the situation of the debtors was the most tragic. The laws concerning imprisonment for debt had been inherited from the English debtor system, of which Voltaire once remarked that "if a poor fellow cannot readily pay a little money when his hands are at liberty, the better to enable him to do it, they load him with handcuffs." The statistics of those who were thus thrown into prison were (and remain) startling. From January 1787 to December 1788 it was stated that 1,162 persons had been incarcerated in the City Jail for debt, and of these 716 had been imprisoned for debts that were recoverable before a justice of the peace. Frequently the debt did not exceed twenty shillings (about $2.50). This meant that during this brief period almost one out of every seven free male New Yorkers above sixteen years of age had been confined in the Jail for nonpayment of some debt. A debtor might go through bankruptcy proceedings, but only if the persons holding three quarters of the debt agreed to this legal release. Efforts made to correct this curious legislation came to nothing. With the postwar depression new pressure was exerted, but to little effect.

When the New York Assembly was about to adjourn in 1787, Robert Lansing asked the attention of the legislators while he read the list of persons confined for debt within a few blocks of where the Assembly met. He said that there were ten men, whose total debts amounted to £24, who were rotting away without any hope of release. The members of the Assembly agreed to his suggestion that they each contribute one day's salary to succor them. The New York *Packet* reported on March 6, 1787, that there was one prisoner, among two dozen in all, who had been in jail for more than a year and for a single debt which he might have paid in far less time had he been at liberty. The apparent answer was that his creditor was a man in the same business who thus wished to eliminate competition. The debtors were thrown into the same quarters with hardened criminals and were subjected to all the abuses of an antiquated system.

Perhaps the most onerous feature of it all was that debtors were forced to pay for their own food, fuel, and clothing while thus imprisoned. Public concern for the confined debtors became articulate in January 1787, when the New York Society for the Relief of Distressed Debtors was formed. But less than two years later the funds of this philanthropic group were exhausted and the clergy were solicited to appeal for contributions. The state legislature responded in 1789 with a law that provided that persons owing £10 or less might not be imprisoned more than thirty days. But the debtors remained bitter and forlorn. Some of them took the contributions of charity and sent them to their families so that not *all* need starve. Despite the modification of the laws, Marinus Willett, a former sheriff of the city who had again visited the Jail in 1790, reported of the debtors that "the wretchedness there is past my power to attempt a description—if distress ever claimed legislative assistance . . . the confined debtors in this place demand attention." The society continued its activities; in May 1789 it acknowledged the anonymous gift of 1,500 pounds of fresh beef. During December 1789 the prisoners in the Jail gave thanks to the President of the United States for having contributed fifty guineas for their relief, but the secretary of the society informed the public that the President had wished to have no publicity connected with his donation. The society lobbied in the legislature with some small effect, so that in 1791 it forbade the sale of liquor in the Jail by the warden, who had for many years thus consoled his prisoners and enhanced his personal profits. Two of the most curious publications in American newspaper history arose from the plight of debtors. On March 24, 1800, William Keteltas, a debtor in the Jail, began publication of the *Forlorn Hope,* in which he denounced the "injustice, impolicy and inhumanity" of the whole system of imprisonment for debt. He declared that the debtors would starve were it not for the efforts of the Humane Society (the new name for the Society for the Relief of Distressed Debtors). Within six weeks Keteltas found that he had a journalistic rival, the *Prisoner of Hope,* published for expected profit by William Sing, a relative of his and a person who was also intimately acquainted with the conditions of which he spoke. Both publications disappeared within a few months, but the problem of the insolvent debtor remained—and received no adequate remedy until the new legislation of 1819 and 1831.

Before closing any brief survey of the state penal code as it existed in 1789, two additional features are worthy of note. On February 18, 1789, the legislature passed an act which regulated in detail the fees of all officers of justice within the state. It not only established very low fees for all the officers of all the courts as well as for the sheriffs, but it fixed proper charges for the attorneys engaged in virtually all legal actions. For example, in any case in the Supreme Court the lawyer could charge a retaining fee of only twenty-nine shillings, ten shillings for the arguing of every special motion, two shillings for every attendance in examining a witness out of court (at the rate of eight shillings to a dollar!). The manuscript records show that the court costs in many cases did not amount to more than sixpence or several shillings. Thus it would seem that litigation was cheap in 1789.

Certainly this was the clear and laudable purpose of the legislators. The court fees in many cases were most moderate, but the private papers of several lawyers indicate that they and their clients were little bound by the prescribed charges for legal services. Brissot de Warville observed that "the fees of lawyers are out of all proportion; they are, as in England, excessive." Brockholst Livingston once succeeded in keeping a case in the Court of Chancery so long that the final bill for his services was £200. When Alexander Hamilton resigned from Washington's cabinet and returned to his law practice, his annual income was soon reported to be $15,000, of which a considerable part was derived from retainers and consulting fees. But even if there had been a law to cover every possible service of a lawyer, who, indeed, would have been foolish enough to engage one who did not know enough to circumvent the legal regulations?

If you did not wish to pay a lawyer you might, at your peril, plead your own case. The same act which regulated fees (Chapter XXV of the Twelfth Session) also provided that any person might carry on or defend his suit in any court of the state "without the aid of any attorney, solicitor, proctor, advocate or counsellor at law." This, however, was enacted when the laws were neither so complicated nor the lawyers so well organized.

The second feature reflected the spirit of economy which reigned over the purse of the eighteenth-century taxpayer. It was that spirit which dictated early trials for all accused persons who could not give bail, because it cost the public to feed some of the inmates of the Jail (those imprisoned for debt had to feed and warm themselves). It was the same spirit which said that it was better to hang or whip or brand a culprit and be rid of him than to confine him for long periods at the public expense. But the act of 1789 also provided that in all criminal cases the accused, if he possessed any property or wealth whatsoever, was compelled to pay the costs of transporting himself to prison. In addition the accused was forced to pay the salary of the guard employed to guarantee his confinement. This was a bit of irony which only the imprisoned could best appreciate. And, unless he was ultimately put out to work at hard labor, he had ample time to meditate upon the strange ways of the world.

Of local laws—ordinances passed by the Common Council— there was more than a plenitude. They regulated in detail the public markets, the sale of bread, firewood, hay, lime, and charcoal. Their supervision covered the activities of cartmen, ferrymen, and all those who used the wharves and slips of the city. Slaughterhouses, tanneries, and lumberyards did not escape the formal attention of the city fathers. Peddlers and hucksters were curbed and officially admonished to deal honestly. Gunpowder could be stored within the city limits only as the Common Council decreed. Reckless driving and racing on the streets were prohibited. The firing of guns and the use of dangerous fireworks were forbidden.

The ordinary property owner was charged with the building and the maintenance of both the sidewalk and the street upon which his property fronted. He had to pave them and keep them clear of dirt, snow, or other encumbrances. He could not plant a tree in front of his house (if he lived south of Freshwater and Catherine streets); he could not erect a canopy, awning, porch, or portico that protruded more than one tenth of the width of the highway; nor could he build a hitching post in front of his residence. He was forced to keep his chimneys clean and to keep available the proper number of regulation-size fire buckets. For all New Yorkers there were detailed regulations for the observance of the Sabbath. Even the churches did not escape the attention of the city fathers in an early anti-noise campaign. The prolonged and excessive pealing of church bells for numerous funerals brought forth, in August 1789, "a law to regulate the ringing or tolling of the Bells of the Several churches in the City." An ancient New York institution had already quietly fallen victim to the public demand for noise abatement. The official town crier was now silent if not subdued. In 1788 the Common Council paid John Porterfield eight shillings for having "cryed" throughout the city the law against shooting off firearms on New Year's Day. After that he merely "notified" the inhabitants of municipal regulations by house-to-house visits or the new ordinances were simply published in the newspapers.

There were, however, some creatures that were oblivious of or indifferent to the august decrees of the mayor, the aldermen, and the commonalty. They were the dogs, cows, pigs, swine, and goats that leisurely roamed the streets of the metropolis. In 1785 the Common Council legislated against "the Mischief which may arise from distempered or mad Dogs in this city." Hogs were a more constant and difficult problem. Twenty shillings was the fine for the owner if he permitted his hogs "to go at large in any of the streets." The high constable and his assistants were charged with the enforcement of this measure. If the action of the city fathers did not seriously perturb the swine, it did inspire a newspaper rhymester to:

Oyes! Oyes! Oyes!
This is to give notice,
To all Hogs, Pigs, Swine and their Masters,
That from the first of February, '89,
If any person suffer his, her or their swine
To gallop about the streets at large,
Full twenty shillings is the charge
  For each offence;
To be paid (by firm and special order
Of our good Aldermen and Recorder)
To the informer's use, with all expence;
Otherwise, HE shall have free leave to dine
Upon the said arrested swine,
Send them to jail, or give t' the poor,
For which—"The Lord encrease his store."

Since it was uncommonly difficult to identify the owners of the hundreds of pigs that roved the streets, there were few if any fines. The constabulary did not greatly limit the nuisance, although cash rewards were paid for each stray pig delivered to the Almshouse. In 1795 the council declared a civic warfare against stray goats, which had hitherto enjoyed a certain inattention and immunity. For some years, however, pigs and swine and goats roved the highways and helped clean the streets of filth and rubbish—and for years the late New Yorker audibly swore as he stumbled over them in the darkness of the night. There is no record that the cows were disturbed. When, in the 1790s, Milbourne engraved Condit's drawing of Government House, the artist shows two cattle calmly parked in the center of the driveway approach.

Scores of regulations and laws abridged and defined the freedoms of the citizen, but there was no general complaint. The New Yorker of 1789 reluctantly admitted that some restrictions were perhaps necessary and inevitable in the daily life of an expanding metropolis.

CHAPTER XVI

Oyez! Oyez!

DESPITE the relative simplicity of life in New York and the presence of numerous officers of the law, it remained a difficult problem to preserve the peace. Months after the British had evacuated the city, Mayor Duane complained that "the tranquility of the Inhabitants hath been disturbed by an idle and profligate Banditti who continue to rob and steal in defiance of the vigilance of the Magistrates and the severity of frequent and exemplary Punishments and by other abandoned Vagrants and Prostitutes whom the ordinary Process of Justice hath not awed nor reclaimed." In 1784 the grand jury called attention to "the numerous receptacles for the vicious and abandoned" in what was then known as "Canvas Town" and later as "Topsail Town"— the burnt expanse of the city between Whitehall and Broad streets.

In many taverns the guests were pilfered as they listened to news of the town—and to tales of the prevalence of petty larcenies in less respectable inns. The ringing of the city fire alarm was a signal not merely for the firemen but for thieves to gather. In 1786 there was a fire at the house of Diego de Gardoqui, minister of Spain to the United States; when it was all over, the delighted envoy sent a formal letter of thanks to the mayor expressing his astonishment that his home had not been stripped of all its valuables. Street riots on a major scale were not infrequent, and minor brawls were the order of the day and night. Houses of prostitution were numerous but generally were not disturbed unless other lawbreakers notoriously congregated in them. From time to time a dissatisfied city mob would anticipate the officers of the law and demolish a house of ill fame; for other reasons the sheriff would occasionally step in and dismantle a disreputable house. Constables and watchmen were frequently assaulted and battered—and Mayor Varick was once a victim of several thugs who gave him a thorough pummeling. Attempted assassinations dot the record. But what was to be expected of the common citizenry when many of the most prominent persisted in dueling—a more gentlemanly form of assassination, but equally against the laws of the state? What of respect for the laws in general when the laws were openly broken by: Brockholst Livingston (later a member of the United States Supreme Court), General Samuel B. Webb, William Livingston, Jr., Captain Thompson (harbor master of the port), William Coleman (the fiery editor of the *Evening Post*), Aaron Burr (then Vice-President of the United States), and Alexander Hamilton (one of its leading citizens)?

Lawbreakers were like the fish in the sea: there were many more than were ever caught. But enough were apprehended to throng the courts and overcrowd the Jail and the Bridewell. Mingling with them in the tribunals were many plaintiffs and defendants in civil cases. In the courts we may observe justice in its ultimate operation.

The most numerous judicial officers were the justices of the peace, inherited from the old English System. An act of 1787 empowered the mayor, recorder, and the aldermen to act as justices of the peace; in the same year five assistant justices were created to care for the increased press of business. In 1789 they were: James M. Hughes, George Bond, John Keefe, Nathaniel Lawrence, and William Wilcox. Their duties were numerous. They arranged for the support of "bastard children" (seizing property when necessary for the purpose), witnessed oaths, bound out poor children as apprentices, prevented "private lotteries and games of chance," attended and presided at "every town, precinct and district meeting." They were instructed to summon before them every person who broke any law or ordinance or any person who was suspected of having done so. They had power to summon juries to inquire into each and every breach of the laws; they might officially inquire into the conduct of all minor officers of the law. They held court (with or without juries) and could order punishments in any case under grand larceny; they might settle any civil case under £10. And they could always order persons committed to jail pending the action of a higher tribunal. They were a busy group, but few specific records of their activities have survived to give us any detailed picture of their contributions to law and order.

The coroner was a busy officer; in 1789 he was Ephraim Brasher, a goldsmith who lived at 79 Queen Street. The state law of 1787 gave him many duties: he "shall go to the places where any be slain, or suddenly dead, or wounded, or where houses are broken open, or where treasure is said to be found" and then summon at least twelve "good and lawful men of the same county" to inquire into the matter. He was charged with the investigation of all the pertinent details. He was also to inquire fully concerning "all them that die in prison or be killed by misfortune." If any person was wounded, "especially if the wounds be mortal," he was enjoined to ascertain the "length, breadth, and depth, and how many wounds there be, and with what weapons they were made . . . and who are guilty." The coroner of 1789 had the investigating and the arresting powers of the modern district attorney in addition to the duties of the coroner of a later age. His records show that deaths by drowning were frequent all along the waterfront; there were many others. On October 6, 1789, he made "an inquisition on the body of one Hannah Roberts" whereby it was found that she "being intoxicated with Strong Drink died of an Apoplexy." Almost in the same category was one William Becker who, "being intoxicated with Strong Drink died in the Street near the fly Market by a visitation of God." Accidents to children were also included. It was, according to the coroner's records, on November 10 that

"Catherine Walker in Company with several other Children being a playing on Boards near a certain pile of Boards sticked up, the same fell upon the Body of the said Catherine Walker and much bruised her, of which accident" she instantly died. Since the coroner's duties included the investigation of all houses that were robbed, his records contain the circumstances as well as the penalties that were finally meted out to the culprits, but these grim facts are part of the chronicle of the Supreme Court—to which the coroner reported his findings.

Beyond the justices of the peace and next in rank above them was the Mayor's Court (also known as the Court of Common Pleas). It was the oldest court in the city, and under the jurisdiction of Mayor Duane it became the most esteemed court among both litigants and lawyers—a tribunal from which appeals were seldom taken. It was empowered to hear all actions, real, personal or mixed, that arose within the county of New York. It was composed of the mayor, the recorder, and the aldermen, or any three of them—of which the mayor or recorder should always be one. This was to try civil cases, but the same personnel constituted the Court of General Sessions which was held for a session of a week beginning the first Tuesday of February, May, August, and November to judge criminal cases. This same group of judges might be convened in a Court of Special Sessions at almost any time, especially if the person accused of a criminal offense could not give adequate bail or surety. The taxpayers reasoned that it was cheaper to convene the judges than it was to detain the prisoner at the expense of the municipality. Hence justice was speedy whether the accused was eager or not.

These three courts were really only several aspects of the same court. Although they met at different times and for several purposes, the judicial personnel was the same. Before these august judges came a motley collection of plaintiffs and defendants. Many of the cases were for assault and battery—49 out of a total of 137 for the year 1789. Take the complaint of Jane Hutchinson against one John Winnick. Both were servants in the household of Antoine René Charles Matharin de la Forest, one of Louis XVI's diplomatic agents to the United States. She alleged that on October 20 the said John Winnick raised his foot and "planted it firmly at or near her middle posterior." The accused denied the charge but admitted that it was sometimes necessary to be firm with obstreperous females. The plaintiff was said to have created a disturbance in the kitchen. Thereupon Winnick was commanded by his master to lay his hands gently upon her and persuade her to desist. Witness Ann McGwire testified that she saw him slap this troublesome Jane but added that he used more than his hands. Delicacy seemingly forbade the plaintiff to testify. The recorder charged the jury to find for the defendant, Winnick was vindicated and order restored to the kitchen of the French envoy.

Those guilty of assault and battery were ordinarily not heavily fined: the usual fine being from £2 to £5. Exceptional cases, however, increased that customary penalty. William McFall assaulted Mayor Varick and was penalized £10. Paul Micheau assaulted a Mr. Dunlap as he was coming out of church and paid £20. Only one person went to jail on this charge: John O'Brien, who had struck Ann Gray in the market, was incarcerated because "he was too poor and unable to pay any fine." The others were only lightly assessed: Moses Levy, forty shillings for having beaten John Godwin until "Godwin cryed murder"; Angelica Mallet, 3s. 6d. for an attack upon John Gibeau, etc.

These were criminal actions. Civil actions for assault frequently brought higher fines. In the case of Brown *vs.* Bloom the damages were fixed at £50. There had been a fishing party off Long Island. Brown, a member of the party, raided Bloom's peach orchard and was about to make off with a few peaches when he was accosted by Bloom and his son. Thus apprehended, Brown declared himself quite willing to pay for the fruit, but the Blooms demanded satisfaction of a different kind. They set upon poor Brown and gave him a thorough beating, which cost the belligerent Blooms £50 and sixpence—the sixpence representing the court costs.

The manuscript records of the court have also preserved the testimony in the case of Sylvester Van Buskirk *vs.* Patrick Shays. Samuel Barnet testified that a dispute happened at the City Tavern and the defendant struck the plaintiff twice. He was so hurt that "he kept his House several days." Edward Bardin testified that, while he did not see any blows, he did hear a noise and saw the bloody plaintiff and "gave him raw Oysters to wash his Eyes with." Dr. Frederick Hermans said that Van Buskirk "was blind . . . his eyes were closed being much swelled . . . for two days." The jury awarded the plaintiff £10:16:6. Once more the costs were sixpence. But when George Van Buskirk was set upon by Peter Van Arden and several others in the entry of Bardin's Tavern, the court said, in effect, that such brawls were sometimes inevitable and advised the plaintiff to remain at home if he wished to escape them.

Houses of prostitution were scattered throughout the city, but they were especially numerous in the lower sections of Broad Street and in the several blocks between St. Paul's and Columbia College. It was concerning this latter section that a statistical-minded visitor had noted, in 1774, that the entrance to the college "is thro' one of the streets where the most noted prostitutes live. This is certainly a temptation to the youth that have occasion to pass so often that way . . . above 500 ladies of pleasure keep lodgings contiguous within the consecrated liberties of St. Paul's." The manuscript records indicate that this area still had a very considerable and special population after the war. The officers of the law regarded these activities with a genial indifference—unless houses of ill fame became very noisy or were known to harbor criminals.

The testimony of three branches of the law-enforcement machinery was involved in the case of Hugh Doyle, who was charged with keeping a disorderly house. This case, determined in the summer of 1789, shows that the police were almost too intimate with the establishment. James Culbertson, the high constable and one of the captains of the watch, testified thus: "Knows defendant—has often been at his house—entertained lewd women, thieves and bad men—has seen them in bed together—has often driven them out of the house." Then James Scofield, a member of the watch, said that last summer he had heard a great noise at the defendant's house and "went there—some people at the door gave notice that the watch was coming—found a woman with her clothes torn—she said two thieves were in the house and had escaped out of the back door and that they had torn her clothes because she refused to lay with them." Bartholomew Skaats, the city marshal, said that he knew the defendant and "he kept a bad house." The verdict was hardly in doubt, but there had been some delay, for the "mayor charged the jury, who find the defendant guilty, and he having been in jail since the 1st. September last the court sentence him to be imprisoned for one month." This was in effect a sentence of a year, for the case did not come to trial until August of 1790. Charles Wood, who kept a more refined house at 5 Chatham Row, was found guilty and fined £12. It cost Giles Parks £10 for harboring loose women in his establishment, but James Irwin escaped with a penalty of only £5.

Slander, libel, and extortion were against the law. John Gibeau, he who was slapped by Angelica Mallet, paid £20 for having called William Bayleport a thief and having stated that he had stolen "from me £130 hard money." Isaac Glover was fined £13 for having declared Isaac Michaels "a damned rogue and a thief." Alderman Wylley made the mistake of charging too much for a peace warrant and was fined £50 by the court of which he was a member.

Apprentices often brought court actions against their masters. Thus Martin Hill was restored, by judicial order, to the bosom of his family because he successfully charged George Cork, his master, on four counts: "1. For not clothing him. 2. For playing cards with him. 3. For his wife's enticing him to lay with her.

4. For employing him in servile labour not concerning his trade."

It should be added that the courts of 1789 had no place for heart balm, mental anguish, and similar afflictions. An untold amount of mental suffering might be involved in an attempted assault, but if you wished to prosecute your assailant successfully it was wise to stand by and accept a few of the blows—preferably, of course, in the presence of your friends or other good witnesses. Consider the sad example of one Flinn who on an October day raced up Nassau Street pursued by a piratical-looking assassin. Some said that the pursuer had a dirk in his hand; others maintained that it was a cutlass (this point was hotly disputed); all agreed that the pursuer "howled like a dervish." Flinn was more nimble on his feet, dashed into Mooney's Shop and thus saved his hide. But he thus lost his case, because when he prosecuted it he was unable to show any wounds and the assassin was set free—to the probable future terror of the plaintiff. To prosecute your persecutors you had to have a good wound to display to the court and the jury.

So great was the business of the Court of General Sessions that by January 1797 Mayor Varick and his colleagues urged that a session of one week be held the first Tuesday of every other month, beginning in April. In writing to Governor Jay, Mayor Varick added that—

> none of the Magistrates have for some time past appeared willing to sit & try any Man at a *Justices* or *Bridewell Court*. And I [have] expressly declared that I will much rather *Resign my Office* than again sit in a Court where *myself & my Brethren* may stand accused before the Assembly of this State by the *Perjury* of *any Rascal* in the Community or be the object of private prosecution thro the *contemptible & officious Zeal* of even an Alexander Hamilton himself . . .

They all agreed that two more sessions were desirable; but the request was finally granted by the legislature only in 1800. The belligerent mayor was himself accused of maladministration of the laws, but the grand jury gave him a thorough vindication during the November session of 1790.

Ranking next above the Mayor's Court and the Court of General Sessions in the judicial scale was the Court of Oyer and Terminer. It consisted of any one member of the Supreme Court sitting with the mayor, the recorder, and the aldermen—or any three of them. They met in New York at the same time as the Circuit Court and heard cases which embraced robbery on the highway, larceny (even of amounts as low as forty shillings), forgery, receiving stolen goods, and similar offenses. This was the court which meted out the heavy punishments—from public whippings to death by hanging. At the end of each session it might transfer any unfinished cases to the Supreme Court. But the governor might seemingly direct special sessions of the court to relieve the overcrowded jails. In November 1798 Mayor Varick appealed to Governor Jay—

> to know whether a Commission of Oyer and Terminer is out for this City & County? & if so whether your Excellency can & will be pleased to direct Chief Justice Lansing (if Permission can be obtained from his crabbed peevish Wife) or Judge Lewis, if he can be impressed with a sense of Duty & the Necessity of obeying the Laws, to hold an Oyer & Terminer here by the 17th December to deliver our Gaol. All our System is calculated to increase the Number of Vagabonds, Rascals & Convicts in our City & will do so, until such fellows can again be soundly flogged 39 lashes twice or thrice told.

Mayor Varick was articulate in his opinions.

Beyond the Court of Oyer and Terminer was the Supreme Court of Judicature. It was not quite so lofty or final as its title might seem to imply. In 1789 it had a distinguished roster of judges: Richard Morris as chief justice and Robert Yates and John Sloss Hobart as associate justices; John McKesson was the clerk of the court. It met in New York twice a year: the third Tuesday in January for a term of two weeks and the third Tuesday in April for a term of three weeks. The justices heard a wide variety of cases: murder, rape, petty and grand larceny, riot, grave robbing, bigamy, counterfeiting, receiving stolen goods, assault and battery, and inquisitions submitted by the coroner.

There were many other specialized courts that seldom came into public prominence. The Court of Admiralty, in 1789 under the direction of Judge Lewis Graham, had jurisdiction over all maritime cases in New York, New Jersey and Connecticut. It might also try cases of murder, of mayhem arising on vessels in or "hovering in the main stream of great rivers or nigh to the sea." With the organization of the Federal government, the United States District Court supplanted the Court of Admiralty. Chancellor Robert R. Livingston had long presided over the Court of Chancery, but the business of this tribunal was so small that it was usually transacted at Livingston's house at 3 Broadway. Despite the paucity of cases there were also two masters in chancery, a register, and an examiner—until the court was finally abolished in 1847. The Court of Probates possessed jurisdiction over wills and the administration of wills. Peter Ogilvie was its judge from 1787 to 1799; during that period the surrogate was David Gelston. The United States District Court, presided over by Judge James Duane (who had resigned as mayor to take the new office), first met in New York on November 3, 1789, admitted several attorneys, and adjourned for want of other business. The justices of the United States Supreme Court had been appointed in 1789. The first meeting of the court was not held until February 1790 in New York, but there were no cases before the court, and after much ceremony, the admission of attorneys, and a dinner it adjourned.

In the light of the subsequent history of the United States Supreme Court there is one New York court—indeed, the highest —which deserves more than a passing glance. The state constitution of 1777, hastily written in the midst of a revolution, contained a provision for establishing "a Court for the Trial of Impeachment and Correction of Errors," but it was not until November of 1784 that the legislature defined its powers in detail. It was the highest court in the state; it was composed of the president of the Senate, the senators, the chancellors and the judges of the Supreme Court, "or the major part of them." The Assembly had the sole right to institute impeachment proceedings which were to be tried by this court. But its other powers were more important, for it might correct and revise any decision of any important lower court, including the Supreme Court. This was a curious mixture of the judicial and the legislative branches of government and was established before the doctrine of "separation of powers" became popular. It was never invoked to override the decisions of a conservative judiciary, because in 1789 the senators were far removed from any democratic control or influence. But the machinery was there, and as the ballot was gradually extended to the masses, it might have made unnecessary any later attempt to "pack the courts" by any chief executive eager to respond to an alleged majority of popular opinion.

An examination of the details of all the available manuscript records of the cases that passed through the tribunals of 1789 gives a very clear impression: the problems of justice were comparatively simple, and their settlement was usually prompt. To the law officers of that era their tasks seemed difficult and unending. But what were the actual crimes that came before the courts? Murders were rare; there were but few cases of counterfeiting or of serious riot. Most of the criminal cases were for petty or grand larceny, the keeping of disorderly houses, assault and battery, and grave robbing. Crimes were committed by persons who were simply lewd and dissolute, persons who were desperately poor, or by drunks in a festive or belligerent mood. There were no prostitution, gambling, bootlegging, or dope rings. There were no labor problems, no picket lines to be supervised, no organized extortion to curb; nor were there any bombings. "Murder, Incorporated" was far in the future—a development of a century and a half of progress. The primitive, but celebrated, early "gangs of New York" were also institutions of the future. It was not until 1792 that Coulter's Brewery was erected on the banks of the Old Collect and began to dispense an honest and worthy brew that quickly commanded public esteem. But the building itself became more famous, for in 1837 the dilapidated structure joined the dregs and became the most famous tenement in the history of the city: the heart of the renowned "Five Points" district. Here, in their time, flourished the Chichesters, Roach Guards, Plug Uglies, Shirt Tails, and the Dead Rabbits— a motley collection of thugs into whose midst the police seldom ventured. And while the tavernkeeper of 1789 may have winked from time to time at the revenue laws and pocketed an illicit shilling, the venerable American institution of the speakeasy (first disguised as grocery stores) did not appear until some three decades later. The American talent for organization had produced a Federal Constitution, but it had not yet applied itself to the field of crime.

The impartial chronicler must admit that the distance from the courts of justice to the jail is often only a few brief steps. Public opinion in 1789 held that it was not desirable to send convicted culprits to jail. They might be fined or set in the stocks; they might be branded or whipped or hanged. But if possible they should be kept out of jail, because the penal institutions of the city were inadequate and overcrowded and—more important— they were expensive for the taxpayer.

In spite of this the Jail was to many New Yorkers a terrifying and familiar, if not an intimate, institution. In the year 1789 at least one out of every six adult white males was in it or had only recently been released. By virtue of the debtor laws some of the "best people" in the city were either there or were about to enter. The great William Duer, darling of the speculators, was confined there in 1792 after he had failed his obligations of almost three million dollars. He, more than his fellow inmates, found within its walls a certain security, for outside lurked a crowd of creditors who yearned to hang him to the nearest tree. In 1797 a casual visitor might have found the attorney general of the state among the prisoners. Over in Philadelphia, Robert Morris, the financier of the Revolution, languished in a debtors' prison for more than three and a half years.

The Jail, or debtors' prison (better known as the New Gaol, although it was built in 1759), was a rough stone building of three stories with a cupola and a bell. It was located at the northeast corner of the Fields (now City Hall Park). It was originally designed to confine debtors and persons awaiting trial, but it later became thronged with vagrants and convicted criminals. West of the Jail was the Almshouse or Poorhouse. Its purpose was explicit in its name, but in November 1789 the commissioners complained that it had "become too much of a common Receptacle for idle, intemperate Vagrants, many of whom have no lawful residence in this place and who by pretended Sickness or otherwise, often impose on the Magistrates of the City, by which means the House is overcrowded with numbers of abandoned characters greatly incommoding those who are really objects of Charity." West of the Almshouse was a more modern and imposing building: the Bridewell. Begun in 1775 and finally completed ten years later, it was designed to house some four hundred guests: vagrants, the disorderly, the idle, prostitutes, and servants and slaves locked up at the request of their masters. Those guilty of misdemeanors or petty larceny might be sentenced to hard labor in the Bridewell. Their services might be sold to private individuals or devoted to public works: manufacturing nails, cleaning drains, repairing streets, or improving public property. Hardly in the category of hard labor were the activities of those who were sometimes assigned to fish in the Hudson to augment the Bridewell larder.

An official report on the Bridewell complained (even in 1802) that the prisoners "are all mixed together, without any discrimination of character; and by associating so many vicious persons . . . they corrupt each other, and render the prison a mere sink of depravity; after remaining some time in dirt and the most vitiating society, they are sent forth, fit candidates for the state prison."

This was understatement, for the conditions of the prisons provide one of the sorriest and most dismal aspects of eighteenth-century America. A prison was a place of punishment, not of reform. It was to be run as cheaply as possible. Penology did not exist. There seemed hardly any common decency.

All the unfortunates were tossed together: men and women, young and old. The same lice that attacked the debtor who owed three dollars fed upon the fornicator and the robber; hardened criminals jostled the neophytes in crime, and both corrupted the simple victims of misfortune. Prostitutes openly plied their ancient trade within the prison walls, and the warden sold liquor at fancy prices to the inmates. Debtors were forced to feed and warm themselves; the city doled out a meager subsistence to the others. But clothes were not provided, and rags were the style of the day. There were enough beds for almost half the inmates. Toilet facilities were in the category of luxuries; prisoners went months without washing or shaving. Disease and vice took their toll. And to all this profound distress was added the presence of the insane. For them there was no medical care, no hospital, no understanding. The state law of 1788 provided that lunatics be securely locked up and, if necessary, chained. Keepers sometimes quieted a madman by hanging him up by the thumbs and flogging him to the point of exhaustion. In many institutions they were not segregated from the other prisoners, but a beginning was made in New York in 1785 when several small rooms in the attic of the Bridewell were set aside for the confinement and the chaining of the mentally ill.

The wonder is that the ordinary prisoner retained a semblance of his sanity; certainly many preserved only the memory of morale and of hope. Fortunate was the culprit who was flogged or branded and then turned loose. He had his scars, and perhaps his liberty was precarious, but at least he was not rotting away in the filth and the debauchery of the Jail or the Bridewell.

CHAPTER XVII

Against Foreign Enemies

TO BE (and remain) unprepared against the threat of invasion by a foreign foe is a venerable American tradition even more ancient than our national government.

The strategic advantage afforded by the possession of New York City (and the valley of the Hudson, if possible) was properly understood by the British at the beginning of the Revolution. Although they were never able to sever New England from the remainder of the revolting colonies, they did occupy New York longer than any other great American city. And today, in the files of the general staff of every potentially hostile power, is a detailed plan for the invasion and occupation of the metropolis that is a thousand times more important in the twentieth century than it was in the eighteenth. Today it is miserably defended, almost as poorly as in 1789. Its defense has always been a paramount problem for the inhabitants of the city. How were New Yorkers prepared to defend themselves against foreign attack in the eighteenth century? Where were the army and the navy of the United States? Behind these poignant questions is a simple but meaningful story.

When Lord Cornwallis surrendered his hosts at Yorktown in October 1781, there was a vast sigh of relief—a comfortable conviction that the war was over. The fighting was indeed ended, although the formal peace was a matter of many months and many negotiations. The morale created by the tension of foreign danger was relaxed. Some army officers now began to entertain more seriously their just resentment against the shabby treatment they had received from the Continental Congress. Meanwhile certain members of Congress, who had only half concealed their inveterate distrust of the military, became bolder. As the dangers of war disappeared they became—in their civilian fashion— braver and more belligerent.

While delegates debated in Congress and diplomats began to maneuver towards a peace, there were ominous rumblings in the army. In the spring of 1782 Colonel Lewis Nicola sent Washington a letter fraught with the highest mischief. The colonel discoursed on various forms of government and concluded that a limited monarchy was the best; he referred to the habitual ingratitude of republics and suggested that the same great talents which had commanded an army might well rule a nation. Nicola's proposal that Washington become king provoked the majestic wrath of the great Virginian. He replied at once that "no occurrence in the course of the war has given me more painful sensations than your information of there being such ideas existing in the army, as you have expressed, and I must view with abhorrence and reprehend with severity." His ire mounted: "I am much at a loss to conceive what part of my conduct could have given encouragement to an address, which to me seems big with the greatest mischiefs, that can befall my Country. If I am not deceived in the knowledge of myself, you could not have found a person to whom your schemes are more disagreeable." Then came the solemn admonition: "Let me conjure you, if you have any regard for your Country, concern for yourself or posterity, or respect for me, to banish these thoughts from your mind, and never communicate as from yourself or any one else, a sentiment of the like nature." Washington was writing not merely to Colonel Nicola, but to posterity. With this in mind he summoned two aides, had them attest a true copy of the original, and carefully filed it among his private papers.

Of Colonel Nicola no more was heard, but during March 1783 there was circulated in the camp of the main army at Newburgh an anonymous address, replete with the effective and logical exposition of undeniable facts. Bold and inflammatory, it urged a rebellion, if necessary, to compel the Continental Congress to express some tangible gratitude for the army which had fought through a long war. It called for action, for a meeting of the officers. But Washington quickly convened a meeting of his own. "Gentlemen," he said, as he arose and took from one pocket his written address and fumbled in the other for his glasses, "you will permit me to put on my spectacles, for I have not only grown gray, but almost blind, in the service of my country." There were few dry eyes and little effective spirit of rebellion in the audience which heard his plea for still a little moderation and forbearance.

Washington had scotched two sinister movements against the republic. But a third burst forth while men were still pondering the ominous aspects of the Newburgh Addresses. Some raw recruits of the Pennsylvania line in camp at Lancaster mutinied and marched into Philadelphia to collect their long-awaited pay —either from Congress or from the bank itself. On June 21 some two hundred men, joined by a few veterans, assembled before the State House where Congress was in session. There was no serious disturbance until strong drink had made the rounds too often; then came some broken windows, taunts, coarse jokes, and obscene jests. Congress twice besought the council of the state of Pennsylvania (then sitting under the same roof) to call the militia for protection, but the chief officer said he did not dare summon them. Congress quickly dissolved, fled the city. Several days later the members found more tranquil quarters in a college building at Princeton. Regular troops put down the rioters, but Congress had no desire to return to the scene of its humiliation. To some this all seemed high comedy; to others, the first act of a tragedy.

With the coming of peace the Continental Army was rapidly disbanded. When General Knox (who succeeded Washington) had reduced it to fewer than seven hundred men, Congress declared that "standing armies in time of peace are inconsistent with the principles of republican governments, dangerous to the liberties of a free people, and generally converted into destructive engines for establishing despotism" and ordered the discharge of all but eighty. These men made up the regular army of the United States; two dozen were to guard the military stores at Fort Pitt, and the remainder were to garrison West Point—to cut the grass and to oil a few cannons of doubtful value. The following day Congress recommended that Connecticut, New York, New Jersey, and Pennsylvania raise seven hundred militia to garrison the frontier for one year. Washington and other military leaders had often declared that the attempt to substitute a short-term militia for a regular army would always prove "illusory and ruinous." But Congress knew better, and in 1784 the regular army, with the exception of the eighty glorified watchmen, disappeared. With the sale of the *Alliance* in 1785 the American navy no longer existed. This true disarmament should have satisfied both those who dreamed of universal peace and those who insisted upon absolute economy.

The good gentlemen who disbanded the army and literally sold the navy had reliance upon the various state militia. The law which prevailed in New York in 1789 was substantially the law passed on April 4, 1786. It provided for military service for every able-bodied male citizen "of the age of sixteen and under the age of forty-five"—with stated exemptions for state and city officials, judicial officers, clergymen, schoolmasters, the professors and students of Columbia College, postmen, certain stage drivers and ferrymen, and "the actual attendant of every grist mill." A special provision enabled Quakers to escape service and training by the payment of forty shillings a year. Each citizen subject to militia duty was required, within three months of formal notification by the captain of his beat, "to provide himself, at his own expence, with a good musket or firelock, a sufficient bayonet and belt, a pouch, with a box therein to contain not less than twenty-four cartridges suited to the bore of his musket or firelock, each cartridge containing a proper quantity of powder and ball, two spare flints, a blanket and knapsack."

These things each militiaman assembled and brought with him when called for duty. If he was merely called to exercise he might leave his blanket and knapsack at home. One might volunteer for one of two light-infantry companies—in which event it was necessary to purchase a prescribed uniform. Each trooper supplied his own horse and equipment. In fact the state furnished nothing beyond the regulations, the compulsion, the occasion, and —to the artillery—a few ancient cannons. The law provided that all the militia "rendezvous four times a year" and established a schedule of fines for those who failed to enlist or absented themselves from exercises. All commissioned officers in the disbanded Continental Army were exempted from any service.

There was no concern about the uniform of the ordinary infantryman, but for all non-commissioned officers and the privates of the volunteer companies of light infantry the style was prescribed: dark blue coats with white linings, collars and cuffs, and white underclothes. General officers wore dark blue coats with buff facings, linings, collars and cuffs, yellow buttons, and buff underclothes. Regimental officers were entitled to the same uniform but with white trimmings; staff officers were entitled to the uniform of the general officers, but their coats had neither facings nor cuffs. The several companies of grenadiers in the New York City militia splashed the colors about more freely. The second company of grenadiers of the 1st Regiment thus accoutered itself: blue coats, yellow waistcoats and breeches, black gaiters, and cone-shaped caps faced with bearskin. Another company of grenadiers did better with a combination of blue coats faced with red and embroidered with gold, white waistcoats and breeches, black spatterdashes buttoned close from the foot to the knee, and cocked hats with white feathers.

If half the time consumed perfecting sartorial elegance had been devoted to serious military training, the militia might have been a formidable as well as a resplendent army. Only a few of the officers of the militia had received any considerable experience during the Revolution, and there was hardly an opportunity to communicate that little to the rank and file. The "rendezvous" required four times a year by the state law usually meant a parade down Wall Street, up Queen, and thence to the raceground in Bowery Lane for maneuvers and "a variety of evolutions." On July 4, 1789, the New York City brigade paraded over the raceground at six in the morning and then marched into the city and past the house of President Washington. The general, although ill, acknowledged this mark of respect by appearing in his full regimentals. At noon several cannons at the Fort boomed a salute, and at four the officers repaired to dinner, wine, and music at Fraunces' Tavern. The privates had already dispersed to their favorite taverns. The New York military had been called twice earlier this year for reception duty: on April 23, when Washington first arrived in the city for the inaugural ceremonies, and on April 30, the day of the inauguration. But 1789 was an unusual year in the history of the city. The annual inspection of the brigade was made by Adjutant General Nicholas Fish on July 29. The parade and review of September 28 was marked by the death of Lieutenant John Loudon, accidentally killed by the discharge of a ramrod from the gun of one of his men.

Service in the militia was seemingly more of a frolic than a chore. It usually came but four days a year; the parade was colorful and the citizenry appreciative; the maneuvers were not strenuous, and the banquets which often concluded the exercises were events worth attending. Certainly there was matter for a parade but little for a military officer to review. Useful in quelling local riots, the militia could never, as Washington said, "acquire the habits necessary to resist a regular force in modern war." It was fortunate that no foreign enemy appeared in 1789. There was no American navy; and this was the army available for defense.

Armed men alone are not an adequate defense. Where were the fortifications of New York City? The answer in brief: they did not exist. Fort George, a vast sprawling structure just south of Bowling Green, was a fort in name only. It had never been completed; and in 1789 it was deep in dilapidation and decay. It had offered no obstruction to the British capture of the city during the Revolution; now it was definitely an obstruction to the growth of the city. To the west and the south, beyond its heavy masonry and extending almost to the water's edge, was the Battery or Mall. It contained the remnants of an earthwork and several cannons still valuable for ceremonial salutes. The Battery, with its fine view of the river and the harbor, was a promenade ground for the city.

It was clear that the Fort, if it had ever merited that description, must go. Real-estate values would be augmented and the Bowling Green and Battery would gain a fresh beauty. New Yorkers wished to make the city the permanent national capital, for it brought them both honor and profit, and so proposed that the state erect an appropriate residence for the President. Negotiations to raze the Fort, begun in the summer of 1789, were rapidly concluded. The state agreed to demolish parts of the Fort to extend the line of Broadway to the river; the city was to construct bulkheads to utilize the dirt from the Fort to increase the area of the Battery. By late fall demolition was under way; it continued through the greater part of the following year. Down came the parapets and the bastions, the thick walls of masonry and the great mounds of earth. Some of the stones were used in the President's house which fronted on Bowling Green. Before the house was completed the national government had moved to Philadelphia, and "Government House" was the residence of the governors of the state until Albany became the new capital. Wood from the old Fort was distributed to the poor, for the winter of 1789–90 was bitter.

New York had no alarms of war, but it clearly heard the echoes of Shays' Rebellion in Massachusetts and of later Indian troubles on the Western frontiers. Along the taverns of the waterfront and in the halls of the old Continental Congress (which met in New York from January 1785 until the new government began its operations) went stories of American seamen who had been captured and enslaved by the Barbary pirates. Congress was without money. General Knox had raised private subscriptions to enlist men to put down the rebellion in Massachusetts. Congress had no navy to speak the language pirates understood; it was without money to redeem American citizens from the auction block in Algiers. Various members of Congress did, however, express their sympathy.

When Washington became president a little vigor was introduced into national defense measures. General Knox was made secretary of war. Senator Maclay grumbled about the idiocy of appointing a secretary of war in time of peace and insisted that Knox was only conjuring up phantom dangers in order to provide employment for the War Department. That department then consisted of Secretary Knox and one clerk. In the Indian wars of 1790 hundreds of militia without training and sometimes without weapons were slaughtered and frontier settlements laid waste; it was not until 1794 that a trained army under General Wayne ended the menace. But the frontier was far away, and New Yorkers were not perturbed; nor did New York militia take any part in suppressing the celebrated Whiskey Rebellion in western Pennsylvania.

It was the French Revolution and the bitter struggle between France and Great Britain that made New Yorkers rise to the sense of foreign danger with a sudden start. So great was the danger of American involvement that Washington issued a Neutrality Proclamation in April 1793; then came the difficulties of enforcement. On June 14 the New York militia seized a French privateer; by midsummer the war itself was brought to Sandy Hook. A duel was arranged in New York between the British frigate *Boston*, Captain Courtney, and the French 36-gun frigate *Ambuscade*, Captain Bompard. Hundreds of excursionists sailed down the bay and through the Narrows to witness the battle on August 1 during which Courtney was killed and his ship badly shattered. The *Ambuscade,* which suffered more than forty casualties, lay at the Battery for almost two months making repairs.

During 1794 New York City made feverish preparations for defense. The city gave "Bedlows or Ellis's Isle" to the state that it might be fortified. The city fathers began to search for a supply of muskets and cannons. They remembered that 522 "musquets & Accoutrements" had been taken from the basement of the City Hall by the Continental Army in 1775; the Corporation petitioned Congress to pay for them. Inventors came forth to help; one submitted plans for a device "for heating shot red hot in one-half the usual time." It became fashionable for patriots to contribute their services in erecting the wooden and sand barricades on Bedloe's Island. Every day for more than three weeks the patriotic citizens in numbers of fifty to a hundred contributed their services with shovel and wheelbarrow. Groups and societies appointed a special day for their joint labors: the cartmen, Tammany Society, Democratic Society, the English Republicans, the professors and students of Columbia College, the Republican Ship Carpenters, Journeymen Hatters, the St. Andrew's Society, the cordwainers, the Patriotic Grocers, the lawyers, and the Peruke Makers and Hair Dressers. One John Hillyer had secured the rights to the only ferry to the island just as the procession began; he had a tremendous business but no profit, since his franchise provided that all "fatigue Parties" be carried "gratis."

There came a lull in preparations, and it was not until the "X Y Z Affair" and our undeclared war with France that the war fever again seized the city. Young men were trained on the military drillground on the Battery three days a week from five until eight in the evening. Citizens again volunteered their services. Cannons were mounted on the Battery; breastworks of planks and masonry were built in spite of the protests of some citizens that the fashionable promenade on the Battery was being destroyed.

Congress at last authorized the beginnings of an adequate army. Washington emerged from his retirement as commander in chief, and Alexander Hamilton became second in rank. A marine corps was organized and the Navy Department created in 1798. By that year the navy possessed three new frigates, each destined to become famous in history: the *United States,* the *Constitution,* and the *Constellation.* This was so serious a beginning that some Britons became alarmed. The Duke of Gloucester quickly proposed that Great Britain "lend" the United States some line-of-battle ships, frigates, and other vessels.* America was to pay a subsidy, man the ships, and agree to build no more war vessels. This suggestion was never consummated, but in the autumn of 1798 the British did lend the United States the guns of a captured French ship together with eighteen hundred shot. It would seem that Great Britain also offered to provide convoys for American ships.

Because of the British navy and because of President Adams' determination to avoid an open war with France, no hostile fleets appeared to bombard American cities and there was no attempted invasion.

Once the danger of war seemed past, all interest in defense lapsed—hardly to be revived until the country was in the midst of the next crisis.

The winter of 1804 was bitter cold. Fuel was scarce in New York. So it was ordered that all the wood from the forts be taken and converted into firewood for the destitute.

*Though this suggestion was never carried out, it might well be noted that the Duke of Gloucester was the first to suggest a "lend" if not "lease" arrangement between Great Britain and the United States. In substance his idea was a "lend-lease" arrangement.

CHAPTER XVIII

Municipal and Social Services

THE New Yorker of August 1940, casually reading his newspaper, possibly found a temporary distraction from the summer heat in a headline of a news story such as appeared in the *World-Telegram:*

JENNINGS WANTS ZOO ANIMALS
TO HAVE COMFORTS OF HOME

And beneath it the reader discovered that Allyn R. Jennings, the progressive director of the New York Zoological Society, was asking Robert Moses, the eminent park commissioner of the city, for funds to eliminate many cages from the Bronx Park Zoo so that animals might be viewed in surroundings closely resembling their native habitat. No longer would the animals be separated from the visiting public by iron bars; moats would take their place. The society was asking the taxpayers of the city for the sum of $135,000 for the 1941 program, of which $72,000 was to be spent for "barless bear dens." For the 1942 program more funds were asked, and of these it was proposed that $28,000 be spent for a model farmyard "to satisfy the curiosity of children and the nostalgia of adults."

Messrs. Jennings and Moses were men of vision and of action. Presently moats were dug and iron bars were ripped out. Both lions and bears should have exulted in what was apparently a new measure of freedom. The expenditure brought forth no public protest; on the contrary, it was regarded as a wise and humane measure.

Several weeks after the report of Mr. Jennings' letter the same newspaper reader might have observed in the *Herald Tribune* the summary of a routine report by the Citizens Budget Commission thus captioned:

PER CAPITA DEBT

OF CITY UP $135

IN LAST 20 YEARS

The commission cited an increase of New York City's per-capita debt of $180.87 in 1919 by approximately $135 in 1940; one of the report's fifty-six statistical tables showed an increase in the city's per-capita disbursements from $46.79 in 1919 to $107.70 in 1939. The commission did not specifically object to "barless bear dens" (possibly Mr. Jennings' request was too recent), but it did ask for some curb upon municipal improvements, because the net debt of the city had mounted to the sum of $2,024,214,925, including $300,000,000 of transit-unification bonds.*

The members of the Budget Commission were men of vision and also of caution. Between the lines of the printed pamphlet of their report loomed the specter of impending bankruptcy of the world's greatest city. With the release of this report came a few lugubrious editorials, but there is no record of any riot of taxpayers. Although its information touched the vital interests of hundreds of thousands it never became a best seller. Perhaps the average taxpayer had been so beaten down through the years that he had lost the stamina and the will either to protest or to resist.

These and other similar clippings are available for the contemplation of modern readers. But what would be the reflections of any well-informed city father of the late eighteenth century upon these two random items?

*By June 30, 1942, the net long-term debt of the city had risen to the sum of $2,443,856,715. For 1941–42 the per-capita debt had increased to $324.94.

In the first place he would be greatly puzzled to know just what a "zoo" might be, why any animal should be exhibited at the public expense and why any exhibition of any kind should be housed in the Bronx, then relatively a wilderness—perhaps not completely a wilderness, but the long journey would certainly be prohibitive to the great majority. And was not this business of exhibiting strange animals a matter for cheap theatrical promoters—certainly not a problem for the sedate city fathers!

He might well gaze in astonishment upon the magnitude of the sum of $135,000 for the 1941 program of the Zoological Society; from any point of view this was a vast amount of money. The per-capita expenditures of the city for 1790 were approximately $1.87. Even with a population of approximately 30,000 souls, this meant that some official was proposing to spend more than twice the total expenditures of the city of 1790 to support and improve a "zoo," an institution of which he had never heard. As for the sum of $72,000 for a new kind of bear dens—this one item was still more than the usual total annual expenditure of the city. Certainly there was still a bounty for the killing of wolves, if not bears, in the northern regions of the state. They were a menace, not a curiosity.

The good city father would be completely puzzled to understand this expensive solicitude for a collection of wild animals that had no practical value anyway. He would recall that his own era threw petty debtors (thousands of them) into jail to fend for themselves or to rot, while the insane were locked up as a penalty for their perversity. There were no adequate funds to care for the sick and the lame; not enough funds to provide food and clothing for the poor. How many thousands discovered how simple it was to find themselves in an eighteenth-century jail; how very few thought or cared about the squalor or misery those jails contained! Certainly our city father of Washington's day would be bewildered by this manifestation of a later and more curious era in which vast sums of money and some of the best talents are devoted to the problem of concealing from the animals the hard fact of their imprisonment.

For the $28,000 item for a model farmyard our city father would have had no answer whatever. He would have been speechless. Many New Yorkers had yards and gardens and horses and cows and stables. And for those who did not possess them there was a stream of cows and horses and pigs through the streets of New York. Much of the extent of the city was rural; certainly there was no nostalgic desire or any great curiosity to see a farm.

He would neither understand nor believe the reading of the figures of the Budget Commission. A per-capita debt of $316.57! Within his memory that per-capita debt had never exceeded three or four dollars. Annual per-capita disbursements of $107.70! He might well remember that for 1790 they were approximately $1.87, which caused some citizens to carp about the extravagance of the city officials.

There is a striking disparity between the New Yorkers of 1789 and those of today—in both per-capita debt and per-capita annual expenditures. Roughly calculated, the average New Yorker of 1941 owes and spends (through his city government) at least one hundred and seventy times more than his frugal ancestor of 1789. What explains this great difference? There are several good explanations.

The thrifty citizen of the eighteenth century paid very little in taxes and received very little in municipal services. Some contemporaries said that he received even less than that for which he grudgingly paid, but this type of taxpayer we have with us always. The average New Yorker had a very limited vision of what the city government ought to and might do for him. Many believed in the Jeffersonian theory that society was best served by as little government as possible. Whole fields of activities (present and needful to the civic well-being even in the age of Washington) were left entirely to the benevolence or the enterprise of individuals and institutions supported by charity. A century and a half of change has created municipal problems undreamed of by Mayor Duane or by Mayor Varick.

Even if there had been any group of New Yorkers who foresaw a few of the needs that were to arise and who wished, by municipal improvements, to anticipate some of the problems of the immediate future, little could have been accomplished. Such improvements require both imagination and money. There was little imagination and there was no money. The city fathers entertained a belief (odd as it may seem to the twentieth century) that you should pay as you go; the citizenry generally agreed that expenditures should be restricted to the approximate revenues. Those revenues came from several sources: rents from ferries, docks, water lots, a few houses, the public slaughterhouse, and the public powder magazine. Added to these were market fees, court fines, tavern licenses. When a deficit threatened they sold more city property in the form of building lots. For special expenditures the city fathers were sometimes empowered to hold a public lottery. But these sources did not provide enough for growing needs.

The city had no authority, without a special act of the legislature, to levy any real or personal property taxes. And each such concession by the legislature was reluctantly given—and for but a single year. For the fiscal year 1788–89 the city was given authority to levy a property tax of about $25,000; for the following year permission was granted to raise a similar sum. The city sought unsuccessfully to avoid the necessity of an annual appeal to the legislature for the right to levy a property tax; by 1794 it was permitted a yearly tax of approximately $50,000 on property within the city and county.

The taxpayers paid little. What did they get in return? Possibly—even probably—they got what they paid for; surely no more.

Certainly the taxpayer received no free public schooling for his children. We have already discovered that the only elementary school in 1789 supported by taxes was for the youthful inmates of the Almshouse. How large it was is not known, but three years later we glimpse a dim picture of one schoolmaster, one schoolmistress, and some sixty-five pupils. These children were given some rudimentary training not because education in itself was a good thing. A little of it would increase their later chances of self-support and thus lighten the taxpayer's burden. Otherwise the municipal government spent no money for education. Today education commands millions of every New York City budget; then it cost virtually nothing.

We know, too, that the New Yorker of 1789 enjoyed little effective police service. True, indeed, there were constables, watchmen, marshals, and sheriff—sometimes picturesque, many times desultory. A special criminal might arouse extraordinary activity. In grave emergencies there was the militia of the state. But day in and night out the citizen received a meager, spasmodic protection against those who aimed to pilfer his purse, his house, or his tranquillity.

Thieves and disturbers of the peace were troublesome enough, but fire was a danger more insidious, constant, and complete. A few dwellings might be burglarized during a night, but a single good fire might consume a block of buildings or even a third of the city. Omnipresent were stories and memories of the holocausts of 1776 and 1778. Even in 1789 some of the blackened remnants remained—a reminder and a warning.

To prevent fires and to reduce their possible spread, the state legislature had passed many building regulations, but many structures continued to be built of wood because it was far cheaper than brick or stone. City ordinances attempted to regulate the erection and repair of stoves, fireplaces, pipes, and chimneys. Fines were established for failure to have chimneys properly cleaned or the lack of the proper number of fire buckets. Each householder had to provide from two to six of these buckets, depending upon the number of chimneys in his house. When the church bells rang to give the alarm, the householder threw his buckets into the street to be picked up by the volunteer fire fighters. When the fire was over, the chief engineer supervised the collection of buckets and their removal to City Hall, where they might be reclaimed. But there was much confusion in buckets. Some were never thrown out for the volunteers, others were lost in the confusion, and many were never retrieved by their rightful owners.

The city passed many regulations but spent very little money in fighting the menace of fire. The firemen were volunteers and were paid nothing, except by infrequent cash rewards for bravery and exceptional service. By 1790 there were some three hundred men who had been appointed by the Common Council from among the freeholders or freemen of New York. They received no wages, but they were exempted from constable, jury, and militia duty; they basked in the knowledge that they were performing an important civic duty. The firemen, directed by a fire engineer and several assistants, were organized into seventeen companies and two hook-and-ladder brigades.

A fire in New York was a resounding and picturesque event. The church sextons rang bells and watchmen cried with megaphones to alarm both firemen and householders. The aroused citizenry tossed fire buckets from doors and windows. Some of the firemen rushed forward to tug their primitive engines to the scene of the blaze; others began to collect buckets and to form the citizens into bucket lines. The sheriff and other law officers appeared to protect property and to control the activities of numerous thieves who had arrived as early as the first firemen. The mayor, the recorder, and the aldermen were there to direct the volunteer firemen; for this purpose they were equipped with five-foot white wands topped by a gilded flame. Also present were the members of the Hand in Hand Company, a voluntary organization formed in 1780 to remove valuables from burning buildings.

The fire engines, pumped by hand, had a capacity of less than two hundred gallons of water; the little streams they squirted were more symbolic than effective. Water was supplied by bucket lines of citizens which extended from the engine to the nearest well, pump, or even down to the river's edge. The buckets of water were passed frantically from hand to hand, the contents finally poured into the engine and then pumped at the fire. Sometimes there were not enough buckets, at other times not enough citizens to pass them. The engines were so clumsy and inefficient they could cope with nothing beyond a minor blaze. It was not until several decades later that the city began to acquire a reasonably effective force to fight fires. An irreverent critic of all this was said to have declared that God must have been a member of the volunteer fire companies of 1789—otherwise the city would have burned down many times over.

For all their tugging and pushing, the "brave fire laddies" sometimes found difficulty in making their way through the narrow, winding streets. It was especially irksome when winter snows clogged the passage. During one fire in the winter of 1786 the householders had to come forward to remove the accumulated snow in front of their properties.

This little incident was typical of the entire traffic situation in 1789. Every modern city assumes the responsibility for the building and maintenance of clear traffic lanes; indeed New York goes further and builds tunnels, subways, and superhighways to guarantee adequate transportation facilities. But the maxim of the city fathers of 1789 was: "We will do nothing which costs money; let the property owner do it directly; in fact, *make* him do it."

The city controlled several ferries, but these were leased at a profit. Many of New York's streets needed widening or paving; these things were done at the expense of the owners whose property fronted on the improvement. Any repairs were made directly by and at the expense of the same persons. There was one exception: the improvements to Broadway were made by the city.

Sewage problems were essentially private problems. The city

was concerned about the question of sanitation, but did little about it beyond establishing detailed regulations for the citizenry. Along some of the streets were "open sewers," but these merely carried off surface water. In 1789 there were six official "scavengers" and one superintendent (at $62.50 a year) to keep the streets clean. But the appetite of numerous hogs was considered by some the cheapest solution to the problem of disposing of the garbage and the filth; although one group of the city fathers maintained that the hogs did not dispose of this refuse, but merely scattered it. The latter school of thought prevailed by a vote of six to five, and hogs were formally relieved of their civic duties and were forbidden the freedom of highways and lanes. The goats were untouched by any ordinance; and the hogs were not perturbed by this official discrimination.

To clean up the city for the inauguration the Common Council decreed in April that each householder or property owner shall "before the hour of ten in each day, cause all the dirt and filth in their respective cellars and yards, and in the street, opposite to each of their respective buildings and lots, and between such buildings and lots in the middle of the street, to be swept or collected together and laid in heaps near the gutter, in order that the same may be removed. And it shall be the duty of such respective inhabitants to cause such dirt or filth to be removed and carried away before the hour of twelve on the next day." The penalty for failure to have the heaps removed was five shillings a heap. This was only one of many ineffectual regulations. Worse, perhaps, was the condition of the docks and slips: no traveler could pass by these without nausea.

If the city did not seriously try to clean the streets, it did make some effort to light them. This item was one of the largest of all municipal expenditures. Before the Revolution whale-oil lamps on street posts had been introduced, but many years were to elapse before any satisfactory improvement was effected. One of numerous irate citizens complained in a letter to the newspapers that the street lamps are "so poorly trimmed and cleaned that instead of a full body of light, they exhibit the somnified gloom of a sepulchral taper; but even this little nocturnal comfort is abridged, if the moon is expected to appear." When these flickering sentinels of the night were absent there was grave danger of falling over a pig, knocking yourself out against a pump handle, colliding with a post, or being pilfered by nocturnal bandits. From the numerous complaints it would seem that when the city fathers did spend money it did not produce any general satisfaction.

Perhaps no situation better illustrates the melancholy state of municipal service in 1789 than the problem of the water supply. Water? A modern person might easily assume that there could hardly have been a long period of time in the history of New York when the water supply was a critical issue. Yet there was a constant shortage of water, and almost a total lack of good water, during the closing decades of the eighteenth century.

There was no running water in houses or buildings; there was no system by which it might be piped through the city. There were numerous wells, both public and private; a few were operated by windmills, others by pumps or by the simple dipping of buckets. But this water was generally inferior. The majority of New Yorkers bought their water from "tea-water men" who hawked it through the streets or who delivered it regularly under contract. "Tea-water" was good superior water and was so termed because a satisfactory tea might be brewed from it. The best and most famous source of supply was "The Tea Water Pump" on Chatham Street, a short distance from the Collect (or Fresh Water Pond). The owner or lessee sold this water to the dealers at threepence a hogshead of 130 gallons, and they peddled it about the city at a penny a gallon. Between one hundred and two hundred hogsheads were drawn each day from this well which never went dry. There was a good reason why it did not. The well, located about a hundred yards south of the Collect, had originally been a spring which was fed by the waters of the near-by pond.

After its conversion into a well the same waters continued to supply it. As the Fresh Water Pond became polluted, the "tea-water" became worse, although it long remained the best in the city.

The city fathers realized the need of an adequate water supply, but they felt helpless in the solution. The grand scheme of Christopher Colles had been interrupted by the Revolution and was never revived. The city took steps to repair and protect the old wells and pumps and offered a small subsidy for the sinking of new ones. But these were not the answers, and the shortage continued. Official "scavengers" could not have found the necessary water, even if they might have desired to wash the streets with regularity; firemen sometimes had difficulty in finding enough water to fight a fire, especially when far removed from a river. With little knowledge of the causes of diseases and with no knowledge of how to purify or sterilize his water, the New Yorker sipped or gulped his glass and invited disaster. Equally ignorant, but unconsciously wiser, was the citizen who slaked his thirst with wine or something stronger.

The lack of sanitation, the scarcity of good water, and the medical ignorance of the times made the population easy prey to illness and epidemics. A wave of influenza (said to have been the first in America) struck the city in 1789 and again the following year. But yellow fever was more destructive than influenza, smallpox, diphtheria, or typhoid in a city which had many swamps and hordes of mosquitoes. No one then suspected the cause of yellow fever; it was more than a century later that Walter Reed and others finally ended the scourge. The mild epidemic of 1791 claimed only a few victims; the city established an emergency committee and isolated patients on Governors Island (then known as Nutten Island). The scare in 1793 led to preparatory measures the following year. These were of no avail when yellow fever paralyzed New York in July 1795. Thousands fled the city; until their return with the coming of cold weather the city seemed deserted. Many of those who re-

mained smoked tobacco, took garlic and vinegar, or burned tar
and gunpowder to ward off the plague; others merely prayed.
The dead numbered 732 in 1795. Three years later, in spite
of all additional precautions, the yellow fever returned and
killed more than two thousand persons. Several of the health
commissioners, feeling that their first duty was to preserve
their own health, fled with thousands of other New Yorkers to
neighboring towns and to the country.

It is not difficult to understand the panicky and often futile
activities of the public officials when epidemics so quickly became dread calamities, as in the 1790s. During this period notable
progress was made: hospitals were established, health boards
reorganized, and quarantine regulations made more effective.

In 1789 there was not a hospital in the entire city. The Society
of the Hospital in the City of New York (the New York Hospital)
had been founded in 1771 and two years later began the erection of a building. Completed in 1775, the interior was quickly
gutted by fire. It was rebuilt but not used according to plan,
for it served as a barracks during the Revolution. Lack of funds
hampered the work of the directors after the war. By 1788 a
part of the building was being used as a dissecting room, but
during the "Doctors' Riot" the mob stormed and stripped it. In
1789 the building was offered as a possible meeting place for
either the legislature or the courts; it was not until two years
later that it was opened as a hospital. It was a semipublic institution. Beginning in 1788 the state made an annual grant
of £800, increased to £2,000 in 1792. Less than a month after
the New York Hospital admitted its first patients, another non-
profit medical institution began its services. This was the New
York Dispensary, under the presidency of Isaac Roosevelt. Its
purpose was to minister to the sick poor "unable to procure
medical aid at their own dwellings" and "so circumstanced as
not to be proper objects for the Alms House or New York Hospital." In 1798 Dr. David Hosack began a public subscription
for a lying-in hospital, but this project was later made a part

of the New York Hospital. Work was begun in 1794 on the buildings for "the hospital at Belle Vue" for the treatment of fever patients. Out of these meager beginnings has grown the most extensive municipal hospital system in the world.

For those who suffered from mental disorders there was no treatment beyond simple confinement. The insane were merely apprehended and locked up; if unruly or violent, they were securely chained in "strong-rooms" in either the jail or the poorhouse. The New York Hospital admitted its first mental patient in 1792; these cases became so numerous that another building, known as the Insane Asylum, was opened in 1808 for the treatment of those who gave some promise of recovery. For the deaf, the dumb, and the blind there were no separate institutions either attempting to alleviate their afflictions or to teach them useful occupations.

CHAPTER XIX

Inaugurating a Nation

WHEN John Adams was on his way from Massachusetts to Philadelphia to attend the first meeting of the Continental Congress he stopped off in New York. He had never before visited the city. He tried to get some understanding of the politics of New York, but after a time he concluded that they were "the devil's own incomprehensibles." The visitor of 1789—one with vastly less perspicacity than the first Vice-President—would have had no similar difficulty. There were conservatives and there were mild radicals; there were men of property and others of no property. But, in 1789, they were not aligned in political parties. And since the struggle for the ratification of the Constitution had been ended the previous July there were no burning political issues to stir either curiosity or excitement.

Municipal elections were not calculated to stir the passions of the electorate. The most important city officials—the mayor, recorder, clerk, and sheriff—were not selected by ballot, but were nominated by the governor and formally confirmed by the state Council of Appointment. The governor had been remarkably non-partisan in the filling of these appointive offices—especially the mayoralty. In 1784 the Common Council had urged the appointment of the conservative James Duane upon the governor; Clinton agreed in this recommendation and Duane served until late in 1789 when he was succeeded by the even more conservative Richard Varick. During this period municipal politics were controlled by the merchant-lawyer-Federalist group. By a series of restrictions and property qualifications only about 10 per cent of the adult male population was entitled to vote for the few city officials who were elective. Many of the qualified voters were apathetic, so that municipal elections tended to be unimportant and dull. The Tammany Society was still a social club; Aaron Burr had some plans, but he had not yet turned the society into an effective political machine. Municipal politics gradually became democratized toward the end of the century, but it was a slow process. The mayor of New York was not elected by popular vote until 1834.

Nor did any great issues disturb the state politics of 1789. There had been a bitter struggle over the re-admission of former Tories to political life. This battle Alexander Hamilton and his friends had won; the Tory issue was now a dead issue. While the merchants effectively controlled city politics it was rugged George Clinton and his agrarian followers who controlled the state government. Clinton had been elected the first governor of the state and he had been governor ever since. It had almost ceased to be an honor and had become a habit. There would be no serious opposition to Clinton until the election of 1792, when the candidacy of John Jay became so threatening that Clinton and his followers had to resort to technical trickery to filch the governorship from the man who really won the office.

National issues overshadowed both state and city issues. Hamilton and Jay had been instrumental in the creation of sentiment for the calling of a Constitutional Convention, but once it had assembled in Philadelphia neither New Yorkers nor the New York delegation played a vital role in the deliberations. Yates and Lansing, Clinton's men, were aghast when they discovered that the Convention was determined to write a new constitution rather than merely patch up the Articles of Confederation. So they left the Convention and returned to New York. Hamilton alone remained to represent New York State and sign the finished document.

The Fathers of the Constitution were conservative men, but they were persuaded of the imperative need for action. And in taking that action they became the radicals of the day. They calmly and deliberately prepared to destroy the government of the United States under the Confederation—and to substitute a new government under the Federal Constitution. The Founding Fathers were the true radicals of 1787.

The Convention had been called "for the sole and express purpose of revising the Articles of Confederation" so that an adequate national government might be secured for the nation. The Convention did not revise the Articles; it provided a plan for a new government. The Articles of Confederation providing for a perpetual union could not be altered or amended without the unanimous consent of all the states. But the framers of the Constitution provided that when only nine states had ratified the Constitution it would go into effect among those states which had ratified it. In a word, the nine states would secede from the existing national government and form a new one.

This was not a mere technicality or quibble. Mr. Madison was so concerned about it that he devoted a considerable part of Number 43 of the *Federalist* Papers to its consideration. He states that "to have required the unanimous ratification of the thirteen States, would have subjected the essential interests of the whole to the caprice or corruption of a single member." Then he continued:

Two questions of a very delicate nature present themselves on this occasion: 1. On what principle the Confederation, which stands in the solemn form of a compact among the States, can be superseded without the unanimous consent of the parties to it? 2. What relation is to subsist between the nine or more States ratifying the Constitution, and the remaining few who do not become parties to it? The first question is answered at once by recurring to the absolute necessity of the case; to the great principle of self-preservation; to the transcendent law of nature and of nature's God, which declares that the safety and happiness of society are the objects at which all political institutions aim, and to which all such institutions must be sacrificed. . . .

Mr. Madison said but little more on this point. One need reflect but a moment on his justification to observe that this reasoning is one that might justify any revolution, violent or otherwise, anywhere. To the second question Mr. Madison merely replied that "it is one of those cases which must be left to provide for itself."

Rhode Island, with that independence of judgment and that charming perversity which have distinguished so many of her actions, declared that she would never ratify the Constitution. She announced that she alone was the United States, because every other state had seceded from the original United States and left her in full control. She had logic on her side, but she was forced into the new union when the other states threatened to exclude her from all commercial intercourse with themselves. But she did not ratify until a year after Washington had been inaugurated.

If the conservative interests of the nation scored a triumph in the writing of the Constitution they scored a more important victory in the struggle which brought about its adoption. It seems certain that if the debated document had been submitted to a popular referendum it would have been rejected. As in the writing so it was in the ratification: New York State did not play a conspicuous part. The Poughkeepsie Convention ratified the Constitution only after nine other states had indicated their approval. New York could not afford to remain aloof from the new government after it had become a certainty. New York City and the southern regions of the state had threatened to secede from the state if the Convention did not vote its approval. While the Convention was debating at Poughkeepsie there were turbulent protests and a great victory parade in New York City. When the news of New York's ratification reached the city a mob marched to the office of Greenleaf's *New York Journal* and joyously wrecked the press that had opposed the Federalists.

Even those who had fought the adoption of the Constitution were flattered when New York City was chosen as the first capital of the new government. It was a matter of great prestige; it was also a matter of good business.

There was no doubt in the mind of any with the exception of John Adams, who was somewhat partial to John Adams, that George Washington was the man ideally fitted to lead the new republic through the difficult years of its new beginning. The only doubt was whether or not he would accept the responsibility. When the nation had won its independence on the field of battle and at the tables of diplomacy, he had gladly retired to Mount Vernon to take up again the life of a country squire. He was singularly without personal ambition in the field of politics. His one ambition was to spend the closing years of a full life in simple family life and rural retirement. But the voice of duty to country (a note which rang clear to an eighteenth-century gentleman) could not be denied. Alexander Hamilton, John Jay, and a host of other intimate friends had written him, in tones of flattery and of desperation, that he was the single, greatest hope of the new government. And he had reconciled himself to a series of fresh responsibilities for which he freely admitted he had almost no qualifications.

Across the wind-tossed waters of New York Bay the guns of the Fort in lower Manhattan boomed out on the sunset of March 3, 1789. They sounded the end of the government of the United States under the Articles of Confederation, the instrument of government devised and adopted during the Revolution and since found sadly wanting. On the following day the lingering echoes of that salute were answered by the thunderous peals of eleven guns that announced to an expectant world that a new government was about to take its place in the family of nations. Eleven states of the old Confederation had ratified the new Union.

On April 6, 1789, it was announced that George Washington had been elected President of the United States of America. Charles Thomson, long the faithful secretary of the Continental Congress, was selected to carry the formal notification to Mount Vernon. The next day, a Tuesday, he left New York and traveled as fast as a thundering horse would carry him. Two days later he was in Philadelphia, by Sunday in Baltimore, and at half past twelve on Tuesday at Mount Vernon. There was no formal ceremony. Thomson merely greeted General Washington, exchanged a few pleasantries, and handed him the notification of election. Washington sat down and sent to the president pro-tem of Congress a note saying that he would leave as quickly as possible.

But a few things had to be done. A few letters had to be written. And he had to borrow a little money to pay the expenses of the journey and to take care of a few bills. He wrote to General Knox:

> In confidence I tell you (with the *world* it would obtain little credit) that my movements to the chair of government will be accompanied by feelings not unlike those of a culprit, who is going to the place of his execution; so unwilling am I, in the evening of a life nearly consumed in public cares, to quit a peaceful abode for an ocean of difficulties, without that competency of political skill, abilities, and inclination which are necessary to manage the helm. I am sensible that I am embarking by the voice of the people, and a good name of my own, on this voyage; but what returns will be made for them, Heaven alone can foretell. Integrity and firmness are all I can promise. These, shall the voyage be long or short, shall never forsake me, although I may be deserted by all men. For of the consolations which are to be derived from these, under any circumstances, the world cannot deprive me.

A month earlier he had visited Fredericksburg and paid his respects to his mother; for her he had only a polite and formal affection. So there was no need of returning there. But he did visit his banker and arrange for a loan. And on Thursday, April 16, at about ten o'clock, he kissed his wife and waved to his servants a fond farewell. Secretary Thomson and Colonel Humphreys and Washington left Mount Vernon for a voyage into the future. As the party neared Alexandria he was met by a delegation of friends who escorted them to Mr. Wise's tavern (and a right good tavern it was). Among the thirteen toasts there presented and drunk, the twelfth was to "The American ladies; may their manners accord with the spirit of the present Government." Just what this meant was never exactly defined, and there is no extant testimony by the ladies of Alexandria. But to any who knew Washington this must have been toasted with a significant twinkle in the eye of the President-elect. And then the chairman said, among a dozen other admonitions: "Farewell! Go, and make a grateful people happy."

There were other celebrations, other dinners, other speeches. In our history there has never been any lack of them. Grateful throngs lined the roads and hailed the new leader and the old hero. From Alexandria to Georgetown to Baltimore to Havre de Grace and to Wilmington. Then, after a tedious experience in Wilmington, the party went on to Chester and to Philadelphia. Here the city went wild. There were processions and wreaths and banquets and speeches and the mounting and parading of all the local military units. It was a fine evening—so fine that Washington was not prepared to get under way until almost ten the next morning—an extremely late hour for a person who usually arose at six. More troops, more escorts, more uniformed dandies—and old warriors too. But it was raining, and Washington sent them back. Then came Trenton, with triumphal arches and little singing girls, ladies and dignitaries, and punch and food. There was even poetry in Trenton on this day. It has never happened before; it may never happen again. And General Washington thanked them, among many things (including the insidious fish-house punch), for "the innocent appearance of the white-robed Choir who met me with the gratulatory song."

Then came Brunswick and Woodbridge and Elizabeth Town.

General Washington breakfasted at the hotel of Samuel Smith (later a part of the Sheridan House), where he held a brief reception for the citizens of Elizabeth Town. At the tavern he partook of a repast provided by the good people of the town, and he then proceeded to the elegant mansion of the Hon. Elias Boudinot, where he met the Committee of Congress. This committee consisted of John Langdon of New Hampshire;

Charles Carroll of Maryland; William S. Johnson of Connecticut, of the Senate; Elias Boudinot of New Jersey; Egbert Benson of New York; Theodorick Bland of Virginia; Thomas Tudor Tucker of South Carolina; John Lawrence of New York, of the House of Representatives.

After spending half an hour at Dr. Boudinot's residence, he rode to Elizabeth Town Point, attended by a vast concourse of people. He then reviewed the escorting troops and took leave of his escort of Jerseymen.

With the committee, Colonel Humphreys, and Mr. Thomson, about twelve o'clock noon, he entered a large boat elegantly adorned, and manned by thirteen skillful pilots of the harbor, all dressed in white sailor costume, Thomas Randall acting as cockswain. The barge had a 47-foot keel and made a splendid appearance as it came out of the Kill van Kull into the bay, followed by other barges bearing the various members of Washington's suite and others of the committee of welcome. The craft was rowed by thirteen master pilots of the harbor, carried two flags astern, and was greeted as it proceeded up the bay with salutes and every manifestation of joy. A sloop that ran out from Elizabeth Town to join in the gala was filled with a collection of the fair daughters of Columbia, who enlivened the scene by singing a variety of expressive and animated airs.

Passing Staten Island, Washington was saluted from the shore, "when the oarsmen rowed half-minute strokes; a great number of vessels were out to meet him, which all fell astern."

The passage from Elizabeth Town Point to Murray's Wharf is described in a letter written by Elias Boudinot, chairman of the Committee of Congress:

> You must have observed with what a propitious gale we left the shore. . . . The appearance of the troops we had left behind and their regular firings added much to our pleasure. When we drew near the mouth of the Kill a number of boats with various flags came up with us and dropped in our wake. Soon after we entered the Bay, General Knox and several other officers in a

large barge presented themselves with their splendid colors. Boat after boat and sloop after sloop, gayly dressed in all their naval ornaments, added to our train and made a most splendid appearance. Before we got to Bedloe's Island a large sloop came with full sail on our starboard bow, when there stood up about twenty gentlemen and ladies and sang an ode prepared for the purpose to the tune of "God Save the King," welcoming their great Chief to the seat of government. Another boatload sang a second ode. . . . As we approached the harbor our train increased, and the huzzaing and shouts of joy seemed to add life to the brilliant scene. At this moment a number of porpoises came playing amongst us, as if they had risen up to know what was the cause of all this happiness. We now discovered the shores to be crowded with thousands of people. . . . From the Fort to the place of landing . . . you could see little else along the shore, in the streets, and on board every vessel, but heads standing as thick as ears of corn before the harvest.

The vessels in the harbor made a superb appearance indeed, dressed in all their pomp of attire. The Spanish ship of war, the Galveston, in a moment on a signal given, discovered 27 or 28 different colors of all the nations on every part of the rigging, and paid us the compliment of thirteen guns, with her yeards all manned, as did also another vessel in the harbor, the North Carolina. We had a like compliment from the battery of eighteen pounders. We soon arrived at the ferry stairs where there were many thousands of citizens, waiting with all the eagerness of expectation, to welcome our excellent patriot to that shore which he regained from a powerful enemy by his valor and good conduct. We found the stairs covered with carpeting and the rails hung with crimson.

The President, being preceded by the Committee, was received by the Governor and the citizens in a most brilliant manner.

As the presidential barge passed the Battery en route to Murray's Wharf at the foot of Wall Street, a Federal salute was fired. The salute was repeated as General Washington landed near the City Coffee House, where he was greeted by Governor George Clinton, Mayor James Duane, and the principal officers of the Corporation. A somber, dignified figure in the midst of the elaborate festivities, Washington was simply dressed in a plain suit consisting of blue coat, buff waistcoat, and breeches.

Forming the central figure in an impressive procession, he moved between banks of cheering men, women, and children to the Franklin House at No. 3 Cherry Street, which had been elaborately prepared for his residence. The line of march was as follows:

1. Troop of horse.
2. Artillery and residue of the Legion under arms.
3. The military officers in uniform who were off duty.
4. The President's guard, composed of the Grenadiers of the First Regiment.
5. The President, the governor, and their suites.
6. The principal officers of the state.
7. The Mayor and Corporation.
8. The clergy.
9. The citizens.

As the parade moved through Queen Street, to the Franklin House, bells were rung, colors were displayed from the Fort and from the vessels in the harbor and from buildings in the city. After being formally ensconced in his new home, General Washington was conducted to the house of Governor Clinton, where he dined.

The city was brilliantly illuminated that night. The joy and satisfaction universally expressed at the arrival of the new President clearly evidenced the high esteem and devoted affection in which he was held by his countrymen.

If the inaugural journey was a triumphal progress from Mount Vernon to the capital of the United States of America, it only foreshadowed brilliant scenes to follow.

Reports coming into New York from towns along the route told of Federal salutes and military parades, the ringing of bells, and huzzas of the admiring throngs. New Yorkers were all agog. The town was full of visitors taxing every available stopping place and tavern. Private mansions overflowed. One young woman wrote as follows to a friend:

> We shall remain here if we have to sleep in tents as many will have to do. Mr. Williamson has promised to engage us rooms at Frauncis's but that was jammed long ago, as was every other decent public house; and now, while we were waiting at Mrs. Vandervoort's in Maiden Lane till after dinner, two of our beaux are running about town determined to obtain the best places for us to stay at which can be opened for love, money, or most persuasive speeches.

New York had never before housed a gathering of such magnitude. Everybody wanted to see Washington. The aged declared their readiness to die if they could once behold his face. The young described him as looking more grand and noble than any human being they had ever seen.

On the day following his welcome in New York, Washington was host to the members of the Senate and the House of Representatives who congratulated him on his safe arrival at the seat of the Government.

On Saturday, April 25, the Chamber of Commerce met at the Coffee House about half after eleven o'clock, in consequence of a special call from the President. From the Coffee House they proceeded in form to the house of His Excellency the President of the United States, headed by John Broome, Theophylact Beach, and John Murray, Esquires.

On their arrival at the President's, they were conducted into the audience room, and upon His Excellency's entering, Mr. Broome, the president of the Chamber, addressed him to the following effect: that he had the honor, in the name of that Corporation, to congratulate His Excellency upon his safe arrival in this city, under the dignified character of President of the United States, and also to inform him that the members of the Chamber felt a singular pleasure in having a gentleman of his distinguished talents appointed to preside over the Union; and further assured him, that it would be their uniform endeavor, by every constitutional exertion in their power, to render His Excellency's administration prosperous and happy.

To which His Excellency replied to the following effect: that he was greatly obliged to the gentlemen of the Chamber for that mark of their politeness and respect, and that he should be happy at all times, as far as lay with him, to promote the interest of commerce.

After His Excellency's reply, he was introduced by the president of the Chamber to every member present.

During the week that elapsed between his arrival in New York and his inauguration as President, Washington made many new acquaintances, resumed a number of old ones, and was ever the center of acclaim, admiration, and tribute. Senator William Maclay of Pennsylvania was on the point of leaving his room near the Bear Market one day when General Washington arrived to pay a call. So overwhelmed was the solon by the visit that, in writing of it later in his *Journal,* he said:

> I had dressed and was about to set out when General Washington, the greatest man in the world, paid me a visit. I met him at the foot of the stairs. Mr. Wynkoop just came in. We asked him (Washington) to take a seat. He excused himself on account of the number of his visits. We accompanied him to the door. He made us complaisant bows—one before he mounted and the other as he went away on horseback.

April 30 began with gunfire—a salute at dawn from Fort George, near Bowling Green. That salvo woke everyone but the dead, and you at your tavern in John Street were rudely cheated out of a dream that promised to be downright pleasant. No matter. The dream of thousands is about to be realized, the culmination of dreams, in fact. The hero of a hundred battles is about to be made the guardian of their liberties and the visible symbol of a new-found sovereignty.

You, a simple citizen, may be in the city for reasons of your own. An office-seeker, or to put it baldly, hunting a job. You have buttonholed this or that member of the Congress, but you have not yet stooped to join the company of those who importune the President-elect before breakfast, as many are said to be doing. That is going a bit too far. You may have had an office in mind when you made this trek to New York, but—there is no gainsaying it—what you really came to see was the inauguration of George Washington, now the day is at hand.

Thursday, the thirtieth of April 1789, broke bright and clear on Manhattan—a few clouds on the horizon, just threatening enough to make the old folks shake their heads and the young ones snap their fingers. What is a cloud or two on a day like this? Nothing. The great event is scheduled for celebration, rain or shine, and everyone within striking distance means to be there. All up and down the island they harnessed in the plow team and jogged to town, while Long Islanders (outlanders really) came down in droves to Brooklyn ferry or by packet from up the sound, as did the mainlanders, hundreds of them. They filled the city.

But long before the great day people from all points had converged on the metropolis. It was Mecca, the capital of the United States of America (those words now begin to mean something), the seat of Congress and of the government about to be launched under the Constitution, and a President duly elected and notified and now at home in the city was about to take the oath of office.

To those who came from a distance, as many did, and even to those who came from near-by hamlets, the city was a great adventure. It was no sleepy country village, a few horses tied in front of the courthouse, mail stage once a week, church on Sunday, and petty politics. Not at all. Here in the busy port a hundred seagoing ships were anchored; sailors and strangers from all the world explored its shops and taverns; and foreign legations flew the flags of kings. Here was romance and ceremonial and all the pomp of place and parade of fashion of a great city. Here was statecraft in action, government in operation, a sovereign state expressing the declared intention of its makers. To go to New York was indeed going on a journey, and now that you are here your private affairs seem insignificant. Tomorrow will serve. Today you will see the show—the crowds, the military, statesmen, clergy, and other dignitaries, and you will hear the President swear to preserve the Constitution and to faithfully perform the duties of that difficult office.

You are up betimes as custom prescribes, and on this memorable morning the sound of cannonading speeds every move. The whole city is early afoot, hurrying places, getting ready for the day. The committee of arrangements has issued its final orders. The master of ceremonies delivers instructions to his assistants. Lackeys and stablemen put the finishing touches on the coach of state, oil the harness, and polish its fittings. Grooms rub down the horses with an extra flourish, make their coats shine. The horses munch their oats.

Meanwhile you yourself are eating a hearty breakfast, a meat pasty, rasher of bacon, a small fish or two, cheese, bread and jam, and a pint of ale. Jam is said to be sovereign for all ailments of the throat except thirst. The tavern gossip is confined to the day's doings. Colonel Morgan Lewis is master of ceremonies and makes a fine show in regimentals with a spirited horse under him. And his assistants are every bit as fine: General Webb, Colonel Smith, Colonel Fish, Colonel Franks, Major Bleecker, and Mr. John R. Livingston—gentlemen all. Major L'Enfant it seems was also appointed an assistant to the master of ceremonies but declined to serve in that capacity. Piqued. . . . The argument over this incident would on any other day have ended in blows. But not today. Mrs. Fortune, the tavernkeeper, brings them around with a bit of good-natured blarney. If you have not seen the grenadiers, she says, you've seen nothing at all. Every last man of them seven feet high and a foot more, counting their shakos. And the Highlanders now, in kilts, with jaunty air and the bagpipes wailing, a martial music for all it is so sad, and the troopers of Captain Stakes, she babbles, with ensigns streaming—she knows all about the show and you, who have yet to see the sights, must take her word for it.

The streets begin to be crowded at half past eight, and by nine o'clock when the church bells are all set ringing it really looks like a holiday. The sun comes out, and shortly the churches themselves are filled with people gathered there to implore divine guidance in behalf of their elected chief. If you are bent on not missing any part of the celebration you make your way to church or chapel and join in services appropriate to the occasion. And afterwards, afraid of being late for some phase of the event, you hurry around to Federal Hall, crowd your way into the foyer, and watch for signs of a familiar figure. At ten-thirty they begin to drift in, senators and representatives, members of the Congress, the great men of the time.

They come from all over town. Vice-President Adams comes down from Richmond Hill, and Richard Henry Lee comes all the way from Greenwich. Most of them, however, live near by in Maiden Lane, in Wall or Broad streets. Four of the Massachusetts delegation live at 15 Great Dock Street; two of the New Jersey members at 47 Little Dock. Dr. Johnson of Connecticut has quarters at the college; James Madison and four others live at 19 Maiden Lane; and the speaker of the house is stopping with the Rev. Dr. Kunze at 24 Chatham Row. They arrive in clusters, in groups of three or four. It is a great occasion, and they have already discussed it unofficially overnight, and one or two are visibly out of patience. It seems that they can no more agree over the inauguration ceremony than they can about the tariff, the debt, or any other issue that comes up. They do agree, however, on the man for President, and even Maclay, who terms the whole thing an empty, endless business, is not immune from a show of veneration for the President-elect and sincerely wishes him to be first in everything as he has already proven himself to be in so many trying situations.

Through the foyer and into the vestibule of Federal Hall these men of the first Congress pass, still arguing the question

of a title for the chief executive which began again at the breakfast table, a heritage from last night's caucus. Straight ahead
and under the dome of this rotunda they stand in groups for
a parting shot to clinch the argument, and then the senators,
as befits their dignity, mount by a private stairway on the left
to their own chamber, and the members of the Lower House
proceed on across the vestibule to the Hall of Representatives.

This building is much more impressive than you might have
imagined. Its renovating architect was Major Pierre Charles
L'Enfant, and he had done his fertile best at the task. Here
and there a cynic says that his best was not enough—and within
several years Francis Baily will term it the "most clumsy, un-
couth building I ever saw." But he is only a haughty English
visitor, and we have already declared our independence from
England. If you took a vote of townsfolk and visitors—and is
this not an incipient democracy?—the majority would certainly
say that it is handsome and impressive. And if more be needed
to settle the question—well, did it not cost a lot of money? It
did. The alterations cost almost $65,000—a figure more than
the total city budget only a few years ago and a figure twice
the estimated cost. Fortunately that expense is not a charge
against the Federal government, and the arrows of invective
that are sometimes said to fly in both House and Senate cannot
in this instance be leveled at the party of extravagance. The city
of New York itself has footed the bill, or will do so when the
money can be found. The state legislature has authorized the
city to raise the money by extra taxes and by a series of lotteries.
Meanwhile a group of public-spirited citizens has loaned the
city the money (at interest, of course, for this is a property-
minded century) to make the changes. All congressmen are
agreed that this is truly a splendid act on the part of New York
City.

The Hall of Representatives is almost square, and lopping
off the corners gives it an octangular appearance. The floor is
about fifty-eight by sixty-one, and the walls are thirty-six feet

high. The effect is very lofty. The ceiling is arched and rises
in the center to a height of forty-six feet. It is all done on the
grand scale. Its windows are very large and are placed sixteen
feet from the floor, and below the windows a plain wainscot runs
round the room, and into it are set four fireplaces. The Speaker's
chair is on a platform opposite the main entrance. Over the
entrance are two galleries primarily for friends of members. The
public is admitted to an open space behind the rail. There is a
desk and chair for each member. The windows are curtained
in light blue damask and the chairs covered with the same
material. The floor is thickly carpeted. Into this impressive
chamber flock the honorable gentlemen from eleven states, the
roll is called, and the hour is come for them to mount the stairs
and knock at the door of the Senate chamber.

Into this room one hesitates to venture. It is not as large as
the other, but it is filled at the moment with the smoke of debate,
which makes it appear as wide as a battlefield and as dangerous
to cross. Mr. Adams has again asked for an opinion, and the
discussion which follows has raised the question of éclat, titles,
and correct form in a republic to a point which borders on
the absurd. Senators tell him how it is done at court, but, since
he too is familiar with parliaments and ceremony, he has a
definite opinion of his own. It threatens to become a serious
matter when onto the scene of action the clerk of the House
leads his legislative lambs; a temporary decision is then reached
that the head of the state is to be neither Highness nor Excellency
nor Mightiness, but plain Mr. President.

Were we able to gain admittance to the endless debate of the
Senate we might have heard many quaint and amusing discus-
sions. Senator Maclay carefully records one of them that would
compare favorably with some of the best passages in a later
Congressional Record:

The Vice-President, as usual, made us two or three speeches
from the Chair. I will endeavor to recollect one of them. It was

on the reading of a report which mentioned that the President
should be received in the Senate chamber and proceed thence to
the House of Representatives to be sworn: "Gentlemen, I do not
know whether the framers of the Constitution had in view the
two kings of Sparta or the two consuls of Rome when they formed
it; one to have all the power while he held it, and the other to be
nothing. Nor do I know whether the architect that formed our
room and the wide chair in it (to hold two, I suppose) had the
Constitution before him. Gentlemen, I feel great difficulty how to
act. I am possessed of two separate powers; the one in *esse* and
the other in *posse*. I am Vice-President. In this I am nothing, but
I may be everything. But I am president also of the Senate. When
the President comes into the Senate, what shall I be? I can not be
(president) then. No, gentlemen, I can not, I can not. I wish
gentlemen to think what I shall be."

Here, as if oppressed with a sense of his distressed situation, he
threw himself back in his chair. A solemn silence ensued. God
forgive me, for it was involuntary, but the profane muscles of my
face were in tune for laughter in spite of my indisposition. Els-
worth thumbed over the sheet Constitution and turned it for some
time. At length he rose and addressed the Chair with the utmost
gravity: "Mr. President, I have looked over the Constitution
(pause), and I find, sir, it is evident and clear, sir, that wherever
the Senate are to be, there, sir, you must be at the head of them.
But further, sir (here he looked aghast, as if some tremendous gulf
had yawned before him), I shall not pretend to say."

The Senate chamber is, like that of the House, a beautiful
room. You come to it through a long gallery overlooking the
rotunda and communicating with the galleries of the House.
The room itself is forty feet long, thirty feet wide, and twenty
feet high. There are three large windows at each end hung
with crimson damask, those toward the south opening into a
balcony overhanging Wall Street and looking down Broad. This
balcony is twelve feet deep and about thirty feet long, guarded
by an ornamental iron rail and grill, and on this spot the President is soon to take the oath of office. The president of the

Senate sits on a high seat under a canopy of crimson damask.
His chair and those of the senators are covered with cloth of
the same rich hue. The ceiling is arched, blue like the sky, and
in its center is a sun and thirteen stars. The fireplaces are
marble, highly polished, and the floors are covered with rich
carpeting. Desks and chairs are arranged in semicircles facing
the dais on ordinary occasions, but today they are arranged for
company, in two rows right and left of the center aisle. On
these chairs the Congress of the United States awaits the arrival of the nation's chief. There is a slight delay in the arrangements, but you who are not a member need not wait in the
Senate chamber. You can and do make your way to Cherry Street.

Three Cherry Street is the Executive Mansion. To get there
you go down Wall to Queen Street, up Queen past the Fly
Market and on around Queen in a wide crescent to St. George's
Square. It is a good half-mile from Wall Street, and the way
is crowded with holiday-makers, troops with flying banners,
carriages and carts in indescribable confusion. Around the Fly
Market at the foot of Crown there is a traffic tangle which
promises to hold up the procession if not somehow straightened
out. A skittish old horse blind in one eye and with its head
cocked is about to leap into a cart. There are dogs and children
and stolid country folk and excited city belles, sailors, trades-
people, and the military, all in a jostle, going places, edging
their way, a typical crowd at a great public event. You yourself
are one of them and not by any means the least curious. Indeed
you intend to see everything that can be seen by a visitor who
is not wholly without friends in high places and is not squeamish
about elbowing his way into the press and into the very presence
of the great.

St. George's Square is lined with troops. There are coaches
and carriages and officers on horseback and afoot, dragoons
and grenadiers and Highlanders and a crowd of citizens in
Cherry Street. The committee of the House is already there,
and the Senate committee is expected momentarily. It is late

in fact, but it will come. These together constitute the joint committee of arrangements appointed by the Congress. Their chairman is Ralph Izard of South Carolina, and his colleagues on the committees are Richard Henry Lee of Virginia and Dalton of Massachusetts from the Senate; Benson, Carroll, and Ames from the House. It is their business to inform the President-elect that the Congress is ready to receive him.

The house in Cherry Street belongs to Samuel Osgood and has been the residence of the presidents of the Continental Congress. It is not by any means the finest house in the city, and the neighborhood is hardly as fashionable as one would like, but it has been thoroughly overhauled for the President's use. A country squire wants a washhouse and other outbuildings where the necessary work of the household can be efficiently handled; and he wants room for servants. If his family is large, as the President's entourage is certain to be, he wants a big establishment. In that respect this house is admirable. The rooms are large and well arranged. A partition has been knocked out between two of them to make a large reception room. The furnishings are plain, dignified, and in good taste. When Mrs. Washington arrives and has added a few personal belongings and her own presence to this house it will make a very comfortable and convenient Executive Mansion.

It is now past noon, the arrangements are complete, troops and carriages and coach of state are all in line, the Senate committee arrives, and at twelve-thirty George Washington of Virginia is informed that the Congress of the United States awaits his arrival. He is led to the coach, casts a weather eye over the horses and their trappings, the grooms and lackeys and outriders, the gentlemen attendants, takes his place, and is ready to obey that importunate summons. He bows deferentially to the committee, and Colonel Morgan Lewis rides to the head of the column, gives the order to advance, and the inaugural procession is under way.

It is a colorful parade. You take your station at the head of

Queen Street where it debouches from St. George's Square and take careful note of everything that goes on.

At the head of the column rides Colonel Lewis, the grand marshal. He is in uniform, well mounted, and sits his horse like a man who rides to hounds, debonair and gay. He rides alone. Majors Van Horne and Morton, his aides, follow on either side and clear the way of those eager ones who press out too far into the line of march. And now the dragoons are passing with a great clatter of hoofs on the roadway, their banners flying, the clank of swords and champing of bits. Captain Stakes rides at their head, the troopers flaunt their colors, and the horses toss their heads and shy at every passing shadow. After the dragoons comes the artillery under Colonel Bauman, and here come the grenadiers! They are indeed a fine-looking body of men, and Mrs. Fortune was right: they do take everybody's eye. She was wrong, however, when she said they wore shakos. They wear the regulation three-cornered hat and brilliant uniforms of blue cloth with red facings and gold lace ornaments, white waistcoats and breeches, and white spatterdashes close-buttoned from knee to shoe. They hardly need the white feather in their cockades to make them look seven feet tall. They step out to the beat of the drum with all the assurance in the world. It is Captain Scriba's company that wears the shakos. They too are smartly dressed in blue coats, yellow waistcoats and breeches, and black spatterdashes, and their tall hats covered with bearskin make them appear very formidable. Then come the kilties swinging along, in gay plaids and jaunty tams, the pipes wailing. Feminine hearts beat fast and bosoms swell. Then the men of the line, not quite so ornamental but thoroughly reliable, used to gunfire and the ordeal of battle—the light infantry led by Major Bicker and the battalion under Major Chrystie. Then another man on horseback, Robert Boyd, the sheriff of the city and county of New York, and after him the committee of the Senate in carriages, and then the coach of state, drawn by fours, superb horses and bearing the President-elect of the United States.

The coach is a regal affair. There is a footman up behind, a man on the box, and a lackey on one of the wheel horses. It is resplendent in cream-colored paint, decorated panels, and borderings of flowers and cupids supporting festoons. And the man who is being greeted with cheers and applause by thousands on this memorable day is not unworthy of cheers and adulation, dresses quietly in plain dark clothes, doffs his hat and bows, and rides in state like the leader of men he is. At his side on either hand ride three mounted attendants, officers and gentlemen who by look and bearing give every indication of appreciating the high seriousness of the event. Five of them are old campaigners, and the other is a brother of the chancellor, who will shortly administer to their charge the oath of office. As a bodyguard, if he needed one, these men would know how to cut and slash. General Webb has been to the wars. He is a man of fashion, a social figure. Colonel Smith, like Lewis, is a Princeton man, saw service at Yorktown, and is the Vice-President's son-in-law. Colonel Fish was wounded at Saratoga, fought at Yorktown, and is a dashing, gallant man. Major Bleecker is said to be a personal friend of the President-elect. He too was with the army at Yorktown. Livingston and Franks look capable of putting up a good fight. All these men are young, in their early thirties, and are sworn to protect the man in the coach who bows gravely to the applause of crowds.

The coach with cupids passes, and those who do not mean to miss any part of the spectacle hurry down by way of Water Street to Hanover Square at Wall and Queen, arriving there with a bit of luck in time to see the rest of the procession. Colonel Humphries, aide, and Mr. Lear, secretary, ride past in their chief's own coach. The committee of the House passes. Mr. Jay, General Knox, and Chancellor Livingston ride by. The French minister and the Spanish chargé d'affaires pass in carriages and in formal state as befits their diplomatic rank. A line of carriages follow with their distinguished guests. Crowds of eager, excited people are now collecting at Wall and Broad. At that point you see the head of the procession turn up Broad from Great Dock Street, the troops spread out and line both sides of the thorough-fare that in old Dutch days was a canal, Colonel Lewis and the sheriff dismount, the committee of the Senate get down from their carriages, the President-elect descends from his coach, and all proceed on foot up Broad to Federal Hall.

Within this impressive edifice the members of the Congress have been sitting for an hour and ten minutes cooling their heels; they await with some signs of impatience the coming of their committee and in its wake the President-elect. They are relieved therefore when the sergeant-at-arms of the Senate chamber an-nounces that the moment of their arrival has come. Mr. Maclay of Pennsylvania has been and still is visibly perturbed. He might on a different occasion call Mr. Izard a dullard. He controls him-self, however, the members rise, and Mr. Izard conducts their distinguished guest to the spacious seat under its crimson canopy and presents him formally to the president of the Senate. The President-elect has bowed right and left to senators and repre-sentatives as he came up the aisle, and he now bows to Mr. Adams, who asks him to be seated. Standing on that elevated spot he looks very tall, and seated against a background of crimson damask he looks regal. His rich brown clothes, powdered hair, and spotless linen, his own grave countenance against that strik-ing background make an unforgettable picture. There is an awk-ward moment or two, and then Mr. Adams rises to the occasion. Standing at the right hand of the nation's best-loved man, he an-nounces that the members of the Congress are ready to witness his oath of fealty to the Constitution and to faithfully perform the duties of his office as President of the United States of America.

The President-elect at once rises and states that he is ready to take that oath, and with Mr. Otis, clerk of the Senate, leading the way he proceeds immediately to the balcony opening out of the Senate chamber, followed through the central door by Mr. Adams and Chancellor Livingston, Governor Clinton, Roger

Sherman, Richard Henry Lee, Generals Knox and St. Clair and Baron Steuben. Other senators and guests follow through the door to the right while the representatives take that to the left. Major Morton has been hastily dispatched for a Bible, which now rests on a crimson cushion in the hands of Mr. Otis, its pages open to a chapter of Genesis, and on this book the first President of the United States lays his right hand and repeats after Chancellor Livingston the oath which makes him the executive head of the nation, the commander in chief of its military establishment and the officer appointed by popular choice to maintain inviolate its fundamental law. And kissing the Bible he adds in all humility the plea: "So help me, God!"

It is an affecting scene. These men around the President are not weaklings. They are inured to battle, to the thrust and parry of debate, the chicanery of courts, and the wiles of political intrigue, but they are not unmindful that this man has qualities of mind and heart that make him eminently their chief. He is grave, courteous, earnest. He is sincere. They know him to be steadfast. And not one of them would presume to challenge his right to stand there as the man best fitted to compose their own political differences and to make the state endure. The simple and stately modesty of a great man in a momentous hour of history brings tears to the eyes of many.

When Washington has finished taking the oath of office, Chancellor Livingston turns to the vast throng and says: "Long live George Washington, President of the United States!" A signal is given, and the flag of the new republic is raised over Federal Hall. As it unfurls, cannon roar on the Battery and the Spanish man-of-war *Galveston* booms a fifteen-gun salute in the harbor. Church bells peal forth. The dense crowd in Wall and Broad streets, in every doorway and window, on all the housetops, is frenzied with cheering. Some are so profoundly moved that they cannot speak or join the universal shouting: they merely wave their hats. The President bows to the crowd and then is slowly escorted back into the Senate chamber. He takes his place under the crimson canopy and, after a little nervous fumbling, finds a manuscript and prepares to read his inaugural speech to the nation's responsible lawmakers and their invited guests.

The President rises, and the whole company rises ceremoniously. He is nervous. His hand shakes. Hardened debaters who get on their legs in the heat of an argument and pour out a torrent of withering scorn or neat and well-rounded clichés are amazed and somewhat saddened by this lack of oratorical aplomb. Their own facility in speech is the very opposite of this grave, quiet, almost hesitant utterance. They hardly know what to make of it.

Indeed it is not a lively speech. It is not declamatory. There are no flights of fancy, no incriminations of slack or faithless public servants, no loud and ringing declarations of futile and known to be futile policy, no hollow flummery and empty words. It is sincere. It is manfully brave. There is nothing from beginning to end of this speech but a careful consideration of the facts of the situation so far as the speaker understood them, together with a statement of principles designed to effectuate a stable and orderly and solvent government.

Senator Maclay is disappointed and hurt that Washington is "not first in everything. . . . I sincerely, for my part, wished all set ceremony in the hands of the dancing-masters and that this first of men had read off his address in the plainest manner, without ever taking his eyes from the paper." The senator is a virulent republican who likes neither ceremony nor dancing-masters. But he does admire Washington, and it pains him to observe that "this great man was agitated and embarrassed more than ever he was by the levelled cannon or pointed musket. He trembled, and several times could scarce make out to read, though it must be supposed he had often read it before." If Maclay was not properly impressed he was almost alone, for the other members of the audience were deeply moved.

In the composition of his first speech to Congress it is clear that Washington had no assistance such as he later received from Hamilton, Madison, and Jay. It seemed to say but little, yet it said much. For it came from the heart. He stated that he had been called from the asylum of his declining years by the summons of his country, "whose voice I can never hear but with veneration and love." He confessed that he was peculiarly conscious of his own deficiencies because he had inherited "inferior endowments from nature" and was "unpracticed in the duties of civil administration." He asked that his fellow citizens forgive mistakes that he might make and called for the blessings of the Almighty Being who had thus far so graciously favored the establishment of American independence. The most eloquent point of the speech was reached when he declared that "the preservation of the sacred fire of liberty and the destiny of the republican model of government are justly considered, perhaps, as *deeply,* as *finally,* staked on the experiment intrusted to the hands of the American people." There was one small point that was appreciated by only a few of his audience. He declared that from the early days of the Revolution he had refused any pecuniary compensation for his public services. He would not now depart from that fixed determination. The government might pay his necessary expenses as President, but he wished no salary. This came from a gentleman who only a few short weeks before had been forced to borrow some cash to pay his bills before leaving Mount Vernon for the inauguration.

At the conclusion of this address the whole company proceeds in order to St. Paul's Chapel at Broad Way and Chatham Row, a dignified procession headed by Colonel Lewis and the sheriff and the committee of arrangements, followed by the President and his secretaries and bodyguard, members of the Congress, the governor and other officials, the diplomatic and invited guests. The streets are still lined with holiday crowds, windows are filled with eager faces, and all along the way the President is greeted with cheers and blessings.

St. Paul's, a small church, can accommodate but a fraction of those who would attend this service. It faces the river, and its low tower rises above Broad Way. It is simple in design, said to be in the manner of Christopher Wren, and it is now filled with the company from Federal Hall and others especially invited for the occasion. Bishop Provoost presides, the Anglican service is read in its amended form, prayers are intoned, and one special prayer addressed to the high and mighty Ruler of the universe comes home to the heart of everyone, for it asks that the President be blessed with long life and the strength to meet his arduous duties. He is sitting there halfway down the church on the right hand of the bishop, a man in brown clothes, his hair powdered and tied behind, silver buckles on his shoes, a sword at his side. He may rest assured that this petition is endorsed and repeated by uncounted thousands in every town and hamlet and distant outpost of the United States.

The service is over, and out across St. Paul's churchyard, threading through the headstones and at home among them, the parishioners are streaming. The men of Congress and other strangers walk tenderly in this spot, fearful where they step, but those who are at home among these graves are not so careful. They are hurrying to catch another glimpse of this man of destiny as he climbs into the coach of state for the final stage of this short, eventful journey. The military and carriages are in readiness, the sheriff mounts his horse, six gentlemen of distinction mount and range themselves beside the cream-colored coach, and the President of the United States is escorted home to Cherry Street. You may not yourself be moved to actual tears, but you cannot help noting that many are, and certainly you will agree that it has been an impressive ceremony.

Back at John Street where the ale is flowing you pick up an item or two of gossip, give Mrs. Fortune the lie circumstantial as to shakos, and she tells you (in strict confidence) that Captain Scriba out of his own purse equips the grenadiers and offers them to the President. But the President will have none of them—he

being safe in any tavern in the city or on the highways even after nightfall, since none could fail to recognize the gentleman he is by his height and bearing. Nor would he be king, although there are many tavern whisperings of that, and never a king has ruled that took the people's eye as he does or was so fit to be one. Nor titles either—he would have none of them. And what a rare volley of cannonading it was when the chancellor shouted, "Long live George Washington!" It shook the windows, and there will be damages to pay from shattered panes in the Broad Way where the guns were firing. Ran up a flag they did on Federal Hall when the oath was taken, and Captain Van Dyck has a match to his guns before you can wink an eye. You will be taking in the fireworks, Mrs. Fortune says (giving you the wink), and you assure her that you do not mean to miss any part of this celebration.

It has been a thrilling, an unforgettable day, and when the guns at sunset tell the end of it you set out once more to see the town. For the night is just beginning.

You are aware the moment you step outside the door that this is no ordinary night. Your own tavern is all lighted up, the theater a step away is covered with transparencies, and everywhere people are hurrying in carriages and afoot from one illuminated scene to the next, gay and carefree and chattering.

Down at the foot of Maiden Lane the Fly Market is a blaze of color; along Queen Street the windows of aristocracy and humble alike are all aglow; Hanover Square, a fashionable spot, is flooded with lights; and over on Broad Street some clever artist exhibits over a taproom a lifelike and greatly applauded transparency of the President. At the head of Broad the Federal Hall, the center of the day's festivities, is brilliantly lighted and presents by night an even more imposing appearance than by day.

The crowds are enthusiastic. They have never before seen such a display of lights. They exclaim and compliment themselves on recognizing some famous scene depicted, and if an allegory or an allusion proves a little vague they hurry on to the next. For although these decorations are part of the spectacle and not to

be missed, the real attractions are at Bowling Green at the bottom
of Broad Way, where the fireworks are to be set off and where
some very mysterious activities have been going on at the Spanish
Legation. To that spot you hasten along as hundreds of others are
doing and as thousands, it seems, have already done an hour
earlier.

The crowd as you approach Bowling Green is denser than you
remember ever having seen. The whole city apparently is here,
high and low, as a tangle of carriages and coaches and pedestrians
makes plain. And if the fair occupants of these splendid vehicles
are more richly powdered and dressed than those beneath them
in the roadway, that too is part of the show. Indeed, carriage
traffic at this point becomes impossible, and lackeys who have
never been caught in a jam like this are at a loss to know how to
cope with it. Great and small are soon on the same footing and
practice the same elbowing.

This seems to be the very center of the stage: it is the house of
the Spanish minister.

The chancellor's house is a few doors away. The French
Legation is across the street. Senator Izard, chairman of the committee of arrangements, lives next door. Every way you look there
is something to take the eye.

The Spanish minister has done himself and his king proud.
His residence presents a riot of color, gardens of flowers, foliage,
vases and statuary, marble columns and pots with plants in blos-
som. And not content with picturing this bower enshrining as it
seems all the virtues of man, he has placed over it a sky with
shining stars, the sun also shining, and clouds, and in the clouds
a figure with a trumpet in one hand and a flag in the other.
How all this could possibly have been conceived and executed,
many wonder but no one attempts to explain. All are loud with
praise and exclamations of wonder. Some spectator counts eleven
stars, but others correct him. The number is thirteen, of course,
and if two of them are dim, that too is reasonable, since two states
have not yet ratified the Constitution. There is music—and inside

there must be food and drink and entertainment. But these are reserved for the dignitaries of the nation and for their ladies. This is a show in itself for the humble little folk who push and shove and jostle for vantage ground.

If the minister of the King of Spain has deemed it appropriate and wise to open his purse for the great event, the minister of the King of France, our faithful ally in the war for freedom, could do no less.

The Comte de Moustier is said to be very rich in his own right and even more closefisted than rich. He is said to be so stingy that he is economical in spending other people's money. But he had not been uninformed of the preparations that have been arranged by his friendly rival, so he has instructed his servants to make it a memorable event.

They have done so, and the result is a lively pictorial display of scenes in which the President figures, and a Latin tag which compliments the nation's hero with a delicacy truly French. A swarm of bees is pictured buzzing around their queen, and the implication seems to be that this guardian of their happiness is attended by a noisy and admiring throng. A little less attention to Horace and more to Vergil might have helped you here, but since those around you are no more wise your word explains it all. This is really a very fine illumination, and the President himself is said to have remarked about it.

But it is now eight o'clock, and Colonel Bauman with a punctuality which the military always display sets off his cannon and the fireworks get under way. Thirteen guns are fired and thirteen rockets pierce the sky, and the two succeeding hours are packed with thrills, splendor, star clusters, and the thunder of wild applause. A spectacle like this was never before seen by any but a few of these enthusiastic citizens of the republic lately born and today consolidated, and it is doubtful if any had seen so fitting a climax to an event so significant and so fraught with meaning. For two hours there is a constant stream of cascades, rockets, tourbillions, fountains of fire, serpents, fire trees, fire letters, Italian candles, paper shells, crackers, and exclamations of delight and wonder from a thousand throats, and when at the end of the display the cannons again are fired and thirteen rockets break into clusters of kaleidoscopic beauty no one who is there denies that this night goes down in the book as one long to be remembered. It is the first night of the United States of America under the Federal Constitution. It has never happened before; it will never happen again. It has been the President's day, and yours. It is everybody's night. And all along the way to John Street you, and they, make the most of it.

But Senator Maclay does not join these nocturnal celebrants. Since early afternoon he has been suffering from rheumatism and an aggravated attack of republican acidity (an even older ailment with the senator). He remains confined to his lodgings.

But on the morrow he would be back in his Senate chair—objecting to and correcting the many blunders made by Secretary Otis in the Senate journal, listening to "the vacant, silly laugh of the Vice-President," debating and working on a mass of bills and measures. For in spite of delays and obstructions both the Senate and the House did make progress in the establishment of the working machinery of government. Washington was occupied with the appointment of a cabinet and later with the appointment of the Federal justices and judges. Hamilton toiled late into the nights on his financial measures. And even when Jefferson later returned from his French mission to take up his duties as Secretary of State there was no conflict between them. The French Revolution had not yet progressed far enough to alarm and divide political sentiment in the United States; Jefferson had not yet seen enough of Federalist measures to rally his friends in a party of the opposition. Indeed they were friendly enough to come to an agreement on the removal of the Federal capital from New York to the banks of the Potomac in a region to be called the District of Columbia. Jefferson pledged Hamilton enough votes to pass the bill for the assumption of state debts; in return Hamilton promised sufficient votes for the Potomac site. By a majority of one vote the Senate

on June 28, 1790, voted to move the capital to Philadelphia for
ten years and then on to the permanent location on the Potomac.

New Yorkers were gloomy at the prospect of losing the national
capital. But one observer was somewhat more philosophical:

> So Congress has at last determined to leave this city. And what
> then: all public improvements must stop, no more streets will be
> new paved, the new government house must be contracted to a
> smaller scale, the Battery never can be finished, the Lottery never
> will be filled, and we shall not know what to do with Federal
> Hall; there will be no more Levee days and nights, no more danc-
> ing parties out of town thro' the summer, no more assemblies in
> town thro' the winter; the Company of Players will never return
> here again; in short, mirth and sociability and everything worth
> living for, will soon be fled to the banks of the Delaware, our city
> will be deserted and become "a wilderness again, peopled with
> wolves, its old inhabitants."

Well, mused the writer, it's done and now that it is done perhaps it might be a good thing.

> House rents to be sure will fall, the same cause will render our
> markets proportionately cheaper. The loss of the support afforded
> to many whose employments depended on Congress, will be coun-
> terbalanced by the saving in the expences of entertainments,
> which have perhaps exceeded the abilities of many a host. . . .
> We shall revert once more to our old principles of honest Dutch
> oeconomy and plain New York hospitality. . . . The plain citi-
> zen will once more stand a chance of being noticed by the fair fe-
> male, no longer allured by the superior grace and venerable dig-
> nity of a superannuated legislator of the federal government.
> . . . As long as Congress allows old Hudson to roll and empty
> itself into the ocean, I see no reason why we should be in such a
> mighty fever about their going away. . . .

And with the close of the second session of the First Congress
on August 12, 1790, New York City ceased to be the first Federal capital under the Constitution. Its career had been exciting,
however brief. And during those busy months New Yorkers had

witnessed a miracle. The new Federal government was no longer a simple aspiration; it was an actuality. It was no longer merely an idea; it was an operating fact. And if New York regretted that it could not retain the government it was proud to have been the scene of its auspicious beginnings.

Acknowledgments

Every good historian builds upon the work of those who have gone before him. And many who never pictured themselves as chroniclers of their time now rightly appear in the esteemed and honorific role of historians. How shall we rightly thank the humble scribblers and the honest printers of an event or an issue long ago? How shall we express our gratitude to the persons of high and medium estate who took the trouble to sit down and record their impressions of things seen, felt, heard, or yearned for? If the majority of the population—the simple tradesmen, the mechanics, the farmers, the tavernkeepers, the housewives: the little folk—had been literate or posterity-minded enough, our chronicle would have been immensely richer. But we are grateful for the abundance that we have.

To those who had the wisdom to preserve the records of the early years of the Republic we render tribute. That tribute goes forth to the descendants of the men and women of 1789. They are numerous and are highly appreciated by all who treasure our past. Chief among these guardians of our knowledge of our rich heritage are the libraries and historical societies. We are deeply indebted to the New York Society Library, the New York Public Library, the New-York Historical Society, the Sterling Memorial Library of Yale University, the Library of Congress—and their directors and staffs.

A number of individuals have rendered special services: Miss Edith Crowell, librarian, and Miss Marjorie Watkins, curator of rare books and manuscripts, of the New York Society Library; Honorable Edward R. Carroll, clerk of the Court of General Sessions; Mrs. Arthur Iselin of Bedford House, Katonah, New York; Mr. Crosby Gaige; Mr. Milton Halsey Thomas, curator of Columbiana at Columbia University; Mr. Stewart Riddell; Mr. Arthur W. Danziger; Dr. John A. Bryson, Director of Research of the Citizens Budget Commission; Brigadier General Theodore Roosevelt; and the members of the editorial staff of Doubleday, Doran who have patiently persisted through delays typical of a more leisurely century. Our grateful thanks to them all.

THE AUTHORS

The Sources

THE printed materials on the history of New York City are voluminous enough to crowd a small library; a critical bibliography of them would fill a large volume. The following pages contain no effort in this direction. A general bibliography will be found in the monumental work of Stokes; a more restricted one is contained in the excellent volume by Pomerantz. Greene and Morris have published a highly useful guide to the manuscript collections for New York City history. The following list contains merely those volumes most useful in the present study. Additional sources for special subjects are indicated in the brief notes relating to each of the chapters.

The present volume represents our joint labors during a period of more than four years. We have diligently searched for every detail that would contribute to our picture of New York life a century and a half ago, and in our pursuit we have ransacked the many travel accounts, the biographies, memoirs and correspondence of contemporaries, the newspapers and magazines, and the many monographs and special studies devoted to the period. We have constantly sought to utilize the original sources as much as possible. The chapter on the courts is based upon an exhaustive study of the many surviving manuscript minutes. The remarks upon the reading habits of New Yorkers in 1789 are a result of a thorough investigation of the manuscript charging-out book preserved in the New York Society Library. More than nine thousand titles were tabulated and analyzed; the detailed findings, of which this volume presents a summary, will later be published as a monograph. Other studies among manuscripts have yielded up materials for our text.

We have minimized the usual footnotes. The original draft of the manuscript contained (and still contains) hundreds of them, but they fell by the wayside before reaching the printer. No antiquarian surpasses the authors in their admiration for a well-turned and pointed footnote, but for our present purposes footnotes seemed rather like the scaffolding erected to assist in the construction of a building: of immense temporary use, but hardly an ornament for the completed structure. Also we were in no mood to spend time and space in pointing out errors of fact and interpretation as well as typographical lapses committed by previous writers in the field. We hope that those who lament the academic and voluminous footnotes will find some small consolation in the brief remarks which follow the bibliographical list.

THE AUTHORS

Bibliography

(The following books represent only a selected general bibliography of works frequently used; for specialized publications see the bibliographical notes relating to each chapter.)

ALEXANDER, EDWARD P. *A Revolutionary Conservative: James Duane of New York* (New York, 1938).

ANDREWS, WILLIAM LORING. *New York as Washington Knew It After the Revolution* (New York, 1905).

ASBURY, HERBERT. *Ye Olde Fire Laddies* (New York, 1930).

BAYLES, W. HARRISON. *Old Taverns of New York* (New York, 1915).

BEARD, CHARLES A. *An Economic Interpretation of the Constitution of the United States* (New York, 1935).

BOOTH, MARY L. *History of the City of New York* (New York, 1860).

BOWEN, CLARENCE WINTHROP (editor). *The History of the Centennial Celebration of the Inauguration of George Washington as First President of the United States* (New York, 1892).

BOWERS, CLAUDE C. *Jefferson and Hamilton—The Struggle for Democracy in America* (Boston, 1925).

BOYNTON, HENRY WALCOTT. *Annals of American Bookselling, 1638–1850* (New York, 1932).

BRISSOT DE WARVILLE, JACQUES PIERRE. *Nouveau Voyage dans les Etats-Unis. . . . fait en 1788* (3 vols., Paris, 1791). The abridged English translation (2 vols., London, 1792) omits many piquant details of the original.

BROWN, HENRY COLLINS. *The Story of Old New York* (New York, 1934).

BROWN, HENRY COLLINS (editor). *Valentine's Manual of Old New York* (New York, 1920).

BROWN, HERBERT ROSS. *The Sentimental Novel in America, 1789–1860* (Durham, 1940).

BURNETT, EDMUND CODY. *The Continental Congress* (New York, 1941).

CHANNING, EDWARD. *A History of the United States.* Vol. III covers the period 1761–1789 (New York, 1912). Vol. IV treats the period 1789–1815 (New York, 1917).

DAVIS, JOSEPH STANCLIFFE. *Essays in the Earlier History of American Corporations* (2 vols., Cambridge, 1917).

DUER, WILLIAM ALEXANDER. *New York As It Was During the Latter Part of the Last Century* (New York, 1849).

EAST, ROBERT A. *Business Enterprise in the American Revolutionary Era* (New York, 1938).

FITZPATRICK, JOHN C. *The Diaries of George Washington, 1748–1799* (4 vols., Boston, 1925).

FLICK, ALEXANDER C. (editor). *History of the State of New York* (10 vols., New York, 1933–37). Vols. IV ("The New State") and V ("Conquering the Wilderness") are most relevant to the present study.

FRANCIS, JOHN W. *Old New York* (New York, 1866).

GILDER, RODMAN. *The Battery* (Boston, 1936).

GRISWOLD, RUFUS WILMOT. *The Republican Court or American Society in the Days of Washington* (New York, 1856).

HARLOW, ALVIN F. *Old Bowery Days: The Chronicles of a Famous Street* (New York, 1931).

HART, SMITH. *The New Yorkers—A Story of a People and Their City* (New York, 1938).

JANVIER, THOMAS A. *In Old New York* (New York, 1894).

KELLEY, FRANK BERGEN (editor). *Historical Guide to the City of New York* (New York, 1909). Excellent for its maps and as a practical guide to the old sites in the city.

MACLAY, WILLIAM. *Journal of William Maclay . . . 1789–1791.* Edited by Edgar S. Maclay (New York, 1890).

McMASTER, JOHN BACH. *A History of the People of the United States from the Revolution to the Civil War* (5 vols., New York,

1885). Vols. I and II give details on social conditions from 1784 to 1795.

Minutes of the Common Council of the City of New York (New York, 1917–30). Vols. I and II cover the period from 1784 to 1793 (New York, 1917). The splendid two-volume analytical index (New York, 1930) was prepared by David M. Matteson.

MONAGHAN, FRANK. *John Jay: Defender of Liberty* (Indianapolis, 1935).

MONAGHAN, FRANK. "The Results of the Revolution" in Vol. IV of the *History of the State of New York*. Edited by A. C. Flick (New York, 1933).

NEVINS, ALLAN. *The American States During and After the Revolution* (New York, 1924).

POMERANTZ, SIDNEY I. *New York: an American City, 1783–1803* (New York, 1938).

SMITH, THOMAS E. V. *The City of New York in the Year of Washington's Inauguration, 1789* (New York, 1889).

SPAULDING, E. WILDER. *His Excellency George Clinton: Critic of the Constitution* (New York, 1938).

STOKES, I. N. PHELPS. *The Iconography of Manhattan Island* (6 vols., New York, 1915–28). Vol. V contains a day-by-day chronicle of events for the year 1789.

WATSON, JOHN FANNING. *Annals and Occurrences of New York City and State* (New York, 1846).

WECTER, DIXON. *The Saga of American Society: A Record of Social Aspiration, 1607–1937* (New York, 1937).

WILSON, JAMES GRANT (editor). *The Memorial History of the City of New York*. Vols. III and IV (New York, 1893) contain many details of life and institutions in New York in 1789.

Notes

CHAPTER I

Off to New-York

General details of travel in the late eighteenth century will be found abundantly in Seymour Dunbar, *A History of Travel in America* (New York, 1937); Alice Morse Earle, *Stage-coach and Tavern Days* (New York, 1900); Stephen Jenkins, *The Old Boston Post Road* (New York, 1914); and McMaster and Smith. For personal accounts consult the *Correspondence and Journals of Samuel Blachley Webb* (edited by W. C. Ford, 3 vols., New York, 1893–94); François Jean, marquis de Chastellux, *Travels in North-America in . . . 1780, 1781 and 1782* (London, 1787); François Alexandre Frédéric, duc de la Rochefoucauld-Liancourt, *Travels through the United States* (2 vols., London, 1799); Henry Wansay, *The Journal of an Excursion to the United States of North America in the summer of 1794* (Salisbury, 1796); John Davis, *Travels of Four and a Half Years in the United States of America during 1798, 1799, 1800, 1801, and 1802* (New York, 1909); Thomas Fairfax, *Journey from Virginia to Salem, Mass.—1799* (London, 1936); and Brissot de Warville. Curiously detailed maps of the main roads leading out of New York may be seen in Christopher Colles, *A Survey of the Roads of the United States of America* (New York, 1789).

CHAPTER II

Your Room and Board

Besides Smith, Dunbar, and Earle (*Stage-coach and Tavern Days*), rich details will be found in W. Harrison Bayles, *Old Taverns of New York* (New York, 1915) and Elise Lathrop, *Early American*

Inns and Taverns (New York, 1936). For drinks consult Alice Morse Earle, "Old Colonial Drinks and Drinkers," in the *National Magazine,* XVI, 149–59 (New York, 1892).

CHAPTER III

The City on Show

Unfortunately the first guidebook to New York was not written till 1807, a sorry little affair by S. L. Mitchell, entitled *The Picture of New York, or The Traveller's Guide through the Commercial Metropolis of the United States.* The present authors were therefore compelled—a little late in the day—to create their own. Most of the details were taken from Stokes, Smith, Wilson, Hart, Janvier, Pomerantz, Brown, Kelley, and the several city directories. Many details came from various essays in the *Half Moon Series—Papers on Historic New York* (edited by Maud W. Goodwin, Alice C. Royce, and Ruth Putman, 2 vols., New York, 1898–99).

CHAPTER IV

Fourteen Miles Round

Valuable information for this tour will be found in Janvier, especially the first two chapters, and in the papers contained in the *Half Moon Series.* Alfred B. Mason and Mary M. Mason have described Washington's favorite drive in detail, in *Half Moon Series,* I, No. VI; and Washington's own references will be found in his *Diaries.*

CHAPTER V

Shopping Round the Town in '89

Many writers have briefly commented upon shops and styles and kindred subjects of this period, but they have usually been satisfied with a paraphrase of the most convenient previous account. Smith has done well within a few pages, because his quotations are directly from the newspapers. Our remarks upon the merchants and their shops are based upon detailed and somewhat exhaustive research into that most relevant of sources, the newspapers. Photostatic copies of every page of each extant issue of all the New York newspapers for April and May 1789 were made. From these each advertisement was cut out, classified, and filed. These thousands of clippings thus present a detailed and systematic picture of the many things available to the shopper of 1789. Various other facts have been taken from letters and memoirs of the period. As far as possible the original sources have been consulted. With the exception of the newspapers, these sources are scattered and fragmentary. No contemporary felt the need or saw a possible profit from a printed shopper's guide; New Yorkers knew their shops well, and the transient population was not yet large.

CHAPTER VI
The City at Work

The most comprehensive accounts of economic life in New York during 1789 and thereabouts will be found in Smith and Pomerantz. For maritime commerce consult Robert G. Albion and Jennie Barnes Pope, *The Rise of New York Port* (New York, 1939); for real estate, Arthur Pound, *The Golden Earth—The Story of Manhattan's Land Wealth* (New York, 1935); for occupations, the city directories and the newspapers. The story of the good ship *Experiment* is best told in Carl Carmer, *The Hudson* (New York, 1939).

CHAPTER VII
Medical Arts and Wiles

Much material on the state of the medical arts will be found in Smith and in Pomerantz. For the wiles it is best to consult the advertisements in the daily press. Biographical materials concerning the leading physicians have been assembled from contemporary memoirs.

CHAPTER VIII
The Woman's World

Excellent material covering the period has been gathered in Esther Singleton, *Social New York Under the Georges* (New York, 1902);

William Chauncy Langdon, *Everyday Things in American Life—
1607–1776* (New York, 1937); Alice Morse Earle, *Home Life in
Colonial Days* (New York, 1898) and *Child-Life in Colonial Days*
(New York, 1899). The street cries were taken from *The Cries of
New York* (New York, 1931, a reprint of the 1808 edition with five
additional cries from the edition of 1814). Marketing is treated in
Thomas Farrington DeVoe, *The Market Book of New York* (New
York, 1862), and in Smith, Pomerantz, and Stokes. Details on
Washington's expenses while in New York will be found in Smith
and, for liquors, in Hewson L. Peeke, *Americana Ebrietas* (New
York, 1917). The description of the furnishings in the McCrea
home is taken from Mary de Peyster Rutgers McCrea Conger, *New
York's Making* (London, 1938).

CHAPTER IX

The Social Whirl

Griswold's *Republican Court* is the most authoritative of the early
accounts of social doings in the Inauguration Year; but in his as in
every similar case, once a historian undertakes to record gossip he is
in danger of becoming a gossip himself. Dixon Wecter, *The Saga of
American Society* (New York, 1937); Anne Hollingsworth Whar-
ton, *Salons Colonial and Republican* (Philadelphia, 1900) and
Martha Washington (New York, 1897), all give many details of
the social season of 1789. Bowers gives the best picture in brief. For
an annotated copy of Mrs. Jay's "official" list for the 1787–88
season, see Wecter, pp. 199–204. Its catholicity should be noted:
merchants and doctors, lawyers and clergymen, statesmen and diplomats, bankers and professors. It was a Who's Who rather than a
Social Register. What the ladies and gentlemen of importance in
that day looked like may be seen most conveniently in the portrait
reproductions in Bowen's *Centennial*. This work likewise contains
biographical sketches of all the members of Congress who attended
the first session. The origins of the Tammany Society are related in
Edwin P. Kilroe, *St. Tammany and the Origin of the Society of
Tammany or Columbian Order in the City of New York* (New
York, 1913). The account of the programs, anecdotes, and songs of

the meetings in the Great Wigwam are taken from the manuscript minutes in the New York Public Library.

CHAPTER X

Diversions and the Arts

Succinct accounts of the public amusements in 1789 are given by Smith and Pomerantz. The theater is treated at length in the first volume of George C. D. Odell, *Annals of the New York Stage* (New York, 1927); William Dunlap's *Diary* (New York, 1930) has the immediacy of a first-hand account and the defects arising from writing down whatever first comes to mind. Royall Tyler's play, *The Contrast,* was reprinted by the Dunlap Society (New York, 1887). Details on painting, sculpture, and music will be found in Smith, Pomerantz, and Griswold and in many special monographs and articles.

CHAPTER XI

News and Reviews

Frank Luther Mott has done an excellent history of American newspapers in his *American Journalism . . . 1690 to 1940* (1941); for the periodical press the same author's *History of American Magazines, 1741–1850* (1938) is the authority in the field. A most interesting work, *The Sentimental Novel in America, 1789–1860,* was published by Herbert Ross Brown in 1940. It is indicative of the general lack of knowledge of the reading habits of the men and women of the early years of the Republic when one of the best-informed scholars in the field does not even mention the name of the author of *Female Stability,* which ranked so high in the esteem of New Yorkers.

No secondary works can take the place of a thorough examination of the newspapers, magazines, and the books themselves. In this we have tried to be accurate and thorough.

The discovery of the charging-out ledger of the New York Society Library has enabled us to make a pertinent and valuable contribution to our knowledge of the period. It is unique in the knowledge that it supplies, for publishers' records for this period are rare. The study and the tabulation of the entries in this great manuscript volume at the New York Society Library required more than three hundred hours of concentrated effort. We believe that the results provide us with the most realistic and satisfactory approach to the question of what the best read books of 1789 really were. But our answers are neither final nor conclusive. We cannot demonstrate that every book that was borrowed was actually read, or that it was half read, or that the potential reader ever got beyond the tenth page. It is safe to assume that most of the books that were taken from the library were read. These figures are as valid as those for the best sellers of today, for who would venture to demonstrate that every book that is bought is actually read? So we have ventured to call our discoveries the "best read" books of 1789. They were not the "best sellers," because they were borrowed and not sold. But to give high prominence to the "best *borrowed*" books of any period would be too discouraging to authors and publishers, here and hereafter.

The lists of books borrowed by several readers of the New York Society Library may be of interest. In the charging-out ledger of the library each book is given a separate line. To save space we have run them together, but otherwise they are simply transcriptions of the pages of the manuscript volume. John Jay was Acting Secretary of State and later chief justice of the Supreme Court; James Roosevelt was a prominent merchant of the city; and the Rev. Dr. Linn was the chaplain of Congress.

MR. JAY'S LIST:

Fielding; ditto; Anson's Voyage round the world; Animated nature; Peregrine Pickle v. 1, 2, 3; Sully's memoirs v. 1, 2, 3, 4, 5; Irwin's adventure; Bruce's memoirs (travels); Baron de Tott's memoirs v. 1, 2, 3 (travels); Grose's voyage to the East Indies v. 1, 2; Henry Swinburne's travels in the two Sicilies v. 1, 2; Cook's voyage around the world v. 1, 2; Ramsay's Revolution in South Carolina; Plutarch v. 1; Chrysal, the adventures of a Guinea v. 1, 2, 3; Children's friend v. 2; Lady's encyclopedia; Children's friend v. 3; Rollin's Ancient history v. 4; Children's friend v. 4; Marmontel's tales v. 1; Brydone's tour through Sicily and Malta; Sale of authors; Rollin's Ancient history v. 7; Buffon v. 6, 7; Plutarch

v. 1, 2, 3, 4, 5; Life of Putnam; Enfield's speaker; Wilson's Pelew Islands; Hawkesworth's voyages v. 1, 2; Carver's (or Carter's) travels; Independent, a novel; Candide; Arpasia v. 1, 2; Historical miscellanies; Fair Syrian v. 1, 2; Boyle's voyages and adventures, with the story of Mrs. Villars; Fool of quality; Irwin's adventure; Le Bruyn's travels; Campbell's Lives of the admirals; Adelaide and Theodore v. 1; Children's friend v. 3; Adelaide and Theodore v. 2; Children's friend v. 4.

MR. JAMES ROOSEVELT'S LIST:

Gordon's History of the American War, three volumes; Tour through France; Bachelor of Salamancha, two volumes; Smyth's Tour in the United States, two volumes; Hayley's plays; Hume's History of England, eight volumes; Smollett's History of England, seven volumes; Cotton Mather's works; Emmeline, two volumes; Arundel, two volumes; Brydone's Tour through Sicily and Malta; Political magazine, five volumes; Fair Syrian, two volumes; Caroline of Litchfield, two volumes; Modern times, or Gabriel outcast; Cook's Voyages, four volumes; Life of Putnam; Hawkesworth's Voyages, two volumes; Johnson's Anecdotes; Henriade; Zoriada; Lady Luxborough's letters to Shenstone; Beauties of magazines; Pliny's Epistles; Emma Corbett; Temple's works; Wilson's Pelew Islands; Herring's letters; Power of Sympathy, two volumes; Marriage Act, two volumes; Rowe's Callipaedia; Cotton's works; Smith's Universalist.

REV. DR. LINN'S LIST:

Goldsmith's Animated Nature (6 volumes); Sheridan's Art of Reading; Reid's essays; Brydone's Tour through Sicily and Malta; Derham's Physico Theology; Clarissa (four volumes); Alexander's History of Women; Robertson's History of America; Peregrine Pickle (two volumes); Beauties of magazines; Chastellux, Travels in America; Moore's Fables for the female sex; Recess, a novel (3 times); Kames's Art of thinking; Chapone's (Mrs.) Letters on the improvement of the mind; Zelucca (2 volumes); Ela, or the delusions of the heart; Arpasia, or the Wanderer (2 volumes); Fairy tales; Children's friend (3 volumes); Persian tales; Plutarch (3 volumes) ; Clio, an essay on Taste; Beauties of Genlis; Anna, or the memoirs of a Welsh heiress (2 volumes) ; Louisa, or the sisters, by Miss Seward; Fair Syrian; Fielding (2 volumes) ; Platonic Guardian, history of an orphan, by a lady; George Bateman (2 volumes) ; Zoriada, or village annals; Parental solicitude; Vicar of Bray; Beauties of history (2 volumes) ; Matilda, or the efforts of Virtue (3 volumes) ; Lyttelton's History of England; Fingal, a poem; Baron Trenck's memoirs; Burgh's Dignity of human nature.

CHAPTER XII

To School?

No one can write seriously of Columbia College (formerly King's College and, in this period, designated either as Columbia College or the "College of New-York") without recourse to the erudition and generous co-operation of Milton Halsey Thomas, curator of Columbiana. There are already a number of volumes on the history of Columbia; none of them is adequate. *A History of Columbia University, 1754–1904* (New York, 1904) is pleasant, cursory, and woefully inadequate. High attention awaits the forthcoming volume on the beginnings of King's College by Dr. Beverly McAnear. But Columbia deserves a history of the scope and excellence of those published or now being written for Harvard, Yale, and Princeton. An informative catalogue of the academic courses given at the College in 1794 is found in the mistitled pamphlet by Dr. Samuel L. Mitchill: *The Present State of Learning in the College of New York* (New York, 1794). A fragmentary but interesting insight into the life of a Columbia student of 1789 is given in the unpublished diary of John B. Johnson (Columbiana Collection).

Harry R. Warfel's *Noah Webster: Schoolmaster to America* (New York, 1936) is an excellent contribution to the general picture of American education of the period after the Revolution. Mary Sumner Benson's *Women in Eighteenth-Century America: A Study of Opinion and Social Usage* (New York, 1935) gives an understanding of the neglect of formal education for females. There were no schools for education in the professions of law or medicine until the nineteenth century, but an indispensable volume for the understanding of the preparation of lawyers for their careers is Paul M.

Hamlin's *Legal Education in Colonial New York* (New York, 1939), for the colonial practices prevailed long after the Revolution.

Other volumes that make minor but useful contributions to the general picture of education in the New York City of 1789 are: Thomas Boese, *Public Education in City of New York* (New York, 1869); Robert Francis Seybolt, *The Evening Schools of Colonial New York City* (Albany, 1921); Archie E. Palmer, *The New York Public School, being a History of Free Education in the City of New York* (New York, 1905) and Elsie Garland Hobson, *Educational Legislation and Administration in the State of New York from 1777 to 1850* (Chicago, 1918).

There is no one volume (or even several volumes) to which the reader can be referred for a satisfactory view of education in 1789. Smith and Pomerantz present brief treatments, but the materials must be searched in the memoirs, biographies, family histories, newspapers, and periodicals. This chapter covers only the *formal* educational institutions of the time; for others see Chapter XI: "News and Reviews."

CHAPTER XIII

The City at Prayer

The best general sketches of the churches are given by Smith, Pomerantz, and Booth. The general background will be found in Ernest Sutherland Bates, *American Faith* (New York, 1940). Portraits of many of the leading clergymen are painted by Griswold, Mathews, Francis, and Duer. Herbert M. Morais, *Deism in Eighteenth-Century America* (New York, 1934) may be profitably consulted for not only deism but its kindred faiths. Histories of the various Christian denominations and of Judaism in early America are too numerous and well known to require listing here.

CHAPTER XIV

Preserving the Peace

See the *Minutes of the Common Council,* the contemporary newspapers, Smith, Stokes, Pomerantz, and Augustine E. Costello, *Our Police Protectors* (New York, 1885).

CHAPTER XV

Be It Enacted by the People . . .

Thomas Greenleaf of New York City printed a two-volume collection of the *Laws of the State of New-York* . . . in 1792 and added a third volume in 1797. This should be supplemented by the printed *Proceedings* of the state Assembly and Senate. James Parker's *Conductor Generalis: or the Office, Duty and Authority of Justices of the Peace* . . . (New York, 1788) was a convenient handbook for judicial officers and for state and city officials. The *Minutes of the Common Council* do not always give the details of municipal ordinances, but the complete texts were frequently published in the newspapers.

CHAPTER XVI

Oyez! Oyez!

Much of this chapter is based upon a detailed study of the surviving manuscript records. The minutes are available in the office of the clerk of the Court of General Sessions in the Criminal Courts Building and in the New York Public Library. In addition to Smith and Pomerantz see also James W. Brooks, *History of the Court of Common Pleas of the City and County of New York* (New York, 1896); Alden Chester, editor, *Legal and Judicial History of New York* (3 vols., New York, 1911); Charles P. Daly, *Historical Sketch of the Judicial Tribunals of New York, 1623–1846* (New York, 1855); David M. Schneider, *The History of Public Welfare in New York State, 1609–1866* (Chicago, 1938); and the notes for Chapters XIV and XV. It should be remarked that the criminal statistics presented by Henry B. Dawson in the *Historical Magazine* (March 1871, pp. 172–73) are inaccurate and misleading.

CHAPTER XVII

Against Foreign Enemies

There is no detailed history of the United States Army or of the various state militia. Good general summaries are William A. Ganoe,

History of the United States Army (New York, 1924) and Oliver L. Spaulding, *The United States Army in War and Peace* (New York, 1937). For the Navy see Gardner W. Allen, *Our Naval War with France* (Boston, 1909). Samuel L. Mitchill published a brief but interesting pamphlet in 1812: *An Historical Summary of the Several Attacks that have been made upon the City of New-York . . . and of the Measures . . . for its defense.* The official records of both city and state, together with the newspapers and private correspondence, supply abundant details.

CHAPTER XVIII

Municipal and Social Services

Smith has many relevant passages, but they are brief and scattered. Pomerantz is far more detailed; his Chapter VII on "The Finances of a Growing City" is chiefly concerned with the sources of municipal revenues. The various ordinances of the Common Council do not appear in the published *Minutes,* but they are usually given in full in the newspapers. A spirited and informing history of fire fighting in New York City is Herbert Asbury, *Ye Olde Fire Laddies* (1930); this also contains a good discussion of the city water supply of the period. The treatment of the insane can be gathered from the state laws under the chapters dealing with "disorderly persons"; see also Vol. I of *The Institutional Care of the Insane . . . ,* edited by Henry M. Hurd (1916). Allan Nevins has a number of pertinent general remarks on public welfare in his *American States . . . ,* but by far the best in this field is David M. Schneider, *The History of Public Welfare in New York State, 1609–1866* (1938).

CHAPTER XIX

Inaugurating a Nation

There is no volume which treats with satisfactory detail municipal and state politics of the decade after the Revolution. There are accounts of the fight for the adoption of the Federal Constitution. Then there is a lapse until the closing years of the century when the growing power of the Jeffersonians successfully challenges the

Federalists. For a brief picture of the municipal government Pomerantz is excellent. Burr and Tammany have not yet become potent political forces. Spaulding provides a concise picture of George Clinton's role as governor of the state; Alexander gives an all too brief picture of James Duane's activities as mayor of the city. The energetic and vitriolic Richard Varick, the city's second mayor during our period, has never found a competent biographer. Is this neglect partly explained by his miserable handwriting? His voluminous unpublished correspondence, filled with rich, pungent details, is fascinating.

National politics, a predominant interest until local political movements could once more get under way, has claimed the attention of many writers: McMaster, Channing, Bowers, and a host of others. Here, again, Maclay's *Journal* is an indispensable original source of materials.

The events of the inauguration are well treated in T. E. V. Smith and in the massive volume edited by Clarence Bowen. But each of these was published more than fifty years ago, and since that time many new materials, both printed and in manuscript, have been made available. A detailed presentation of these materials was made by Frank Monaghan in *The Inaugural Journey and the Inaugural Ceremonies of George Washington* and a supplementary compilation (both printed, but not published, in 1939). These several hundred pages of research materials were made available to the committees and groups who participated in the re-enactment of Washington's inaugural journey from Mount Vernon to New York City (under the executive direction of Dr. Monaghan). This re-enactment, the first success in several attempts, laid the historical background for the opening of the New York World's Fair on April 30, 1939—the 150th anniversary of Washington's inauguration in New York City.

Index

Account of the Pelew Islands (Wilson), 154
Adams, John, 34, 43, 103, 113, 116, 125, 153, 156, 178, 237, 251, 255, 265, 267, 273, 281
Adams, Mrs. John, 34, 43, 108, 112, 113, 132
Adventures of Gil Blas, 165
Advertising, 47, 48, 51, 52, 54, 64, 70, 81, 90, 123, 141
Albany, 1, 4, 13, 46, 53
Algarotti, Count, 158
Almanacs, 142–3
Almshouse, 24, 35, 168, 198, 201, 213, 226, 243, 249
Amours of Count Palviano and Eleanora, 153
An Account of the Voyages . . . , 153
Animated Nature, 151, 157, 158
Apology for the Life of George-Ann Bellamy . . . , 159, 160
Arabian Nights, 165
Arpasia, or the Wanderer, 161
Art, 132, 133, 134, 195
Articles of Confederation, 252, 253, 255
Astor, Jacob, 20, 48, 65, 69, 72, 73, 130, 190
Arundel, 161, 164

Balloon, Mr. Decker's, 129
Bardin, Edward, 16, 219
Barlow, Joel, 167
Beauties of History, 156
Bedlow, William, 21, 22
Bell, John, 155
Bellamy, George-Ann, 152, 159, 160
Betsy Thoughtless, 153
Bleecker, Anthony L., 47, 55, 70, 71, 264, 272
Boardinghouses, 18, 19, 20
Bold Stroke for a Wife, A, 166
Boston, 1, 8, 10–14, 16
Boudinot, Elias, 117–18, 257, 258, 259

Brickwell, Alexander, 159, 160
Bridewell, 24, 35, 79, 198, 204, 215, 221, 226, 227
Brissot de Warville, Jacques Pierre, 5, 6, 7, 8, 9, 10, 12, 14, 45, 58, 70, 74, 81, 85, 89, 99, 105, 210
Buffon, G. L. Leclerc, Comte de, 158
Burns, Robert, 167
Burr, Aaron, 20, 68, 74, 75, 119, 148, 153, 156, 215, 252
Busybody, The, 166
Butler, Pierce, 31

Candide, 153
Centlivre, Mrs. Susannah, 166
Cervantes Saavedra, Miguel de, 165
Chastellux, Marquis de, 111, 131, 153, 156
Children, 100, 101, 215, 216, 242, chap. xii *passim*
Children's Friend, The, 153
Childs, Francis, 33, 138
Chinese Traveller, 154
Chrysal, 151, 164, 166
Churches: Baptist, 180, 190; French Huguenot, 180, 187; German Calvinist Reformed, 180, 190; Independent Congregational, 180, 192; Jewish, 180, 184; Lutheran, 180, 187; Methodist, 180, 191; Moravian, 180, 190; Presbyterian, 180, 185, 188, 189; Protestant Episcopal, 180, 185, 186, 187; Quaker, 180, 187; Reformed, Dutch, 180, 182, 183, 187; Roman Catholic, 180, 191; Universalist, 194
Cincinnati, Order of the, 118–19
Clinton, George, 105, 108, 113, 117, 125, 133, 134, 178, 200, 201, 251, 252, 259, 260
Colden, Cadwallader, 156
Collect Pond, 28, 30, 36, 37, 68, 82, 101, 225, 247, 248

Colles, Christopher, 2, 83, 84, 129
Columbia College, 170, 171, 173, 174,
    176–9, 184, 188, 219, 231, 236
Common Council, 32, 82, 192, 199,
    200, 211, 212, 244, 246, 251
Commons Debates, 148
Congress (Continental), 106, 229–31
Congress (Federal), 183, 236–7, chap.
    xix *passim*
Congreve, William, 166
Connections (Prideaux), 159
Conquest of Canaan, 167
Constitution (U.S.), 85, 192, 225,
    251, 253, 254, 282
Cook, Captain James, 154
Courts: Admiralty, 223; District
    (U.S.), 223; General Sessions, 198,
    217, 222; Impeachment and Errors,
    223–4; Mayor's, 198, 217, 222;
    Oyer and Terminer, 204, 222; Pro-
    bates, 223; Special Sessions, 217;
    Supreme (N.Y.), 217, 222–3, 224;
    Supreme (U.S.), 223
Coxe, William, 155
Crime, 35, 36, 195, 198–202, 204, 214,
    216, 224, 225, 226
Currency (and coins), 3–4; 48–9

Dafoe, Daniel, 164
Daily Advertiser, 13, 15, 33, 77, 87,
    105, 119, 123, 124, 125, 127, 136,
    138, 140, 141, 192
Daily Gazette, 115, 131, 136, 138, 140,
    142
Dancing Schools, 131, 132, 141
Debtors, 76, 77, 78, 131, 208–210,
    226–7, 240
Declaration of Independence, 183, 192
*Decline and Fall of the Roman Em-
    pire*, 153, 154
Defence of the Constitution . . .
    (Adams), 156
Deists, 180, 192, 194
DeLancey, James, 15
Dentists, 88, 89
Description of China (Grosier), 154
Dialogues of the Dead, 153, 156
Diderot, Denis, 149
Directory (N.Y.C.), 143–6
Disease, 85–91, 248, 249
Doctors, 85, 86, 87–8, 90, 91, 200

*Domestic Memoirs of a Pennsylvanian
    Family*, 156
Don Quixote, 165.
Dow, Alexander (translator), 154
Drinking, 4, 5, 6, 8, 16, 18, 22, 24–26,
    44, 45, 46, 48, 65, 66, 71, 99, 102,
    111, 112, 114, 118, 119, 120, 205,
    209
Dryden, John, 153, 166
Duane, James, 145, 214, 217, 223, 242,
    251, 259
Dwight, Timothy, 167

Edwin Mortimer, 153
Elements of Criticism, 153
Elizabethtown, 13, 257, 258
*Emmeline, or the Orphan of the
    Castle*, 161–4
Empire of Morocco (Chenier), 155
Entertainments, 104–30, 279–81
Essai sur les moeurs, 156
Essay on Man, 159
Essay on Old Maids, 159

Fair Syrian, The, 153
Fairfax, Thomas, 7, 13
Farquhar, George, 166
Fashions, 46–67; Men's, 3, 53, 55, 57,
    58, 61, 62, 63, 102, 109, 111, 133,
    232, 271, 277; Women's, 55, 56, 57,
    58, 59, 60, 61, 63, 102, 124
Federal Hall, 10, 33, 94, 125, 135,
    148, 186, 265, 277, 278, 282
Female Stability, 160, 161–4, 166
Fielding, Henry, 149, 152, 153, 161
Fires, 197, 214, 243–5
Food, 6, 7, 8, 12, 16, 18, 22, 23, 71,
    98–102, 111, 112–14, 118, 264
Franklin, Benjamin, 4, 16, 98, 138,
    192
Fraunces, Samuel (Black Sam), 15,
    76, 96, 98
Fraunces' Tavern, 8, 15, 119, 120,
    132, 186, 233, 261
Fulton, Robert, 12
Furniture, 94–6

Games, 80, 81, 115, 177, 205
Gardoqui, Diego de, 34, 191, 214
Gazette of the United States, 139
Gibbon, Edward, 153, 154
Goethe, Johann Wolfgang von, 161

Goldsmith, Oliver, 151, 156, 157, 158
Gordon, William, 154, 155
Grandison, 161
Grose, John Henry, 154

Hamilton, Alexander, 20, 33, 74, 87,
106, 107, 119, 121, 134, 139, 145,
148, 153, 173, 189, 210, 215, 221,
252, 255, 276, 281
Hamilton, Mrs. Alexander, 108, 117
Harte, Walter, 155
Hawkesworth, John (comp.), 153
Hayley, William, 159
Helvétius, Claude Adrien, 149, 159
Henriade, 153
Hindoostan (Dow), 154
History of China (Duhalde), 154
History of Greece, 153
History of Gustavus Adolphus, 155
History of the American War, 154,
155
History of the Five Nations, 156
History of the Herculean Straits, 155
*History of the Late Revolution in Swe-
den*, 155
History of the Province of New York,
156
Hitchcock, Enos, 165
Hooke, Nathaniel, 154
Hospitals, 249–50
House of Representatives, 183, 188,
281
Housing, 37, 80, 92, 93, 94, 95, 97,
101, 102, 178
Humphreys, David, 156

Independent Journal, 90, 110, 129,
138, 139, 186
Inns and taverns: Adams, 8; Adamson's, 42; Bardin's, 219; John Bat-
tins', 24; Bliss Tavern, 8; Brannan's,
44; Bull's Head, 40; City Tavern,
15, 17, 170; Cummings' Florida
Gardens, 39, 44; Dog and Duck, 41;
Dove Tavern, 42; John Francis, 15,
24; Fraunces', 8, 15, 119, 120, 132,
186, 233, 261; Halsey's, 10, 84;
Mrs. Haviland's, 10; Hitchcock's, 7;
Michael Huck, 19, 24; Hyatt's, 10;
Little's, 23; Merchant's Coffee
House, 20, 24; Montagnie's Gar-

dens, 24, 36; Zeno Parsons, 8;
Jonathan Pearsee's, 24; Ranelagh,
36; Rawson's, 24, 82; John Sim-
mons, 24; United States Arms, 6;
Vauxhall, 44; Williamson's, 44
Insane, treatment of, 227, 240, 250
*Interesting Letters of Pope Clement
XIV*, 159
Inventions, 12, 81, 82, 83, 84
Isle Inconnue . . . L', 153
Izard, Ralph, 34, 270, 273, 279

Jail, 24, 35, 77, 197, 200, 201, 204,
208, 209, 211, 215, 225, 226, 227
Jay, John, 33, 50, 77, 104, 106, 107,
114, 119, 134, 135, 138, 145, 148,
151, 164, 200, 201, 221, 222, 252,
255, 272, 276, 299, 300
Jay, Mrs. John, 34, 35, 107, 113
Jefferson, Thomas, 8, 105, 116, 156,
166, 170, 192, 241, 281
Jews, 28, 175
Johnson, Dr. Samuel, 142, 152, 154,
156, 159, 172, 174, 179, 265
Johnstone, Charles, 151, 164, 166
Journey to China and the East Indies,
(Osbeck), 154

Kames, Lord (Henry Home), 153
King's College, see Columbia College
Kissing Bridge, 10
Knights of Malta (Vertot), 155
Knox, Henry, 34, 60, 93, 108, 145,
230, 235, 256, 258, 272, 274
Knox, Mrs. Henry, 34, 35, 60, 61, 107,
108
Kunze, John Christopher, 18, 187–8,
190

Labor, 76, 77, 80
Lafayette, Marquis de, 118
Land values, 72, 73, 74
Law, 37, 203–27
Law of Nations, 135, 138, 147, 148
Lawyers, 68, 74, 75, 146, 203, 210
Lend-Lease (in 1798), 237
L'Enfant, Major Pierre Charles, 264,
266
Le Sage, Alain René, 165
Libraries, 147–54, 156–67
Life of Cook (Jones), 154

Life of Putnam, 156
Linn, Rev. William, 150, 153, 180, 183, 184
Literature, 148–67
Lives of the Poets, 152
Livingston, Robert R., 112, 117, 272, 273, 274
Locke, John, 149
Lyttleton, George, 153, 156

Maclay, William, 18, 27, 32, 39, 43, 44, 78, 85, 94, 105, 109, 110, 113, 118, 126, 174, 188, 193, 194, 235, 262, 265, 273, 275, 281
MacPherson, James, 167
Madison, James, 192, 253, 254, 265, 276
Magazines, 146, 147, 165, 169
Mante, Thomas, 156
Markets: Bear Market, 98; Catherine Market, 98; Exchange Market, 98; Fly Market, 10, 98; Old Swago (Oswego), 35, 68, 98; Peck Slip, 10, 98
Marmontel, Jean François, 165
Marriage Acts, The, 164
McCormick, Daniel, 33, 34
McFingal, 167
Memoirs (of Sully), 159
Memoirs of the Bloomsgrove Family, 165
Memoirs of the Turks and Tartars, 154
Military affairs, 228–37
Mitford, William, 153
Moll Flanders, 164
Monkland, Mrs., 161
Morning Post, 138
Morris, Gouverneur, 74, 171
Morris, Robert, 32, 74, 225
Morton, Mrs. Sarah Wentworth, 165
Moses, Robert, 30*fn.*, 238
Moustier, Count de, 34, 113, 117, 280
Music, 65, 116, 125, 129, 130, 131, 141

Natural History, 158
Negroes, 28, 31, 33, 78, 79, 87, 168, 187, 191, 200
Newport, 13, 14
Newspapers, 47, 50, 52, 54, 57, 59, 64, 81, 90, 115, 116, 123, 129, 130, 131, 136, 138, 139, 140–2, 209, 254
Newton, Sir Isaac, 159
Newtonian Philosophies . . . , 158
New York Society Library, vii, 135, 146, 147, 150, 152, 156, 165
Notes on Virginia, 156

On Air, 158
On the Prophecies, 159

Packet, The, 82, 115, 116, 139, 208
Palmer, Charlotte, 160, 161–4, 166
Pamela, 149, 161
Pease, Levi, 4, 7
Peregrine Pickle, 149, 165
Philadelphia, vi, 1, 3, 4, 11, 12, 13, 17, 137, 141, 146, 282
Phyfe, Duncan, 96
Pindar, 167
Platonic Guardian . . . , The, 153, 164
Plays (by Dryden), 153
Poems of Ossian, 167
Police, 196, 197–9, 202, 207, 215, 243
Politics, 251–4
Pope, Alexander, 149
Postal Service, 21, 140
Power of Sympathy, or the Triumph of Nature, 165
Priestley, Joseph, 158
Printers, 66, 67, 120, 138, 139, 152, 165
Prisons: Almshouse, 24, 35, 168, 198, 201, 213, 226, 243, 249; jail, 24, 35, 77, 197, 200, 201, 204, 208, 209, 211, 215, 225, 226, 227
Prostitution, 37, 68, 141, 144, 195, 198, 202, 214, 219, 220, 226, 227

Quincy, Josiah, 5

Reading habits of New Yorkers, chap. xi *passim*
Real estate, 47, 71, 72
Rent, 73, 97
Revolution in Fez and Morocco, 155
Richardson, Samuel, 149, 161
Rochefoucauld-Liancourt, Duke de la, 103, 170
Roman History, 154
Roosevelt, Isaac, 72, 73, 249
Roosevelt, James, 28

Rousseau, Jean Jacques, 149, 159

St. Paul's, 29, 34, 106, 119, 178, 184, 185, 186, 276, 277
Sanitation, 30, 31, 36, 245, 246
Schools, 168–79, 242
Science, 83, 84, 158, 176
Seixas, Rabbi Gershom Mendez, 184, 188, 190
Senate, 186, 281
Servants, 92, 93, 96, 97, 98, 123, 125, 205, 217, 218, 226; indentured, 77, 78, 80, 102
Shebbeare, John, 164
Sheridan, Charles Francis, 155
Slaves, 28, 77, 78–80, 96, 141, 168, 205, 226
Slums, 37
Smells, 27, 31, 35
Smith, Adam, 158
Smith, Charlotte, 161, 164
Smith, William, 156
Smollett, Tobias George, 149, 153, 164, 165
Smyth, J., 156
Social life, 103–18, 124, 126, 280, 281
Sorrows of Werther, 161
Stagecoaches, 4
State of the Jews in Morocco, The, (Addison), 155
Sterne, Richard C., 161, 164
Steuben, Baron, 112, 117, 118, 190, 201, 274
Street lighting, 38, 246
Street vendors, 32, 97
Stuyvesant, Peter, 40
Sully, Maximilien de Béthune, Duc de, 159
Swift, Jonathan, 149, 152
Swinburne, Henry, 153

Tales (of Marmontel), 165
Tammany, Sons of St., 119–22, 252
Temple, Sir John, 33, 62
Theaters, 118, 123–7, 137, 141
Topsail Town (Canvas Town), 37, 68, 101, 214
Tott, Baron de, 152, 154
Tour from London to Petersburgh and Moscow (Richard), 155
Tour in the United States, 156

Travel (in 1789), chap. i *passim*
Travels from Petersburgh in Russia to Asia, 155
Travels in Africa (Carver), 160
Travels in Germany, Russia, etc. (Bruce), 155
Travels in Louisiana (Bossu), 156
Travels in Poland, Russia, Sweden, and Denmark, 155
Travels in the Two Sicilies, 153
Travels through the United States, 156
Trinity Church, 106, 170, 185, 186, 187, 200
Trumbull, John, 132, 133, 167

Union Library, 148
Unitarian Society, 194
Universal History, 153, 156

Varick, Richard, 215, 218, 221, 222, 242, 251
Vattel, Emmerich de, 135, 138, 147, 148
Vision of Columbus, The, 167
Volney, Constantin, 6
Voltaire, François M. Arouet de, 149, 152, 153, 156, 208
Voyage Round the World, 154
Voyage to the Coast of Africa in 1785–1787 (Mathew), 155
Voyage to the East Indies, 154

Wages, 75, 77, 80, 96, 97, 98
War in America, 156
Washington, George, v, 6, 7, 10, 15, 16, 30, 32, 40, 41, 42, 43, 82, 87, 88, 93, 94, 96, 98, 99, 105, 106, 107–11, 113, 114, 116, 119, 124–8, 133–8, 142, 148, 149, 157, 178, 179, 184, 186, 192, 209, 210, 229–35, 240–1, 254–5, 259–66, 270–81
Washington, Mrs. George, 105–8, 110–13
Wealth of Nations, 158
Webb, Samuel B., 12, 14, 104, 156, 215, 264, 272
Webster, Noah, 34, 70, 104, 147, 165, 171, 188
Wonder, The: A Woman Kept a Secret, 166